GEOFF HAMILTON
GARDENERS' WORLD
PRACTICAL GARDENING COURSE

The Complete Book of
Gardening Techniques

BBC

Published by BBC Worldwide Limited,
Woodlands, 80 Wood Lane,
London W12 0TT

First published 1993
Reprinted 1993 (twice), 1994 (twice), 1996 (three times)
New edition published 1998
Reprinted 1998
This edition first published in paperback 2000
© Geoff Hamilton 1993

The moral right of the author has been asserted

ISBN 0 563 36267 7 (hardback)
ISBN 0 563 55163 1 (paperback)

Designed by Grahame Dudley Associates
Illustrations on pages 134–7 by Gill Tomblin
All other illustrations by Will Giles and Sandra Pond

Set in Goudy Old Style by Ace Filmsetting Ltd, Frome, Somerset
Printed and bound in Spain by Gráficas Estella, S.A.

Colour separation by Daylight Colour Art, Singapore

CONTENTS

ACKNOWLEDGEMENTS

Though my name sits on the cover of this book, it was very much a joint effort.
All the team at Barnsdale took part in growing the plants and building the
gardens that were the subject of the photographs. So I must thank Ian Spence,
Carol Woods, Lorraine Shone and Sue Jeal, who helped to grow the plants,
and ace landscaper Adam Frost.
Thanks too to my eldest son, Steve, who displayed patience I didn't believe he
had in taking many of the photographs, and to editors Nicky Copeland and
Ruth Baldwin for their sheer professionalism and that vital attribute when
working with me – a sense of humour.

INTRODUCTION

ONE OF THE supreme joys of gardening is sharing it with friends. There's great pleasure to be had discussing your triumphs and your failures, perhaps over the garden fence, and we all pick each other's brains unmercifully. There are few greater satisfactions than being able to give away an admired plant or to allow the snipping of a cutting or two. And the lending of the lawnmower or fork has become more or less traditional.

So you can imagine the great thrill it is for me to be able to share my own lifetime's experience of gardening with you. I just hope you get as much out of it as I have!

I should warn you that the gardening methods within these pages are strictly personal. If you're an old hand you may not agree with everything I say and you may find some of my techniques peculiar. In a way I hope you do, because it's by constant theorising, discussion and argument that gardeners through the ages have learnt and progressed. But this I can assure you: I have written about nothing that I haven't actually *done* with my own hands and found to be successful.

The knowledge I've been lucky enough to gain is the result of a lifetime of growing plants. I've never done anything else nor ever wanted to. I've loved every minute of getting my hands dirty and I hope I can pass on some of that enjoyment to you. If I can, I shall be a happy man and you're in for a lifetime of sheer joy.

Unlike some of my other books, this one is meant to be purely a work of reference. It has been arranged to make it quick and easy to look up the relevant information and, where possible, I've illustrated the various techniques. I have deliberately avoided being too scientific and botanical, though I do firmly believe that dipping a toe in the botanical bath will not only help newcomers learn about plants more quickly, it'll make gardening that much more successful and enjoyable too. All those Latin names may be a pain, but once you get into them you'll probably find them as fascinating as I do.

I hope that my book will be a constant companion and will become a trusted friend. If you're new to gardening it should lead you reasonably painlessly through the various techniques you'll need to create a beautiful garden. If you're an experienced gardener, I think you'll get something out of it too, since like me you'll have learned that no gardener, however experienced, can ever know everything about this multi-faceted subject. Perhaps with another half-a-dozen lifetimes we could get somewhere near!

But the wonderful thing about gardening is that, with determination, we can all get there in the end; we can all create a work of art right there in our own back yard – with a little unsolicited help from nature, of course.

CHAPTER 1
PLANTS AND HOW THEY GROW

HOWEVER YOU MAY design your garden and whatever
you may want to use it for, the basic reason for it will be
to grow plants. The key to a successful relationship with
plants, as with anything else, is to understand them.
Find out how and why they grow and you're three-
quarters of the way to success.

Modern gardens have become so sophisticated that
most of them grow many plants that really belong to
foreign shores. My own garden grows plants from as far
afield as China and the USA, New Zealand and the high
mountains of Russia. So it naturally pays to discover
both where a plant comes from and the kind of
conditions that prevail in its native habitat.

Some alpines, for example, while as frost-hardy as you
could wish, suffer in my garden because of the damp of
the English winter. They have to be protected – not
from frost but from excessive rain, while Germany's
native swamp iris needs the moist soil of the bog garden.

All plants require light and air, water in varying
amounts and different quantities of food too. A
successful gardener will need to know how and when to
supply those needs. It's not necessary to have an
honours degree in botany, chemistry or physics to grow
a good garden. But a basic understanding of these
subjects is sure to help you become more successful.

Most gardens are home to plants from many different parts of
the world.

Plant classification

All garden plants are classified into groups, depending on certain characteristics. There are some 'grey' areas – when does a large shrub become a small tree?; how woody must a plant be to become a shrub rather than a herbaceous plant? – but the vast majority fit conveniently into twelve groups.

Climber A plant that naturally scrambles over shrubs or up trees. The term is sometimes applied to wall shrubs which grow erect but don't naturally cling. Examples are clematis (such as 'The President', shown here) and climbing roses.

Shrub A woody plant with several branches but generally no central stem. It may be up to several metres high. Examples are forsythia and privet (the golden type is pictured). Some, like holly, are evergreen.

Conifer A cone-bearing plant, usually evergreen, with narrow, spiky foliage. The cones are in fact fruits which bear seed. An example is this *Chamaecyparis lawsoniana* 'Pembury Blue'.

Tree A woody plant generally with a straight stem topped by a bushy head, like this birch, though the modern trend is for 'feathered' trees with branches arising from the main stem right from ground level to form a large shrub. A few are evergreen.

Rhizome An underground stem which will produce shoots and new plants at a distance from the parent. Examples are irises and lily-of-the-valley. Rhizomes are easily divided to produce new plants.

Corm A storage organ made up of a thickened stem and therefore solid. What scales it does have are thin and just for protection. Examples are gladioli and crocus.

Perennial This strictly applies to all plants that live for more than a year, flowering and seeding annually. But in gardening terms it's generally restricted to soft-stemmed herbaceous plants like campanulas, lupins, delphiniums and penstemons.

Alpine Strictly a herbaceous perennial or shrub that naturally grows in mountainous regions, though the term has become used for any plant suitable for growing in the rock garden. Examples are saxifrages, stonecrops, houseleeks and some of the smaller bellflowers.

Tuber A storage organ made from a thickened stem or root. It differs from a corm in having no membranous coating. Examples are potatoes, dahlias and begonias.

Bulb This is really a modified bud with a series of leaves or scales compressed together to form a food storage organ below or at the surface of the soil. Examples are daffodils and onions. Bulb catalogues generally also include corms, tubers and rhizomes under the same heading.

Biennial A plant that is sown in one year, flowers and seeds in the next and then dies. Examples are canterbury bells and sweet williams. Some perennials like pansies are often grown as biennials because they're best in their first flowering year.

Annual A plant that flowers and seeds in its first year after sowing and then dies. There are half-hardy annuals like petunias which are killed by frost and hardy annuals like marigolds that will stand several degrees of frost.

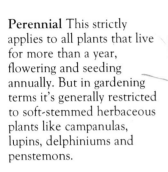

The parts of a plant

All parts of a plant have a specific function. An understanding of these functions will greatly aid the gardener in growing plants successfully.

Leaves The leaves are the plant's food factory. By photosynthesis they absorb sunlight and turn it into plant food. They can also absorb water and nutrients through tiny pores (stomata), and some gardeners take advantage of this to feed plants by spraying plant food on to the leaves. The stomata also allow the exchange of oxygen and carbon dioxide for respiration. Another leaf function is to remove impurities. In autumn the waste can be seen as the colouration in leaves which deciduous plants then lose. Evergreens also lose leaves regularly but continuously rather than seasonally.

Roots A plant has two types of root. The thicker, thongy parts are used purely for anchorage while the thinner roots located at the extremities are used to take up water and nutrients from the soil. These thinner roots are equipped with microscopic root hairs that actually absorb the liquids, so when planting, for example, you should take great care that they don't dry out.

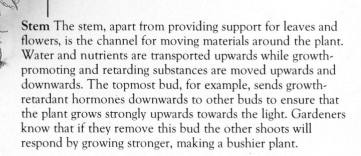

Stem The stem, apart from providing support for leaves and flowers, is the channel for moving materials around the plant. Water and nutrients are transported upwards while growth-promoting and retarding substances are moved upwards and downwards. The topmost bud, for example, sends growth-retardant hormones downwards to other buds to ensure that the plant grows strongly upwards towards the light. Gardeners know that if they remove this bud the other shoots will respond by growing stronger, making a bushier plant.

Fruit The fruit is the part of the plant that carries the seeds. Literally, a pea pod is a fruit, but fruits as gardeners know them – apples, cherries, plums and so on – are seed containers that have been made attractive to birds and mammals as a means of distribution. A bird will eat a cherry, for example, and in doing so will ingest the seed which it deposits somewhere else, thus ensuring that the resulting plant doesn't compete for space with its parent. Other fruits are equipped with different ways of distributing their seeds. Some explode, throwing the seeds huge distances, while others rely on releasing their seeds more gently; these may then be wafted by the wind or picked up on the coats of passing animals.

Seeds All a seed needs are the right conditions for germination, and it's equipped with a number of mechanisms that ensure that it will remain dormant until it has them. Some seeds require the correct temperature or humidity while others need to be frozen. Some have chemical barriers in the seed coat while others have hard coats that need moisture before they'll germinate. Generally it's not too difficult to break a seed's dormancy to make it germinate.

Flowers The flower's function is to reproduce the species. It generally contains both male and female parts, though some plants, like conifers, have separate male and female flowers. In order to produce seed the female ovaries must be fertilised by pollen from a male organ. This is sometimes done by wind but it's very hit-or-miss, so more sophisticated means of transporting pollen have evolved in most flowers. The attractive colouring and perfume of flowers and the nectar at the base of the ovaries are all specifically for the attraction of pollinating insects which quite inadvertently carry pollen on their bodies as they move from plant to plant.

Plant reproduction

In order to ensure the survival of the species, plants have developed a variety of methods of multiplying themselves. They reproduce both sexually (by seed) and asexually (or vegetatively). Gardeners make use of this natural process in order to increase their stock of plants.

BELOW **Seed** All flowering plants increase naturally by seed (though some cultivated varieties produce seed which will not germinate). Garden plants often produce seedlings around the parent and these can be dug up and transplanted to another part of the garden. Alternatively, it's possible to collect seed just before the plant naturally disperses it and this can be sown in a variety of ways to produce new plants (see p. 106). Cyclamen seeds are contained in rounded capsules. When the capsules break the seeds are carried away by ants which are attracted to a substance coating the seeds.

ABOVE **Offsets** Some plants, like sempervivums, will create small reproductions of themselves, usually at the base of the stem. These can be removed, generally with a small amount of root, and grown on to produce another plant.

Runners As an additional safeguard to ensure the continuation of the species, a few plants, like strawberries, produce runners. These are small plants attached to trailing stems called stolons which ensure that the young plants will grow some distance away from the parent, so reducing competition. They will root naturally into the soil and gardeners often peg them down into a pot to produce new plants for planting elsewhere (see p. 322).

Layers Many climbing and scrambling plants and several shrubs (like *Cotoneaster dammeri*) and herbaceous perennials will root naturally into the soil where a shoot bends down and touches it. Sometimes this takes a long time and it is often helped by leaf litter building up around the shoot to bury it. Other plants, such as brambles, will root very quickly. The substances that encourage rooting are generally concentrated in the plant near a leaf joint and gardeners use this fact to layer plants artificially to increase their stock (see p. 120).

Underground runners Some plants, such as *Polygonum cuspidatum*, have vigorous running root systems which naturally produce new shoots some way away from the parent, again to reduce competition. This is often a source of great annoyance to gardeners since such plants are generally invasive, but the natural process is also used to make new plants.

Clump forming Most herbaceous perennials and many shrubs naturally increase their size by producing new shoots around the edges of the plants to form a bigger clump. Generally these shoots can be divided from the parent plant, together with some root, and replanted to form new plants. Indeed, with many herbaceous perennials this is recommended once every few years as the centre of the plant – the parent – becomes old and loses vigour (see p. 122).

Cuttings Plants have an amazing will to live and nature has equipped them with the means to produce roots from many of their parts that are really designed for another purpose. Drop a piece of wandering Jew (*Tradescantia*) on to a wet greenhouse path and it will root in days. Even the leaves of some plants like African violets and begonias will form roots given optimum conditions. The stems contain root-forming hormones mainly in the nodes (leaf joints), and gardeners use this to advantage when taking cuttings to produce new plants (see p. 108).

9

What plants need

It goes without saying that plants will grow best if they are provided with optimum conditions, but it's more difficult to understand just what those conditions are.

Our gardens grow a vast range of plants whose requirements vary enormously, but there are certain basic rules that apply to most.

SOIL

The soil is the gardener's raw material. If you understand what plants require from it and how to provide those needs, you're three-quarters of the way towards growing strong, healthy plants.

Mulch A surface layer of organic matter will help to retain water and inhibit the growth of weeds. It also provides a home for beneficial organisms like slug-eating ground beetles and, it must be said, the slugs too! It will eventually work down to the lower levels to improve fertility, so regular applications round permanent plants are very beneficial.

Topsoil The topsoil is that part of the growing medium which contains life in the form of bacteria and other micro-organisms, earthworms, fungi and so on. Ideally it should contain good air spaces between its particles to allow roots to push through it without difficulty and to enable the free passage of air, water and plant food.

Organic matter This is rotting vegetable matter and is in the topsoil. It is essential in fertile soil to hold water and nutrients without impeding drainage. It also provides food for soil organisms which, in the process of rotting it down, release plant food.

Humus When bulky organic matter like manure rots down in the topsoil, the end product is humus, essential in maintaining fertility. Organic matter rots down more quickly in cultivated soil than when it's undisturbed, so in cultivated soil higher inputs of organic matter are required than nature would normally provide.

Subsoil The subsoil is the layer beneath the topsoil and is much less fertile. It affects the growing conditions mainly in its ability to drain away excess water, with gravel subsoils being much more free-draining than clay. The regular addition of organic matter to the topsoil will gradually work down to the subsoil too and so increase the topsoil depth.

Water table This is the level to which water will normally rise. Its depth fluctuates with the frequency of rain and the time of year. Most plants will not grow in soil that is saturated (except bog and aquatic plants), so the depth of the water table will help to determine the depth of rooting.

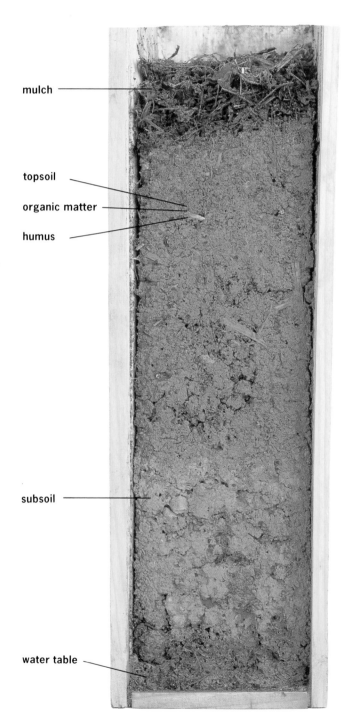

mulch

topsoil

organic matter

humus

subsoil

water table

LEFT Barnsdale soil This soil
was taken from my own
garden at Barnsdale in the
English Midlands. Here I
started with grassland and
have supplemented the
excellent original structure
with plenty of manure and
compost over the years. The
soil is friable, dark in colour,
moisture-retentive and rich
in earthworms.

FAR LEFT Farmland soil Fifty
metres away the same soil has
grown grain for as many years
as I can remember. The straw
has been burned off and no
organic matter has been
added. Chemical fertilisers,
mainly nitrogen, have been
the only input. The soil is
hard and airless and
completely dead. It compacts
so hard it has to be subsoiled
(deep-ploughed) every other
year and strong winds blow it
away in winter. You could
dig it all day and never find
an earthworm.

FERTILITY

There's a wonderful, evocative word that stirs the heart
of any good gardener – *fertility!* It evokes visions of a
soil that's pulsing with life and that's *exactly* what it
means. Unfortunately, modern farming and commercial
growing techniques shun what has been considered an
'old-fashioned' approach, but gardeners do so at their
peril. Even farmers are now beginning to see the folly of
ignoring natural rules.

Nature's great Chain of Life is a very complex
mechanism designed to ensure the continued existence
of all species, with each one relying on the other. While
it is undeniably possible for man to break that chain, it's
always a very expensive thing to do and we are now
learning that it can never be anything but temporary.
For the gardener it is neither necessary nor desirable.

A soil that is rich in organic matter will contain
billions of organisms, most of which have a decidedly
beneficial effect on plant growth. From the bacteria
which break down organic matter and minerals to make
plant food, to the earthworms which aerate soil,
distribute organic matter to the lower levels and
cultivate surprisingly large volumes of soil, all are
helping plants grow. So it makes sense for the gardener
to return all waste to the soil in the form of compost
and to supplement that with extra manure or one of the
alternatives (see p. 68).

Research has also shown that chemical fertilisers can
have an adverse effect on the activities of beneficial
organisms, though to what extent seems unclear. Many
gardeners therefore, myself included, prefer to use
organic fertilisers derived from natural materials.

A good indication of soil fertility is the colour, the
structure and the visible organisms in it. Darker browns
generally – though not always – indicate plenty of
organic matter, while a soil which will crumble easily in
the hand is also likely to be more fertile. But perhaps
the best visual indication for gardeners is the quantity of
earthworms. If you dig a forkful of soil and find half-a-
dozen healthy-looking worms, you can bet your life the
soil will grow good plants. It will pay to keep it that way.

What plants need

WATER

Though requirements vary, no plant can live entirely without water. It serves to help support the stems and leaves and, most importantly, to transport nutrients and other life-supporting materials through the system of the plant. So every plant is continuously taking in water through its roots and, to a lesser degree, through its leaves and passing it out again through the leaves in the process of transpiration. It's essential for the gardener to ensure that there is a sufficient and constant supply.

On the other hand, too much water has an adverse effect, so a strict balance is required. Naturally more water is lost in summer when evaporation and transpiration are faster. In winter many plants lose their leaves entirely and so lose little or no water. Root activity therefore stops and the plants become dormant.

However, evergreens continue to need water because they will be losing it from their leaves all year round. In exposed areas this water loss can be very fast as a result of evaporation by wind, and gardeners may therefore have to protect plants, especially those that are newly planted. With plants like conifers, which have a very large leaf area, the water loss can be so fast that an immature root system simply can't get the water to where it's needed in time, causing eventual browning and loss of leaves. So, though water must be supplied to the roots in dry weather, it's often more important to protect the leaves from water loss.

To make matters more complicated, waterlogging is just as damaging as drying out. The art is to provide the plant with a well-aerated soil that will quickly drain away *excess* water while retaining *sufficient* moisture within the soil particles. In the garden this is done with deep cultivations and the incorporation of coarse grit to aid the drainage of heavy soils and by digging in bulky organic matter to hold water. In the greenhouse the balance is maintained by the use of a well-constructed compost; you will not achieve it by using garden soil in the artificial confines of a pot.

RIGHT Bad drainage is a common cause of winter loss. Plants on the borderline of hardiness will survive a hard winter much better if they are growing in well-drained soil. My own 'Mediterranean' garden at Barnsdale has raised borders with large quantities of coarse gravel dug in. It supports many plants that would otherwise be considered tender in the English Midlands.

Too much water excludes oxygen so the tiny root hairs responsible for absorbing water actually drown. The symptoms are usually a yellowing of the leaves and a general sickly appearance. Plants rarely recover from prolonged waterlogging.

Without water, plant cells lose their turgidity so the leaves wilt. Most plants recover from a short period of wilting but the condition is eventually fatal.

A plant that receives just the right amount of water looks strong, with crisp, self-supporting leaves and a general air of wellbeing.

What plants need

LIME

Calcium, contained in lime, is an important plant food, but lime has a much bigger effect on plant growth than that. Indeed, the amount of lime in the soil will determine the kinds of plants you grow.

BELOW The Victorians' passion for the acid-loving rhododendrons and their resulting preponderance in large gardens still lingers on. Even today some gardeners bemoan the fact that they can't grow them and their like. Yet there are literally thousands of wonderful, lime-loving plants that together will make a superb garden even on the chalkiest soil. This garden proves the wisdom of choosing plants that will grow well on your particular soil rather than waging an unequal war against nature.

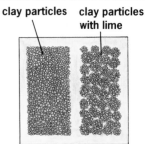

clay particles   clay particles with lime

RIGHT Lime is useful in improving the structure of clay soils, whose particles are so small that they allow little air or water to pass between them. By a chemical reaction, lime sticks the particles together to form larger, better-aerated 'crumbs'.

BELOW Too much lime gives acid-loving plants a sickly yellow appearance and retards growth. If your soil is chalky they're best avoided, though special steps can be taken should you be determined to grow them (see p. 79).

All plants are affected by the relative acidity or alkalinity (chalkiness) of the soil. Gardeners measure the acidity in terms of a unit known as pH. This represents the number of hydrogen ions in the soil, but it's not necessary to understand the complexities. Suffice it to say that pH 7 is neutral while any figure above that is more alkaline and anything below it more acid.

A very alkaline soil tends to make certain minerals, mainly phosphate, potassium, iron and manganese, unavailable to plants and only a few will tolerate such conditions.

Conversely, a very acid soil reduces the availability of phosphate and prevents soil bacteria from converting nitrogen from the air into plant food. Excessively acid soil also makes many plant nutrients more soluble so they're quickly lost by leaching. Very few gardeners will ever experience these extremes but, in fact, quite small variations in the pH will have a marked effect on the growth of some plants.

It's easy to see that it's essential for gardeners to know the acidity of their soil before deciding what to plant. The majority of plants will do well when the soil is very slightly acid with a pH of 6.5. This is also when most nutrients are available.

However, there's a fairly wide margin, with pH 7.5–8 being quite acceptable for all but the acid-lovers, right down to pH 5 when even ericaceous plants begin to suffer.

Nonetheless, before buying expensive plants, it's wise to check the pH of your soil (see p. 78).

ABOVE There are some plants that will grow only on acid soils. These include not just rhododendrons but also others like pieris and ericas. In fact, acid lovers are often referred to as 'ericaceous'.

What plants need

MAJOR NUTRIENTS

All plants need three major nutrients for healthy growth – nitrogen, phosphorus and potassium. They are referred to respectively as N, P and K, and you'll generally see these chemical symbols on bags or bottles of fertiliser. These three nutrients are required in relatively large amounts. Plants will absorb them in exactly the same form whether a 'chemical' or an 'organic' fertiliser is used, though there are advantages to be gained from using purely organic fertilisers (see p. 66).

A healthy, well-fed plant will have a good leaf colour and will bear plenty of flowers and fruit. This requires the separate minerals to be in roughly the right proportion, though there is a wide margin of error.

Nitrogen This is the nutrient responsible for leaf and stem growth. It aids the manufacture of food from sunlight (photosynthesis) and helps build protein. It's quickly washed through the soil by rain, so will need constant replenishment. A deficiency of nitrogen shows up in most plants as an overall yellowing of the leaves, starting at the bottom of the plant. Later leaves produce a pinkish and then purplish tinge, and growth is retarded.

Phosphorus This will ensure good root growth and helps to ripen seeds and fruit. It's not so readily lost as nitrogen and is generally only used on its own at planting time. When plants are deficient in phosphorus, growth is retarded and leaves take on a dull purple or dark blue/green tinge. When pulled up, the root system is generally seen to be stunted.

Potassium Often referred to as 'potash', this is the food used to produce flowers and fruit. It also helps photosynthesis and the production of carbohydrates. Again, it's not so readily washed out of the soil as nitrogen. Potassium deficiency makes leaves scorch around the margins and they can be spotted, mottled or curled and may drop off. Fruits are poorly coloured and potatoes turn black when cooked.

TRACE ELEMENTS

As well as the three major nutrients, plants also need other minerals in varying but mainly minute quantities. So they're known as 'trace elements'. But though only small amounts are needed, they're none the less vital. Deficiencies can have dramatic effects but are rare in soils rich in organic matter. To complicate matters, the deficiency symptoms are sometimes more or less the same. If in doubt about the precise mineral that's deficient, spray with seaweed and try to increase the organic content of the soil by mulching with manure or compost. That should provide them all. Often deficiencies are caused by too much lime in the soil, so try to increase the acidity by adding some organic matter.

Remember that an excess of any of the trace elements is as bad as a deficiency so, though commercial growers sometimes use chemical cures, I consider it best to rely on organic methods. However, it is possible to buy a 'cocktail' of what are known as 'fritted' trace elements. Use them as directed by the manufacturer and they're unlikely to do any harm.

Boron Vital for a whole range of uses. It plays a part in cell division, flowering and fruiting and general nutrition. Deficiency causes brittle stems which crack easily, hollow stems and roots and blackening inside roots and stems. Avoid liming and try to lower the pH of the soil.

Manganese Used as a catalyst in plant nutrition, helping strong growth. A deficiency causes much the same symptoms as magnesium deficiency. There is a general speckling of the leaves. Cure by avoiding the use of lime on chalky soils and by adding organic matter.

Molybdenum Important in the manufacture of nitrogen. Deficiency causes stunting and deformations like 'whiptail' in brassicas. Unlike the other trace elements, deficiency is most common on soils that are too acid and liming will generally cure it.

Calcium Essential for sturdy growth and considered one of the most important of the trace elements. Deficiencies show in a general lack of vigour and the death of growing points. Young leaves are often cupped and deformed and may be blackened at the edges. Calcium deficiency is also responsible for blossom-end rot of tomatoes which causes a blackening of the fruit. Avoid excessive use of potash and water in dry periods.

Magnesium Essential to keep leaves green and for the formation of amino acids and vitamins. Deficiency causes yellowing between the veins of leaves and a mottled or marbled effect. In some plants the edges of leaves remain green while the centre turns yellow. Use magnesian (or dolomitic) limestone when liming.

Iron Helps in the formation of chlorophyll which gives leaves their green colour. Deficiencies show as a yellowing of leaves between the veins. Stems become very weak. This is especially noticed in raspberries and acid-loving plants growing in limy soil. Cure by using sequestered iron at regular intervals, but it's best to avoid growing acid-lovers in limy soil.

What plants need

LIGHT

All green plants need sunlight. They use it to create food through photosynthesis, converting the energy from the sun into sugar and oxygen. This conversion of energy is really the basis of all life, providing sustenance not just for the plants themselves but also for the insects and other animals that eat them and eventually, via the food chain, for us. However, plants' requirements vary, depending on their natural habitat. There is no advantage in putting shade-loving plants in full sunshine in order to increase photosynthesis – they just won't be able to cope. It's important, therefore, to find out the sort of situation particular plants prefer in their native habitat.

RIGHT Plants that normally grow in the shade of trees are restricted in the amount of sunlight they can use for photosynthesis. While the trees themselves are adapted to reach quickly for the light to take full advantage of the sunshine, those plants growing beneath have evolved to grow best in conditions of lower light. The gardener must be aware of these requirements and provide them by planting in a favourable place.

If you provide sun-lovers like this *Rosa pimpinellifolia* with plenty of light by planting them in a sunny border, they'll grow into strong, bushy plants with plenty of flowers.

Plant a sun-lover such as a fuchsia in the shade and it will generally grow an excessive amount of leaf and will produce fewer flowers than usual.

Plants like gazanias (here mixed with purple heliotrope) grow naturally in the strong sunlight of South Africa. In northern countries it's difficult to give them enough light and they should go in the sunniest spot available.

BELOW Lack of light tends to elongate cells within a plant. So plants grown in a uniform condition of low light will grow long and straggly. Where light comes only from one side, the cells on the darker side of the stem elongate while those on the sunny side remain short, so making the stem bend towards the light source.

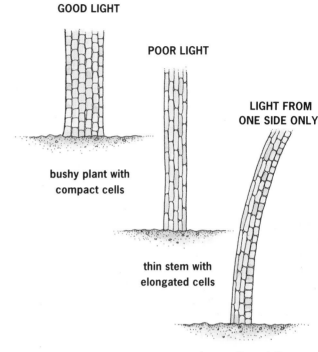

GOOD LIGHT

POOR LIGHT

LIGHT FROM ONE SIDE ONLY

bushy plant with compact cells

thin stem with elongated cells

long cells on left; short cells on right

Most hydrangeas, including this *Hydrangea arborescens* 'Annabelle', are happiest in the kind of conditions they'd find at the edge of a wood, with some dappled shade provided by trees, but not the full shade found deeper in.

Deeper into the wood, plants like ferns, such as this *Dryopteris filix-femina*, would naturally be found and these should be planted in a similar spot in the garden.

The deepest shade, coupled with the competition for water and nutrients provided by plant roots, gives gardeners their most difficult planting problem. However, plants like *Euphorbia robbiae* are naturally adapted to such conditions and will thrive.

What plants need

TEMPERATURE

Just as conditions of light intensity in nature have produced plants particularly suited to them, so temperatures have affected which plants can survive where. The process of evolution always creates plants that thrive in the prevailing temperatures. It would be just as difficult for a cold-loving alpine, for example, to grow in the rain forests of Brazil as it would be for an exotic, heat-loving orchid to survive in Greenland.

So it makes sense for gardeners to grow only those plants that will survive the highest and lowest extremes of temperature likely to occur in the locality of their gardens. Well, that's all very clear and straightforward. What isn't so clear is exactly how you know what is and what isn't hardy in your own locality.

Quite obviously, there will be some things that will be easy to guess. If a plant comes from the hottest areas of South Africa, for instance, you can be pretty sure it won't survive a northern European winter. That kind of information is readily available.

But there are many, many plants of all kinds that are on the borderline of hardiness. What does well in the south of England, for example, may not thrive in the east of Scotland. All you can do really is to give it a try. Obviously you should provide the plants with the best conditions possible (see p. 10), and if you take a few cuttings for insurance against a hard winter (see p. 109) there's not too much to lose.

There is no 'cure' for frost damage. If leaves wilt after a cold night and their surface looks blue and rather watery, you can be sure the cells inside the plant have frozen and will not recover.

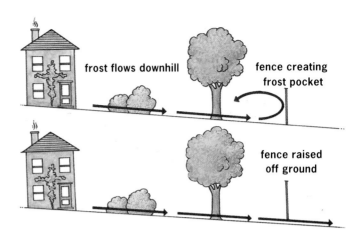

ABOVE Frost tends to 'flow' down slopes and collect at the lowest point. This is known as a 'frost pocket'. Sometimes the effect is created artificially by blocking the frost in with a fence. If you live on a slope, you could well avoid trouble by raising the fence a little off the ground to allow the frost to escape.

ABOVE Frost causes the cells inside plants to freeze and, unless they're naturally adapted to low temperatures, the tissue will be damaged or killed. Scorched leaf margins are a typical symptom of frost damage but, though a few leaves will be lost, the plant could well still survive.

RIGHT If you choose your plants carefully, there is always a wide range that will survive even the coldest garden. Many herbaceous perennials, like this hemerocallis, will die down in winter and become 'dormant', but will return with new growth in the spring.

OPPOSITE Choose plants that can withstand the lowest temperatures of your region.

What plants need

SPACE

All green plants compete with their neighbours for water, nutrients, light and air. In nature only the strongest will survive and this has led to the development of different characteristics such as the ability to climb to the sunshine, to live in the shade of trees or to make do with the minimum of food and water. But in the garden we have created an entirely artificial environment so the gardener will need to act as umpire, restraining the stronger species and encouraging the weaker.

Remember, too, that weeds are natives and, because they're in their own natural environment, will be much better suited and able to compete. It's a completely one-sided battle without the intervention of man, and it's essential to reduce competition either by providing more space or by compensating for the lack of it.

ABOVE Large plants, like shrubs and trees, compete very successfully for water, nutrients and light. So the only realistic way to garden the area immediately adjacent is to grow those plants that can survive with very little of all three requirements. The choice is not large, but here *Geranium endressii* is thriving in competition with a hedge and a tree.

Rampant-growing plants in the mixed border must be constantly restrained to prevent them swamping less vigorous neighbours. This variegated pineapple mint is capable of completely covering the small shrub *Convolvulus cneorum*, so must be cut back regularly. When feeding, the gardener must take account of the density of planting and, though heavier doses are not to be recommended, fertiliser should be applied more often.

If the borders are shaded by a heavy canopy of trees, it may be possible to let in a little more light by judicious pruning. And, though it always goes against a gardener's grain, there are situations where it's much better to remove a tree completely to allow other plants growing underneath to survive and thrive.

ABOVE If the soil is prepared by double digging (see p. 90), to provide a greater depth, and by more frequent feeding, plants can be grown closer together. On 'deep beds' (see p. 244) vegetables are grown much more closely than normal and, though this does reduce the size of the individual vegetables somewhat, the weight of crop per square metre is greatly increased.

RIGHT In established shrub borders plants are bound to grow into each other, so a restraining hand is needed. First decide which of the plants will suffer least from cutting back, then which is the most important and deserves the most space. In this case, for example, the slow-growing maple is the real aristocrat and should remain untouched, while the rampant cotoneaster will shrug off a little pruning and look none the worse for it.

Nomenclature

If there's one thing that sets a new gardener's teeth on edge, it's Latin names. It makes the otherwise fascinating world of plants seem like so much mumbo-jumbo and impossible for the ordinary gardener to grasp. Well, that's a great shame because, in fact, it's not too hard to get acquainted with a bit of Latin and, once you do, plants become much more interesting.

That old, dead, incomprehensible language still spans the continents of the world, providing an international understanding of plants. Even Chinese and Japanese botanists use Latin. And it hides the absorbing history and the thrilling romance of a subject that has fascinated gardeners and botanists for centuries.

Plants and animals are named in Latin purely because the sciences date from a time when Latin was the universal language of the civilised world. A Swedish naturalist, Carl von Linne – who gave even himself a Latin name, Linnaeus – began it all in the eighteenth century when he developed the first system of plant classification. It was, and is, all very simple really.

All plants, like us, have two names. The first name describes the genus or wider classification. All roses, for example, regardless of their colour, habit or size, come within the genus *Rosa*.

The second name denotes the species or specific class. So a rose named after the wife of Sir Joseph Banks is called *Rosa banksiae*. Note that convention demands that the generic or first name starts with a capital letter, while the specific or second name does not.

When a yellow variety (or cultivar) of that rose was introduced, it was given the variety name 'Lutea', which in Latin simply means 'yellow'. Again, convention demands that the variety name should start with a capital letter and be enclosed in single quotes, but niceties like that are only really important to botanists.

However, the Latin name now tells you quite a bit about the plant. You know it's going to be something like the roses you're familiar with; you know whom it was named for, so it's easy to find out when it was introduced; and you can be sure that the flowers are yellow.

Quite a lot of variety names are now in the language of the country where the plant was raised. So you might have a plant with a half-Latin and half-English name, like *Erica arborea* 'Albert's Gold'. The *Erica* tells you that the plant is a heather, because all ericas are. The *arborea* is an indication that it's a tree heather (*arbor* is a tree in Latin), while 'Albert's Gold' obviously says that

the plant was named for an Albert somewhere, perhaps the nurseryman who raised it, and that it's gold in either leaf or flower (in this case, leaf).

Just to make matters more complicated, some hybrids have only the Latin name followed by the variety; thus *Magnolia* 'Elizabeth', named in 1978 after the director of the Brooklyn Botanic Garden where it was raised.

Other names indicate the country of origin. *Wisteria sinensis*, for example, was introduced from China while, slightly confusingly, *Astilbe chinensis* comes from there too. Many new gardeners refer to plants simply as 'Japonica'. That's most confusing of all since this is a specific name that means that the plant originated in Japan – hence *Kerria japonica* and *Chaenomeles japonica* (flowering quince) both different plants with only their country of origin in common.

As far as pronunciation is concerned – well, there are a few plant snobs who pride themselves on the correct Latin they learnt at school, but generally it doesn't really matter. If you say 'tomarto' and I say 'tomater', I'm certainly not going to call the whole thing off! As long as I know what you mean, I'll settle for any pronunciation you like to use. I'm quite sure most sensible gardeners feel the same.

PLANT HUNTERS

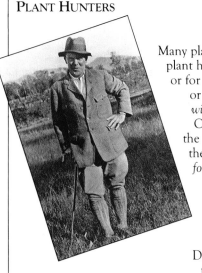

George Forrest.

Many plants are named after the plant hunters who found them or for their friends, colleagues or patrons. Hence *Berberis wilsonae*, introduced from China by E. H. Wilson in the early twentieth century; the beautiful conifer *Abies forrestii*, brought from the same part of the world by George Forrest; and *Berberis darwinii*, introduced by William Lobb but named for Charles Darwin – all little insights that add so much to the interest of the garden.

Most names help the gardener by actually describing the plant and this can be a useful though by no means necessary guide. Most refer to the shape or habit of the plant, the colour of foliage or flowers, or perhaps the shape of the leaves.

NAMES DESCRIBING FLOWERS

campanulata: bell-shaped
floribunda: free-flowering
florida: free-flowering
grandiflora: large-flowered
macropetala: many-petalled
parviflora: small-flowered
pauciflora: carrying few flowers
plena: double
spicata: flowers in spikes

Caltha palustris 'Plena'.

NAMES DESCRIBING PERFUME

aromatica: aromatic
citriodora: lemon-scented
foetida: strong and unpleasant
fragrantissima: most fragrant
graveolens: unpleasant
suaveolens: sweet-smelling

Helleborus foetidus.

NAMES DESCRIBING COLOUR

alba: white
argentea: silver
atropurpurea: red
aurea: gold
bicolor: two colours
caerulea: blue
camea: flesh-coloured
cinerea: ash-grey
coccinea: red
discolor: two colours
flava: pale yellow
glauca: sea-green
incana: grey
lactea: milky-white
lilacina: lilac
lutea: yellow
nigra: black
purpurea: purple
rosea: rose-pink
rubra: red
sanguinea: blood-red
variegata: variegated
versicolor: various or changing colours
violacea: violet
viridis: green

Schizostylis coccinea.

NAMES DESCRIBING HABIT

arborea: tree-like
columnaris: growing into an upright column
fastigiata: the branches grow stiffly upright
fruticosa: shrubby
globosa: rounded in shape
horizontalis: growing horizontally
magnifica: large
major: greater
minor: lesser
nana: dwarf
pendula: weeping
procumbens: hugging the ground
prostrata: growing flat to the ground
repens: creeping and rooting as it grows

Prunus subhirtella pendula rubra.

NAMES DESCRIBING FOLIAGE

angustifolia: narrow
dissectum: finely cut
glabra: without hairs
hirsuta: hairy
latifolia: broad-leaved
macrophylla: large-leaved
microphylla: small-leaved
nitida: shining
palmatum: palm-like
picta: coloured
sempervirens: evergreen

Acer palmatum 'Atropurpureum Dissectum'.

CHAPTER 2

EQUIPMENT

GOOD GARDENING TOOLS should, on the whole, last you for life. Oh, you'll lose several trowels and you'll probably manage to wear out a constantly sharpened knife, but your spade and fork, rake and hoe should, with care, last you well into your eighties or nineties.

But remember that there's no such thing as cheap tools. Unless you can pick them up secondhand, buying the lowest-priced will inevitably cost you more in the end. A much better strategy is to buy only the best, but to collect them slowly, adding to your kit as and when you can afford it. Some equipment, of course, you can make. I find that even when you can afford to go straight out and buy the best, there's a terrific creative pleasure in making your own that money could never buy.

No one knows better than me what a chore it is to be constantly cleaning garden tools. I confess that I'm a great one for putting my spade and fork away covered in soil out of sheer laziness (or often, after a really good day, sheer exhaustion). Nonetheless, there's no doubt that looking after tools not only makes them last longer, but they work more sweetly too. I've therefore devised the quickest, easiest way to do it, I now feel a lot better about tackling the task and my tool kit certainly shows the benefit of a bit of tender loving care.

A few minutes spent cleaning tools after use will ensure that they last and will make them a pleasure to work with.

A starter kit of hand tools

For the first season or so you can get away with the bare minimum of garden tools, which gives you a chance to save up and to drop a few heavy hints around Christmas time. Bear in mind, too, that tools you're going to need only very infrequently, like a shovel, perhaps, or a hedge trimmer, can be hired quite cheaply.

Digging fork and spade The first tool to buy is a good digging fork. It'll double as a spade and a rake, so you could manage the first season with this alone. However, if you have large stones to dig out of a new garden, you will need a spade as well.

Rake A really essential piece of equipment if you're starting a new garden. It'll rake a much finer and more level surface than you'd ever get with the fork.

Dutch hoe This type of hoe is invaluable if you have a large garden. It saves a lot of time where you're growing plants in rows, but in a small garden hand weeding will generally do.

Knife A good knife is essential; I use mine all the time in the garden. It can replace secateurs for pruning small branches and is needed every day for cutting string, dead-heading, etc.

Bucket A plastic bucket doubles as a wheelbarrow for carting weeds, etc., and, used in conjunction with a plastic bottle with small holes pierced or drilled in the cap (see p. 36), makes an effective watering can too.

Garden line This costs next to nothing but is invaluable for landscaping jobs and also for sowing and planting.

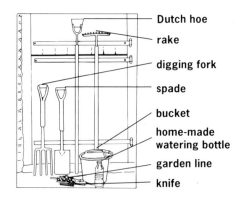

- Dutch hoe
- rake
- digging fork
- spade
- bucket
- home-made watering bottle
- garden line
- knife

Tool maintenance

Buying good tools is pointless unless you look after them. A well-maintained, smooth surface is a joy to work with, but once a spade, fork, rake or trowel becomes pitted with rust, soil sticks to it and gardening becomes a chore.

Wooden handles can be maintained in perfect condition by oiling with a little linseed oil every few weeks. Keep a soaked rag handy for a quick rub down every so often.

Make a point of putting your tools away at night. You need only a few nails banged into the shed wall to keep things ship-shape. If you're not going to use tools for a while, give the metal parts a rub over with an oily rag.

For cleaning tools 'in the field' and before putting them away, make yourself a small wooden scraper that fits into your back pocket. Used regularly while you're digging, it makes life easier and much more pleasant.

Knives and secateurs are worse than useless if they're allowed to get blunt. I keep a small sharpening stone on the kitchen windowsill to give both a sharpen from time to time.

Anything with moving parts like knives and secateurs will benefit from a few drops of oil a couple of times during the season.

Secrets of success

Busy gardeners who persuade themselves that they don't have time to clean tools properly will benefit from the patent, dual-purpose tool cleaner and oiler. To make one, fill a box or tub with sharp sand and pour a bucketful of old engine oil into it. Your garage will throw away plenty so they'll be pleased to let you have some. Before putting digging tools away, shove the blades into the sand

and work them up and down a few times to clean and oil at the same time.

Digging tools

Spade The most used and useful digging tool of all. Buy the very best you can afford. Stainless steel is ludicrously expensive but makes digging a real pleasure, so buy it if you can. Alternatively buy a spade made of forged steel with a good strong socket. Pressed-steel types are useless. For tall people there are now extra-long spades. It's best to try one out first at the garden centre to make quite sure it 'fits'.

Border spade Small spades are available and a much better bet for smaller people. It makes sense to buy a spade you can dig with all day without straining muscles. The same rules apply as when buying an ordinary spade.

Digging fork Very useful, especially for digging heavy soil and for lightly digging between plants. Stainless steel is a pointless luxury unless you're forced to leave the fork out in all weathers. Again, there are pressed-steel types to avoid and long-handled ones for tall people. A potato fork has wider tines and is therefore excellent for digging sandy soil.

Border fork Useful for smaller people and for forking between plants in the border.

Trowel Invaluable for planting small plants, bulbs, etc. Stainless steel is an advantage but bear in mind, before making the extra financial outlay for this material, that trowels have a habit of getting lost. Those with long handles are useful for elderly or disabled gardeners who can't get right down to the ground.

Hand fork Some gardeners find this tool useful, though I never have myself. It is thought to be good for loosening soil when hand weeding. Stainless steel is certainly unnecessary. I know experienced gardeners who use a very-long-handled hand fork for weeding instead of a hoe, but I personally have never been able to get on with one.

Bulb planter Hand planters lift a core of soil, so enabling you to plant bulbs quite quickly. They are useful in soil that holds together well but is not too heavy, since they're quite hard to push into the ground. A larger planter that is pushed in with the foot is much better, especially if planting in grass. I also use one for planting pot-grown wild flowers straight into grass.

Mattock Shaped like a pickaxe with a heavy, hoe-shaped blade on one side and an axe-shaped one on the other. Invaluable for clearing overgrown ground but probably best hired since it won't be used much.

Dung fork A fork with round, curved tines. If you have access to lots of manure you'll find a dung fork extremely useful. For the occasional load, a digging fork will suffice.

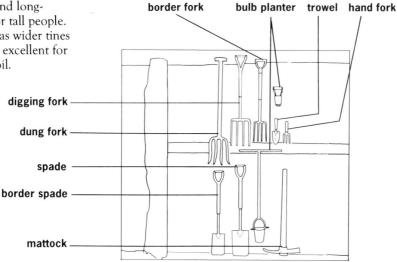

Raking and hoeing

Rake Buy a twelve-to-fourteen-toothed rake with a flat, forged head. Those that look like a strip of steel with nails driven through it are useless. The lighter the rake is, the better. Make sure that the handle's long enough to use comfortably. Much wider rakes are available and are used extensively by landscape gardeners, but though they may appear to make the job easier, they're specialised and difficult to handle.

Springtine rake Used to rake moss and dead grass from the lawn. It's an invaluable tool but it won't be used much, so there's no need to spend a lot of money. This is certainly the best tool for raking in grass seed without altering the levels, so it's best bought early on at the construction stage. Those with plastic or rubber teeth are used for raking up leaves, though the metal ones will do both jobs.

Cultivator A three- or four-pronged tool used to break down clods of soil Especially useful at the beginning of the season when heavy soil has been dug over and left rough. I wouldn't consider one essential, but I know gardeners who swear by them. They're available in several sizes and, as with all tools, it's wise to buy the one that suits you rather than being over-ambitious.

Dutch hoe The most useful of the hoes, this one is used while you walk backwards, leaving the weeds lying loose on the soil to dry out. There are several variations, some with cutting edges on both sides. Most are efficient, but try them out at the garden centre before you buy. Again, make sure that the handle's long enough to allow you to hoe standing up. Keeping the edge sharp makes a great difference to the ease of working, so it pays to file it once or twice a year.

Wheel hoe An excellent, time-saving tool for the gardener with a very large vegetable garden. The hoe can be pushed through rows of plants very quickly indeed, especially if used regularly when weeds are small. Again, it pays to keep the cutting edge sharp by filing it regularly.

Swan-necked hoe Used to draw drills, to ridge potatoes, etc., and to hoe out large weeds with a chopping action. It is a useful but not essential tool, though some gardeners who use one regularly for thinning rows of vegetables achieve a high degree of accuracy and make short work of an arduous task.

Onion hoe This is really nothing more than a miniature version of the swan-necked hoe, designed to be used single-handed. I've found it a most useful tool, especially in small gardens. It enables you to hoe kneeling down near to plants for greater accuracy so that damage is avoided.

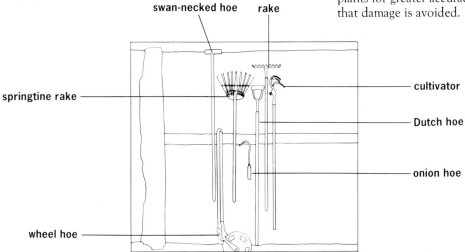

swan-necked hoe   rake

springtine rake

wheel hoe

cultivator

Dutch hoe

onion hoe

Cutting tools

Knife Undoubtedly the most useful of all cutting tools. Nothing fancy with devices for removing stones from horses' hooves is needed, just a good, strong blade. Make sure it's big enough for fairly robust work yet not so big that it pulls your trousers off when you're carrying it in your pocket! But remember that a blunt knife is not only useless but dangerous too. It's *essential* to keep it sharp, so buy a small whetstone as well.

Shears If you have hedges, shears are essential. There are various sizes, so choose a pair that you'll be able to use comfortably for long periods.

Lawn-edging shears Invaluable. A neatly cut edge makes the lawn look much better and spruces up the whole garden. You'll use them regularly and often, so buy a good pair that will last. This is one tool that must *always* be cleaned and well dried after use. Flat lawn shears used for cutting off grass flower stalks are an unnecessary luxury since you can use the hedging shears with a little more effort.

Sheep shears I've found these useful for trimming some shrubs and especially for accurate cutting of the low box hedge that makes up my knot garden.

Secateurs Controversy rages over the parrot-bill *versus* the anvil type of secateurs. I don't think it makes much difference. I prefer the parrot-bill type, but they mustn't be used for branches that are really too big and above all they mustn't be twisted while cutting. Again, keep them sharp. I honestly don't think that there's any evidence to suggest that the anvil type bruises branches.

Loppers I've found these invaluable for dealing with thicker branches. Get a pair with long handles and a cantilevered arrangement of blades which exert more pressure, making the job easy.

Long lopper If you have very tall trees, a long lopper with a saw attachment can be useful. There's even a device for picking fruit from high branches. Generally, though, this is not an essential tool.

Bow saw Useful if you're removing big branches or whole trees, but for most gardens it's used irregularly so is best hired. The smaller saws with a triangular frame are useful for tree-pruning. Blades should be changed regularly: replacements are available for all types of bow saw.

Pruning saw Useful for really large branches. A small folding saw is really all you'll need for most jobs.

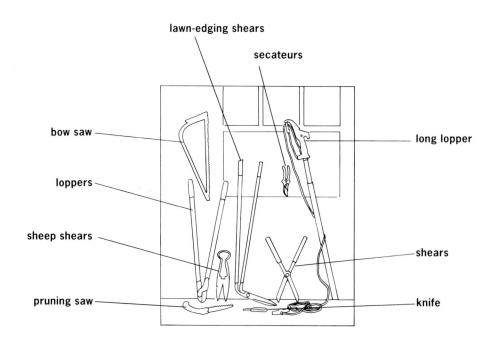

Carrying and watering tools

Bucket What can I say about a bucket? In a small garden it's certainly the best carrying tool there is and doubles as a watering can, at least at first for the novice gardener.

Wheelbarrow The old 'navvy-barrer' is still the best design of all and if you buy it from the builder's merchant it's likely to be the least expensive too. Buy one with a pneumatic wheel which is five hundred times easier to push and make sure that it has a curved strut at the front to enable you to empty it easily.

Sheet A wonderful new invention is the bit of canvas or plastic with a rope handle at each corner. Marvellous for carrying grass cuttings, prunings, etc., with the minimum fuss.

Sack barrow I find a sack barrow with pneumatic tyres invaluable. If you grow lots of tender perennials in large pots which need moving from greenhouse to patio and back again regularly, you will too. They enable one person to lift and cart very heavy weights single-handed.

Watering bottle Make a watering can yourself by piercing holes in the lid of a plastic bottle. A soft cap can be pierced with a large needle, but a hard one must be drilled with the finest of drills. This 'can' has the advantage that no water comes out until you squeeze, so it's ideal in the house where you need perfect control. It's also free.

Watering can In areas where water's short and hosepipes are considered anti-social or are even banned, a watering can is useful outside. In the greenhouse it's essential. Buy a good, long-spouted, plastic one with a fine brass rose.

Water butt In areas of low rainfall a water butt is invaluable. It catches and stores water from the house roof and even bath water can be diverted to it for storage. If you grow acid-loving plants, watering with rainwater will help keep them in good health. Buy a design to suit your house and your taste, but make sure that it has a well-fitting lid to minimise the growth of green algae in the water.

Sprinkler If you have a hose, a sprinkler is essential. You simply can't put on enough water by standing and holding the end of the hose. I like a tall sprinkler on a tripod since this will water over the top of tall plants and so can be used for the lawn, borders and the veg. plot as well.

Hose In large gardens a hose is essential, but in some areas hosepipes are licensed and can be banned in dry weather just when they're most needed. It's much cheaper in the end to buy a better-quality, more expensive hose which will last several years longer than the really cheap ones. In big gardens a hose reel is invaluable too.

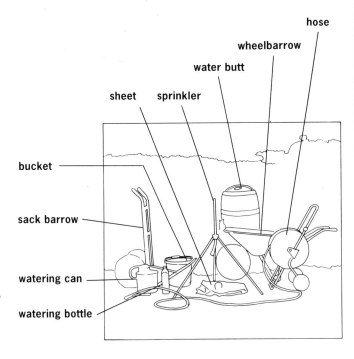

Landscaping tools

Sledgehammer A 3kg (7lb) or so hammer is used quite a lot in the garden for hammering in tree stakes, etc., as well as for construction work, and it's therefore probably best to buy one. There are several different sizes and there's no point in buying one too heavy to handle comfortably and safely.

Bricklayer's line A thin nylon line on two special pins that will neatly slot behind bricks as building progresses. Cheap and worth buying. Many projects have been ruined by the use of a piece of hairy string!

Cold chisel A narrower chisel for cutting stone and for punching holes in walls. Useful to have and will be handy in the house too, so worth buying.

Spirit level Used in almost every landscaping job. It's essential for paving, walling, fencing, etc., and will always be useful so is worth buying. Spirit levels range in length from about 15cm (6in.) to 1.2m (4ft), and if you do a lot of construction it's worth having a short and a long one. But for most purposes buy one about 30–60cm (1–2ft) long and for longer distances use it in conjunction with a straightedge. If you use it when paving or walling, it's absolutely essential to clean it thoroughly after use.

Club hammer There are various local names for the 1.4kg (3lb) hammer used mainly for paving and walling jobs. A useful tool for many other jobs round the garden, so again worth buying.

Bolsters These are wide cold chisels and are used to cut bricks in half. A stone bolster, which is heavier, is ideal for cutting walling stone and paving slabs, though a brick bolster will do at a pinch. They can be hired.

Measuring tape Obviously an essential aid to laying out the garden initially and for any subsequent construction. It's used quite infrequently and is fairly expensive, so it can be hired.

Straightedge For all construction work, a piece of 7.5 × 2.5cm (3 × 1in.) hardwood about 2.7m (9ft) long and planed dead straight is invaluable. The timber merchant will generally be able to machine plane it for you. Keep it dry and lay it flat to make sure it stays straight. Obviously, making do with a piece of timber that's *almost* straight is completely counter-productive.

Bricklayer's trowels A large trowel for handling mortar when laying bricks, stone walls and paving is essential and you'll also need a smaller pointing trowel for finishing work. They'll be used only for construction work, so can be hired, though if you're a do-it-yourselfer too you'll find the smaller one invaluable for jobs in the house. Make sure that you wash every bit of cement off them at the end of each day's work.

Shovel Unless you mix a lot of your own compost, you're unlikely to need a shovel except for construction work. In that case, as with most construction tools, it's best to hire it. The angle of the shovel blade makes it much easier to use than a spade for jobs like mixing concrete, so it's not worth making do. Again, make sure that you wash it well after mixing concrete.

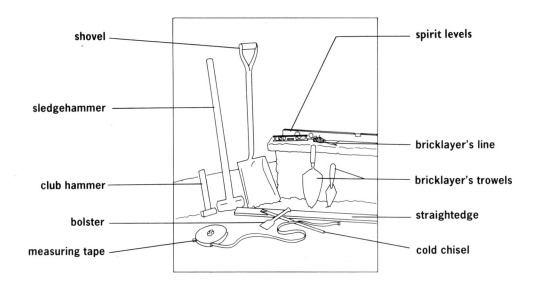

Miscellaneous tools

Line A string line is always useful and I don't need to tell you how to make it, except to advise nylon twine.

Sieve A 6mm (¼in.) sieve is worth having for occasional use in the garden and is essential for the greenhouse. If you don't expect to use it much, make your own: buy a piece of 6mm (¼in.) mesh, knock the bottom out of a shallow box and replace it with the mesh. For really keen gardeners a 6mm (¼in.) mesh and a larger one will always be useful.

Sprayer There are all sizes of sprayer from the tiny pump-action types to the large knapsack sprayers. Generally a pressure sprayer in between is ideal, depending on the size of your garden. However, many garden insecticides and fungicides are now available packed in their own trigger sprayers, so this is a tool that could wait. *Always* wash the sprayer out thoroughly after use.

Spacing board This is an invaluable piece of equipment you can make yourself. I have two and wouldn't be without them. They're home-made from 7.5 × 2.5cm (3 × 1in.) softwood; one is 3m (10ft) long and the other 1.2m (4ft). Centimetres and metres (or feet and inches) are marked with sawcuts and numbered with large-headed nails. I use my boards continually in the vegetable garden where they save a great deal of time and help me achieve neat, perfectly spaced rows.

Edging iron Used for cutting the lawn edges dead straight. With practice you can do the same job with a sharp spade, which is what I use. But it does take practice, so you may feel it's worth buying an edging iron.

Roller A roller's of very little use if you have one on your mower. For rolling new paths you could hire one, but I can think of no other reason to buy one. Some rollers can be filled with water to vary the weight and these make good general-purpose tools.

Lawn spreader If you use granular lawn fertiliser, a spreader will save you hours and will distribute the fertiliser evenly and safely. Most are calibrated to suit one manufacturer's products, so they do tie you down a bit. Again, they can be hired.

Dibber For jobs like planting cabbages or wallflower seedlings, a dibber is very useful. Make your own from a broken fork handle or a couple of bits of wood screwed together in the shape of a T.

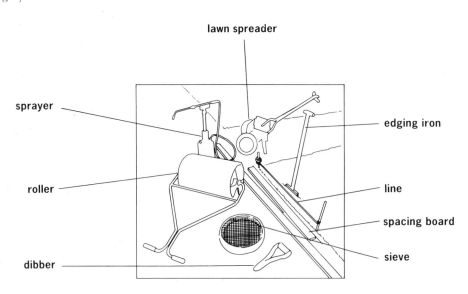

lawn spreader

sprayer

roller

dibber

edging iron

line

spacing board

sieve

Mowers

Most gardens have some grass and, if yours does, you'll need a mower. This is one of the biggest investments you'll make in the garden at one time, so you'll need to choose carefully. Think about the best method of cutting – either with a cylinder or a rotary mower – and the power source, which will be a petrol engine, electricity or plain muscle.

For new gardeners the biggest factor to be considered will no doubt be cost. With mowers, as with everything else, the only way to get a bargain is to buy secondhand, so you may well be forced to buy a cheap machine to start with and progress from there. Nevertheless, properly looked after, even a bottom-of-the-range electric mower should last from five to ten years.

POWER SOURCE
Power will come either from petrol or mains electricity. Battery mowers are also now produced and the rechargeable is just around the corner.

The advantage with mains electricity is convenience. It's just a case of plugging in and away you go. Electric mowers are also cheap and extremely easy to use. For these reasons they have become the most popular machines bought.

The main disadvantage is that, in the wrong hands, electricity can be dangerous. But if you make sure you have a contact breaker at the plug end and that the machine is well maintained and, of course, that you don't mow in the rain or when the grass is wet, an electric mower is perfectly safe. The trailing cable is a nuisance because you must avoid cutting it and it tends to restrict your mobility in a large garden.

Petrol mowers are much more versatile in that they give you the freedom to go anywhere, however big the garden. They're heavier, so the roller does some good and also produces attractive stripes on the lawn. All new mowers now run on unleaded petrol.

Like all petrol engines they can be troublesome to start, though modern engines are greatly improved. They do need constant refuelling and, if you need to refuel while in the middle of mowing, it's vital to take the machine off the lawn as spilled petrol will kill the grass.

Push mowers are relatively cheap, though more expensive than many electric types. For all but the elderly or infirm they're easy to use and good, enjoyable exercise. Using them is completely non-polluting.

CUTTING METHOD
Basically, it's a straightforward choice: if you want a very fine lawn, buy a cylinder mower with as many blades in the cylinder as possible. This type of mower cuts the grass like scissors.

If you have rough grass to cut infrequently, buy a rotary type. This one has a horizontal plate with blades that cut through the grass like a scythe. There's little difference between those with wheels and the hover types that float over the surface on a cushion of air, except when cutting steep banks. Here the hover mower really comes into its own because of its superior manoeuvrability.

For the best lawns you'll need a mower that picks up the grass cuttings. Remember, too, that grass cuttings are easily trodden into the house if left on the lawn.

Push mower Ideal for the young beginner gardener. The push mower with a roller is to be preferred since a sidewheel mower makes cutting right up to the edge of the lawn very difficult.

Wheeled rotary Ideal for cutting long grass infrequently. Some have driven wheels but cheaper models need to be pushed. There are electric and petrol-engined types.

Electric cylinder A very easy-to-use machine and relatively cheap. Ideal for smaller lawns and for gardeners lacking the muscle (or the energy) to push.

Petrol cylinder Probably the most popular and certainly the best for larger gardens with fine lawns.

Hover rotary This can be electric or petrol-engined. Both types are easy to use and the electric ones are cheap.

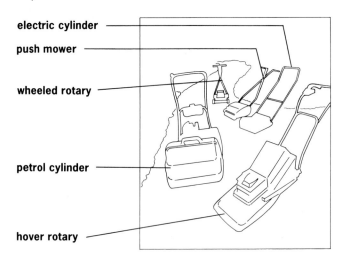

electric cylinder
push mower
wheeled rotary
petrol cylinder
hover rotary

Rotavators and large cutting tools

To anyone with a very large garden or to those who, for one reason or another, find digging difficult, a rotavator will prove invaluable. It's a machine that takes a bit of getting used to and it has its disadvantages, but there's no doubt that it saves a great deal of work.

There are small electric models which can only be regarded as tools for light weeding. For digging, a petrol or diesel-powered machine is essential. Even so, don't expect to dig deeper than about 15–23cm (6–9in.). Remember also that the blades do tend to glaze the bottom of the trench, forming a hard layer, especially on clay soils, so avoid continually rotavating at one depth.

Rotavators are, of course, expensive but can be hired by the day quite cheaply. For the initial cultivation of a new garden, it's worthwhile considering hiring, since one day will be enough to finish even quite a large area.

RIGHT **Rotavator powered through the rotors** Can tend to run away with you until you get used to it. When the rotors hit hard ground and want to run over the top, resist the temptation to pull backwards; instead, push the handles down to press the skid into the soil as a brake.

LEFT **Rotavator powered through the wheels** Easier to use and gives a better finish. Larger types are quite heavy, so make sure that you can manage a particular model before buying or hiring. Some have a reverse gear which is invaluable for manoeuvring in tight corners. At first sight the hire charges seem expensive but a large machine like this will get through a great deal of work in a day. On allotment sites or a new housing estate it's sensible to get together with your neighbours since the transport to the site is a large part of the cost.

BELOW **Smaller rechargeable hedge trimmer** This will last about half an hour between chargings. I think it's a marvellous tool without any of the encumbrance of the mains electric cable or the weight of the petrol engine. And generally you want a change of job after half an hour anyway. Much research continues on this type of tool so new, improved models are becoming available all the time.

Shredder A fairly new introduction, and when you buy one you'll wonder how you ever managed before. There are electric and petrol models of various sizes and, again, they're good candidates for communal buying or hiring. Most will take quite large branches and certainly all the annual prunings and convert them into an attractive mulch (see p. 76).

LEFT **Chain saw** Without doubt the most dangerous machine ever invented. It's impossible to make safe, so if you're considering buying one, my advice is: don't! If you are determined to go ahead, make sure that you take a training course with an expert and that you have all the protective clothing necessary – which will cost you considerably more than the saw. Much better: get a contractor in for the rare times you'd use it.

Electric or petrol hedge trimmer Will save hours of work if you have large areas of hedge. Both types work on a reciprocal action and are quite easy to use but naturally require care and some protective clothing. Gloves and goggles are recommended. With electric machines, make sure that the cable is out of the way over your shoulder and that you work away from it. Naturally, you should also fit a contact breaker at the socket. Don't use electrical appliances outside in wet weather.

Other machinery

There are several machines available that are of only marginal value to most gardeners. Some may be useful for just a very short time in the season, but gardeners with a small plot may find it worthwhile considering a joint purchase with neighbours or persuading their garden club to buy one for use by all the members.

Brush cutter Often available as an extra fitting to a strimmer. It is quite a dangerous tool and not, in my view, to be recommended for the amateur gardener. In any case it would be used very infrequently, so is better hired, preferably with operator. Use one only when wearing heavy-duty footwear, thick gloves and goggles.

Vacuum cleaner For the very large garden, a vacuum cleaner will blow leaves into a pile where they can be sucked into a bag for quick and easy transport. An excellent machine but obviously expensive and a bit of an indulgence even in bigger gardens.

Electric or petrol edge trimmer Useful only for the very large garden. My own garden has over 2km of edge to cut so I find this tool invaluable. However, it has to be said that hand-operated edging shears make a better job and are not too arduous to use in a smaller space. Some strimmers have an edge-trimming facility, making the double-use tool a much more economical proposition. It's important to gear the garden to the machine by keeping deep edges to the borders.

Leaf picker Very useful indeed, but only in the autumn. Certainly no gardener worth his or her salt should waste the leaves that fall in the garden, nor should he or she leave them to rot on grass or plants, where they encourage fungus diseases. This is an excellent candidate for shared buying and the hand-pushed types are easy to use, efficient and not too costly. You'll need to use the machine regularly before the leaves blow into the borders.

Strimmer Useful for cutting areas that are difficult to reach with the mower – around garden statues or ornaments, for example. If you have only a very small lawn and are not too concerned about the quality of the grass, you might consider one instead of a mower. The grass is cut very effectively with a spinning nylon line which wears out periodically but is cheap and easy to replace and is not dangerous. Newer models will automatically pay out more line as it wears out. Petrol and electric models are available with the same pros and cons as mowers (see p.42).

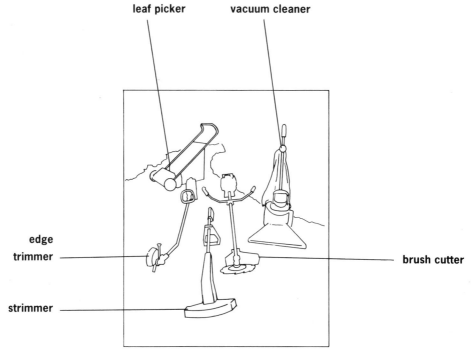

leaf picker vacuum cleaner

edge trimmer brush cutter

strimmer

Sheds, storage and trailers

If you haven't got a garage or you're unusual enough actually to keep your car in it, a shed is invaluable for the garden. Tools and machinery will last much longer if protected from the elements, so it's worthwhile arranging racks and storage space inside to accommodate them. If you can made the shed frost-proof, perhaps by lining it with building paper or hardboard, it will serve to store vegetables and fruit over winter as well as those plants that require little light during the dormant period, like geraniums and fuchsias. Don't forget that a lot of the frost comes through the floor, so an old carpet is the order of the day. A bench and a vice have obvious advantages, particularly for the do-it-yourself gardener.

Standard wooden pent-roof shed Make sure that you treat it with a water- or copper-based preservative to avoid damage to nearby plants. A covering of climbing plants turns a utility item into a real feature.

Metal shed This will last forever and requires no maintenance. The design is perhaps better suited to modern houses.

Large tool chest For very small gardens, it's possible to buy a large tool chest which can stand outside and accommodate all the necessary tools. I have even seen an old wardrobe painted up and planted round and used as a tiny garden shed.

Half-shed, half-greenhouse This type of building is useful where lack of space prohibits the inclusion of both shed *and* greenhouse. While the glass area won't allow quite as much light in as a greenhouse, it will still grow perfectly satisfactory plants.

Car trailer This will soon pay for itself, especially if you have a large plot. It can be used to collect bulky material like manure and straw and will save expensive delivery charges for items that can't be fitted into the car. I also use mine like a rubbish skip to take to the tip any waste that won't rot down.

It's worthwhile checking the law about trailers before use. In the UK, for instance, the lights, brake lights and indicators should be working even if you're using the trailer during daylight hours. There are also rules about the amount of overhang at the back. If you need to carry anything long, fit a cross-bar at the front of the trailer so that any overhang is at the front rather than at the back.

Compost containers

Every garden should have two compost containers. Soil fertility is based on regular additions of organic matter, the cheapest form of which is garden compost made from vegetable waste (see pp. 70–1). Two containers are needed so that one can be filled and then left for the compost to rot down while the other is filling up. Note, too, that it's important to build up heat inside the container so it's best to avoid holes in the sides. Ample air will come in through the bottom. A lid to stop the material getting too wet and to retain heat is essential.

If you're going to build your own, it makes sense to build a double bin, keeping the whole unit neat, tidy and in one place and saving on the cost of one wall. Floorboards make an ideal building material and, if you buy secondhand from a demolition contractor, you'll halve the cost of the container.

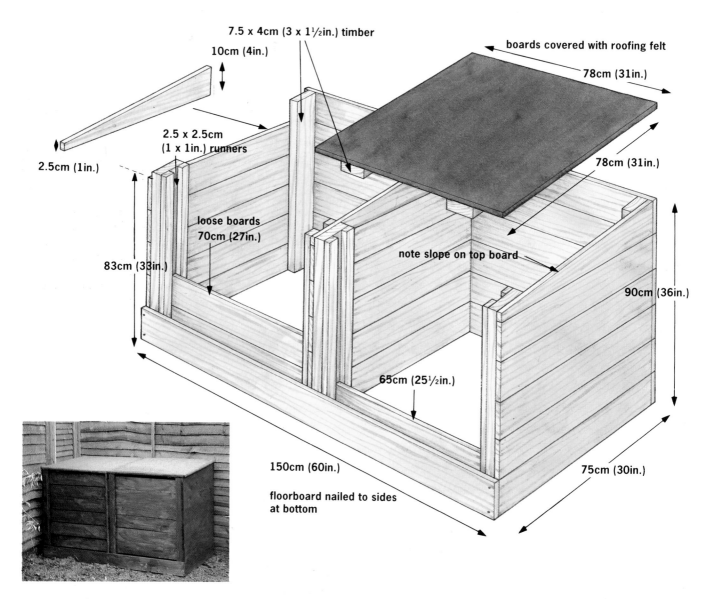

7.5 x 4cm (3 x 1½in.) timber

10cm (4in.)

boards covered with roofing felt

78cm (31in.)

2.5 x 2.5cm (1 x 1in.) runners

2.5cm (1in.)

78cm (31in.)

loose boards 70cm (27in.)

note slope on top board

83cm (33in.)

90cm (36in.)

65cm (25½in.)

150cm (60in.)

75cm (30in.)

floorboard nailed to sides at bottom

The finished container will grace the corner of the vegetable plot.

MAKING YOUR OWN COMPOST BIN

1 Cut all the floorboards for the sides to size and nail them to the uprights. (Secondhand floor joists are ideal as uprights.) Note that there are no spaces between the boards in order to avoid heat loss. Nail on the first slat, taking care to check the right angle.

2 When two sides and the centre wall have been made, set them on end and nail on the boards to make the back wall, checking carefully that they are quite square. Nail into the uprights, not the ends of the boards.

3 Make the runners for the removable sides by nailing two strips on to the front uprights. Check before finally fixing that they are slightly wider apart than the width of the boards, allowing enough room for some swelling when the wood is wet.

4 Cut the loose boards for the removable sides and check that they fit loosely. Then paint all exposed wood with a water- or copper-based preservative. If you're using new wood it's worth having it pressure-treated with preservative.

5 The lids are made with the same material as the sides but are covered with roofing felt held on with large-headed nails.

A home-made container is easy to build but there are plenty of ready-made types too. Plastic bins are good value and take up little garden room. Tumbler types have the disadvantage that they hold only small amounts, so several would be needed.

Cloches

Cloches provide a cheap and efficient means of producing early crops of vegetables (see p. 246), fruit and flowers. By protecting plants from the weather and from flying insects and birds, they can also greatly improve quality. They can be used as an alternative coldframe for acclimatising greenhouse-raised plants to lower temperatures outside prior to planting out and they're invaluable in protecting vulnerable plants from frost throughout the winter. There are dozens of types available and I restrict myself to those I have found most useful.

Tent cloche This type can be made from glass or plastic and, since it really needs only one simple clip to hold it together, is relatively cheap. It has an obvious height disadvantage.

Field frame Ideal for deep-bed growing (see p. 244) and to double as a coldframe. Being large it seems expensive but, on a square-metre comparison, works out quite cheap. It's easily handled by one person.

Barn cloche This type of glass cloche has been around for years, with very good reason. It's tall enough to accommodate most crops for as long as is necessary, it's easy to handle and it's versatile. Its only disadvantage is that glass is expensive and, of course, eminently breakable. It is possible to glaze with rigid plastic or polycarbonate.

Floating cloche The cheapest form of all. It consists of a perforated-polythene or spun-polypropylene sheet that is simply laid over the crop which pushes it up as it grows. Polythene will not protect from frost but will improve quality, while polypropylene will protect from slight frost.

MAKING YOUR OWN SIMPLE CLOCHE

1 A very simple cloche can be made at home. Cut 4 × 2.5 cm (1½ × 1in.) lengths of timber to size to make the base and join at the corners with metal angle brackets to form a rectangle.

2 Drill four holes as shown and bend two lengths of wire or coat hangers to form arcs. Slip the ends of the wires into the holes.

3 Cover with clear polythene, using drawing pins or paper staples to fix it to the wooden base.

MAKING YOUR OWN TUNNEL CLOCHE

A tunnel cloche is about the cheapest supported type available and is invaluable in the larger vegetable garden. The fact that it forms a long, continuous run reduces its versatility and it's not as attractive as a glass cloche, but making your own is very easy.

1 RIGHT Make up a jig using timber 130cm (4½ft) long. Put in bolts, one 15cm (6in.) from one end and another 30cm (1ft) from the other end. Then cut pieces of thick wire the length of the jig. Start with the end of the wire level with the end of the jig and twist it round the first bolt 15cm (6in.) from the end.

2 Twisting round the other bolt will automatically give you a length of wire with two eyelets and two 15cm (6in.) 'legs'.

3 Mark out the position on the ground with two lines 45cm (18in.) apart and push the legs into the ground up to the eyelets. Space the hoops 90cm (3ft) apart.

4 Bury the polythene at one end and drape it over the hoops, pulling tight and burying the other end. Hold it on by fixing string to the eyelets to strain the sheeting tight.

Cloches

MAKING YOUR OWN LANTERN CLOCHE

Cloches are very useful in the ornamental borders as well as the vegetable plot, but there are few, if any, that look attractive enough to use where they'll be seen regularly and for the whole of the winter. The Victorian lantern cloche was ideal but this is now a collector's item and quite expensive. However, an attractive if more modern equivalent can be made quite easily from rigid plastic.

1 Measure the plastic and cut it with a special tool, readily available at do-it-yourself stores. It's best to score both sides before snapping it.

2 Make up a jig with wood strips nailed to a plywood square. Coat the edges of the cloche base with impact adhesive and hold them together in the jig.

The finished cloche is tailor-made for covering small groups of vegetables grown in an ornamental kitchen garden or for protecting individual plants in the borders. Stick to the recommended dimensions as larger cloches are unstable.

3 Glue the top in the same way and finally fix both parts together with adhesive. Tape the edges with outdoor-quality clear tape.

4 Cut a wooden plug to fit inside the top of the cloche, drill it and finally screw in a brass carrying knob.

BIRD'S EYE VIEW OF A JIG

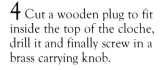

3mm (¹/₈in.) plywood

45cm (18in.)

2.5 x 2.5 x 45cm (1 x 1 x 18in.) wood strips

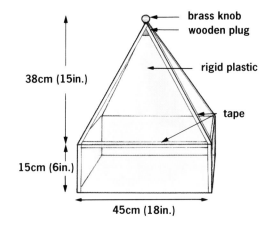

brass knob
wooden plug
rigid plastic
tape

38cm (15in.)

15cm (6in.)

45cm (18in.)

MAKING YOUR OWN DEEP-BED TUNNEL CLOCHE

A tunnel cloche for a deep bed must be much stouter than one made with wire, since it has to span 1.2m (4ft). It can be easily made with alkathene water pipe available at the builder's merchant. It's not quite as cheap but should last literally forever and is easy to store flat at the end of the season. For larger or more permanent structures use larger-bore alkathene pipe and longer dowelling to make the 'legs'.

1 Cut the pipe into 1.8m (6ft) lengths and push a 30cm (1ft) piece of 1.3cm (½in.) dowelling up each end for half its length.

2 Drill and hold it in place with a nail which must point along the line of the cloche or it'll tear the polythene cover.

3 Set the hoops 1.8m (6ft) apart across the bed and, just as with the wire cloche (p. 53), bury the polythene and stretch it across the hoops.

4 Tie a piece of nylon twine to the nail on one side, pass it over the top of the cloche and tie it to the other nail, so tightening the polythene.

5 When access to the crops is needed, simply push up the sides of the polythene.

Secrets of success

For single plants or for taking just a few cuttings in summer, a cut-off plastic bottle is a cheap and easy-to-make mini-cloche. It can get very hot inside, so always leave the top off.

Coldframes

A coldframe will greatly increase the scope of your gardening (see p. 316). There are several types available ready-made, in both wood and aluminium. Most manufactured frames are satisfactory, so choice generally comes down simply to size and price. Strangely the aluminium ones are often cheaper than those made of wood. It's also not too difficult to make your own from floorboards which, if bought secondhand, will significantly reduce the cost. A trip to a local demolition contractor's yard will generally yield quantities of floorboards and also joists which make excellent supports for the corners. However, I find new roofing laths very cheap (and useful for a range of jobs), so I buy them in bundles: they're ideal for the frame lid.

A frame made of aluminium and glass will let in maximum light but tends to be colder than wood in winter.

MAKING YOUR OWN COLDFRAME

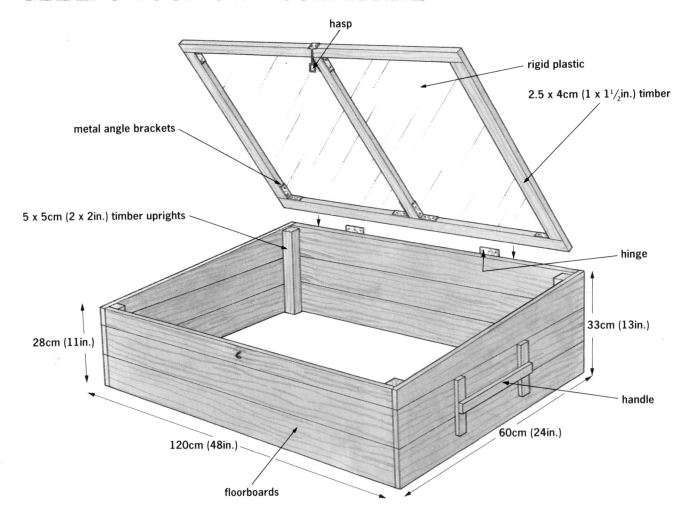

hasp

rigid plastic

2.5 x 4cm (1 x 1$\frac{1}{2}$in.) timber

metal angle brackets

5 x 5cm (2 x 2in.) timber uprights

hinge

33cm (13in.)

28cm (11in.)

handle

60cm (24in.)

120cm (48in.)

floorboards

1 Carefully measure all timbers and cut them to size first.

2 Floorboards are tongued and grooved, so on the top boards only you'll have to plane off the tongue.

3 Hold the boards at the corners by screwing them to the 5 × 5cm (2 × 2in.) uprights.

4 The frame of the lid is made with roofing laths held at the corners with metal angle brackets.

5 Before fitting the lid, fix a handle on each end. Paint the lid with a water- or copper-based wood preservative.

6 The lid is covered with rigid plastic which is screwed on. Note the washers under the screws which help protect the plastic against shattering.

7 Fix the lid with small hinges and finally screw a hasp-and-staple catch to the front.

Secrets of success

The cheapest frame is made from a wooden apple box with a piece of rigid plastic placed on top and held with nylon twine and a strong elastic band hooked over a nail. The shading can be a piece of greenhouse shade netting or even an old onion bag begged from the greengrocer. The frame is small but useful for propagating.

The right clothing

Gardening is by no means a hazardous pastime, though it has to be said that an alarming number of outpatients seen by hospital casualty departments have been rushed there from their gardens. The most frequent accident is the garden fork through the foot, and that's just plain silly. Sensible precautions could almost eliminate accidents and much of the solution lies in kitting yourself out with the right clothes. If you do this right from the start then you'll hardly have to think about being extra careful at all.

LEFT I don't wear any special clothing when I spray, but then I use only harmless seaweed, one completely innocuous caterpillar control or plain water. However, if I can't persuade you not to use chemicals, at least let me convince you of the need to dress for the job. Waterproof gloves are essential and you should still wash your hands afterwards. Rubber boots should be worn and goggles are vital whatever chemicals you spray. If you're using something known to be poisonous, a face mask is certainly advisable. Make sure, too, that you always wear a waterproof jacket.

BELOW Good, strong gloves are also well worth their place in your gardening wardrobe. You'll need them for all hard-landscaping jobs like paving and walling and also for working with some of the more prickly plants. Just try pruning thorny roses without them! Buy tough ones to start with, and if they get wet, dry them slowly to avoid hardening. If you find it more comfortable to work kneeling down, a pair of knee pads or a kneeling mat make it a whole lot more comfortable.

RIGHT I wear stout leather boots for all gardening jobs. They're comfortable, warm in winter and as safe as houses. They're particularly important when you're doing jobs like rotavating, or when you're working with hard materials like paving slabs. Keep them waterproof with a regular lick of dubbin.

LEFT If you use a shredder, you'll need strong gloves and goggles or a face shield. Shredders are very noisy machines, so some form of ear protection is also advisable. I always use a special helmet made for chain-saw use. It incorporates a face guard and ear muffs too, and, of course, protects the head from flying chips. Alternatively you can wear a cap and a pair of cheaper ear muffs. If the latter are not available at the garden centre, try the nearest agricultural merchant or lawnmower dealer.

Winter digging is a great joy, especially when the weather's sharp and clear. But if you work up a sweat you might not notice the cold wind whistling round your exposed back – until the following morning. Always make sure that you wear some kind of sweater or body warmer that keeps the vulnerable small of your back warm – it should be long enough to cover you well even when you're continually bending. I find that the sleeveless types of body warmer protect my back while not impeding freedom of movement.

CHAPTER 3
SOIL AND CULTIVATIONS

THE SOIL is the gardener's raw material. If it's treated with respect, nurtured, coddled and fed like the precious commodity it is, it'll repay you a thousand times over. In ancient times many civilisations worshipped the soil as 'Mother Earth', believing it to be the source of all that was good. They were not far wrong at that.

Mind you, if you've just moved into a new house where the builders have left you with a muddy sea of subsoil growing nothing but a crop of old bricks, bits of wire and hardened cement bags, you may not agree. But miraculously, with a bit of help from nature and a lot of work from you, even that can be brought back into fertility.

Unlike the modern farmer, the gardener should aim to create a *living, breathing* soil. In its natural state it contains billions of organisms, most of which are working away to your benefit to help produce strong, healthy plants. Of course, even the gardener expects far more from his or her soil than nature ever intended, so you'll need to put a lot more back in. But if you build that healthy foundation, a successful, beautiful and productive garden follows naturally and quite inevitably.

Treat your soil with all the respect and care possible and it'll always repay you with healthy, vigorous flowers, fruit and vegetables.

Soil types

There are five major soil types that gardeners may have to contend with and each requires a slightly different management technique. In fact, most soils will be a mixture of two or more types and all garden soil should contain a certain amount of organic matter too, so it's impossible to be too precise. However, the nature of the predominant constituent will determine the type of soil you have to cultivate. Obviously, the first step is to get to know it.

Clay The particles of a clay soil are very small, so they compact together tightly, limiting drainage and air flow. This makes clay soils feel smooth and sticky when wet and hard as rock when dry. Nonetheless, they hold moisture well and, with it, necessary plant food. So, properly managed, clay soils will produce excellent plants in the end.

Sand Relatively large particles put this type of soil at the other end of the range. Sandy soils feel rough and gritty to the touch and are very well drained and aerated. They therefore need constant feeding and watering. But they warm up quickly and can be easily cultivated at most times of the year and always earlier in the season than clay.

Silt This is soil that has been deposited by a river. The particles are small, giving the soil a soft and silky feel when rubbed between the fingers. Like clay, silt has the disadvantages of bad drainage and aeration but can be improved in the same way.

Chalk One of the most restricting soils because the gritty nature and large particles make it free-draining and hungry like sand. Alas, chalk soil is naturally also very limy, so the range of plants it will support is somewhat limited. It has a pale appearance and often white lumps of free chalk can be seen. However, with diligent cultivation and careful choice of plants, chalk soil can still support excellent growth.

Peat Some of the world's best farming land was originally peat bog, so this soil can produce excellent growth. It's dark brown or black and feels wet and spongy to the touch. It can be difficult to manage in that it often lies wet in winter and dries out fast in summer. Its acid nature makes liming necessary for most plants.

Loam This is the common name for a mixture of soils and is what most gardeners will find in their plot. Heavy loams have a predominance of clay, while light loams are mainly sand. All contain organic matter. After a few years of good cultivation, all but the very extreme garden soils will eventually become what gardeners' dreams are made of – good loam.

Treatment of different soil types

Even the heaviest blue clay, the rockiest mountainside or the squelchiest bog can be turned into a beautiful and satisfying garden – eventually. I make no pretence that it's easy or that it's quick. Heavy clay can take at least a couple of years to become workable, while the lightest sand or chalk soils need applications of organic matter every year – forever. But the rewards are great.

Bear in mind, too, that just growing things in any soil will improve it. Roots break up heavy clay and hold light soils together. As they die off and the plants' foliage is incorporated too, they provide a home for soil organisms, all of which contribute to the improvement. So, even if you do nothing at all but cover the soil with plants, it'll improve year by year.

Nothing damages clay or silt soils as much as trampling all over them when they're wet. Try to avoid this by working off boards whenever possible. The first step to improve these types of soil is to incorporate coarse grit into the top levels. The grit should be at least 3mm (⅛in.) in diameter. The amount to use depends on the soil but should be about a barrowload per 2–3sq.m (2–3sq.yds). This will make a permanent physical improvement. After that, incorporate as much organic matter as possible each year and try to keep the soil covered with plants for most of the year.

Sandy and chalky soils can generally be worked very shortly after rain. Improvement consists of continued applications of organic matter whenever possible. On the vegetable garden or where borders are being cultivated, it should be dug in during the autumn and winter. During the growing season, use all kinds of organic matter as a mulch between plants. This will quickly be worked into the soil by worms and weather.

RIGHT It's normally advised that clay soils should be dug in the winter and left rough for the frost to break down. That's good advice, particularly if the garden is plagued with slugs or other soil pests, since it will help kill some by exposure to frost. However, where manure or compost is hard to come by, an alternative is to grow a green manure crop in winter and dig it in during the spring cultivations (see p. 73).

ABOVE Peat soils are high in organic matter, so it's generally not necessary to add any. They are, of course, acid, so you'll need to lime the vegetable plot and to choose acid-lovers for the borders, but that's no problem. Time of cultivation is not important, but peat soils do tend to dry out quickly, so some watering may be necessary. They're also low in nutrients and you'll therefore need to add more than usual out of the bag.

RIGHT Vegetable growers with sandy soil, particularly in dry areas, are advised to dig as soon as possible in the autumn to allow the soil to absorb as much winter moisture as possible. In spring all that's needed then is to rake the surface lightly to avoid, as much as possible, losing water by evaporation. And, of course, adding manure or compost makes a huge improvement.

ABOVE Clay soils can also be improved chemically by a process known as 'flocculation', a complex chemical reaction triggered when lime is added to the soil. It encourages the tiny clay particles to stick together to form larger 'crumbs', so improving drainage and aeration (see p. 14). Bear in mind that the addition of lime will also affect soil acidity, so it should not be used where acid-loving plants are being grown. Here gypsum (calcium sulphate) could be substituted. However, whichever you use, don't expect dramatic improvement. Only the surface of the soil will be affected.

Soil conditioners

There's no doubt that the best soil conditioner of all is animal manure. It varies somewhat, depending mainly on the animal it originally came from, but whichever you can get, grab it with both hands because it'll improve the soil like nothing else.

The animals' bedding provides the bulk which will eventually rot down to form humus, while their waste provides not only the fuel for the rotting process but many plant nutrients too. The resulting humus makes a home for billions of soil organisms which, in their rotting activities, also make nutrients available to plants. If you could acquire enough manure there would be no need to use man-made fertiliser at all but, unless you raise the animals yourself, that's a bit of a Utopian dream these days. All animal manures contain a full range of trace elements (see p. 17). While the nutrient content looks low compared with that of artificial fertilisers, remember that you'll be using very much more manure.

Some animals are bedded on straw, which makes much the best manure. Others rest on wood shavings which, although they rot much more slowly, are still useful. However, both types must be composted in a pile for at least six months and preferably for a year to cool them down and to rid them of any toxins or herbicides that might persist (in the case of straw). In winter cover the heap with polythene to stop plant foods washing out.

Horses bedded on straw provide the gardener with one of the best soil conditioners of all.

Horse manure Excellent and the hottest of all manures, so ideal for use in the hot-bed (see p. 72). It must be stacked for at least six months (preferably for a year) in order to cool it down or it'll scorch young roots and do more harm than good. In some areas it's much easier to come by than other types. Typical nutrient content: nitrogen 0.6 per cent; phosphorus 0.6 per cent; potassium 0.4 per cent.

Chicken manure Very powerful and often dried and used as a fertiliser. However, mixed with straw bedding, it makes an excellent manure. It should be stacked for at least a year, though the very best way to use it, in my view, is to mix it into the compost heap where it will help to rot down green material rapidly. In many areas gardeners with large gardens can keep their own chickens to provide a constantly renewable source of manure. Typical nutrient content: nitrogen 1.5 per cent; phosphorus 1.5 per cent; potassium 0.5 per cent.

Secrets of success

All animal manures are valuable, so it's worthwhile contacting local pigeon fanciers, rabbit enthusiasts and goat keepers who are often only too pleased to dispose of their waste products. Even in small quantities, they're ideal for use as a compost activator, although be careful when using them as they can be very strong, particularly bird manures.

Sheep manure Not normally available like the other types of manure because the animals are not usually housed inside. However, if you have sheep nearby, it's worthwhile asking the farmer if you can pick up sheep droppings from the fields for use as a liquid fertiliser (see p. 84). Typical nutrient content: nitrogen 0.8 per cent; phosphorus 0.4 per cent; potassium 0.5 per cent.

Pig manure Somewhat wet and cold, so perhaps not the first choice on heavy soils, though ideal for light ones. However, if it's a choice between this or nothing, it's still worthwhile. Stack it for a year before use. Typical nutrient content: nitrogen 0.6 per cent; phosphorus 0.4 per cent; potassium 0.6 per cent.

Farmyard manure Made from cow muck, this is probably the best type of all. Though it is not as hot as horse manure, it will compost down to make a light, warm soil conditioner which is full of nutrients and easy to use. Typical nutrient content: nitrogen 0.6 per cent; phosphorus 0.3 per cent; potassium 0.5 per cent.

Alternative soil conditioners

If animal manures are unavailable, you'll have to resort to one of the alternatives, most of which can be bought in bags at the garden centre. Look upon them purely as soil conditioners since their nutrient value is negligible. They're rather more expensive than animal manures but, in the absence of the latter, invaluable for conditioning soil.

Spent mushroom compost
A waste product of the mushroom industry, this consists of rotted horse manure plus a little peat or coir and some lime. It has the disadvantage that it's naturally alkaline, though before selling it for garden use some growers are now skimming off the top layer which contains the lime and it looks as if this will become common practice in the near future. An excellent material in the vegetable garden or on already chalky soils.

Shredded prunings These make a superb mulching material with much the same properties as bark, so don't dig them in. I compost shreddings with all the old potting compost from the greenhouse to make a fine mulching material (see p. 76).

Cocoa-shell A waste product from chocolate factories, this consists of the outer husk of the cocoa bean and is relatively high in nitrogen. It makes an excellent weed-inhibiting mulch and can be dug in. Cocoa-shell is said to repel slugs too. It has the great advantage of a high degree of acidity, so it can be used to acidify limy soil.

Spent hops A waste product from the brewing industry and somewhat hard to come by since many brewers sell them under contract. They can be used as a mulch or composted and dug in.

Seaweed Another excellent conditioner for gardeners who live within access of a beach. It can be used straight away or composted first. It contains an alginate which helps bind soil particles together, thus improving drainage and aeration, and it includes a full range of trace elements.

Leafmould One of the finest of all soil conditioners and best used in the top few inches where it will create a superb seed bed. To make it, collect all the leaves you can and follow the instructions on p. 71.

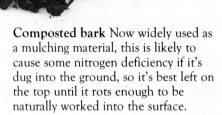

Composted bark Now widely used as a mulching material, this is likely to cause some nitrogen deficiency if it's dug into the ground, so it's best left on the top until it rots enough to be naturally worked into the surface.

Composted straw Straw is composted with liquid cow slurry to make a very good soil conditioner for most purposes, with some nutrients.

Secrets of success

It's worth investigating local sources of organic matter. There are organic wastes, such as wool shoddy, fruit pulps, tea and coffee grounds, potato waste from crisp factories and many more, that may be locally available though not sold on a national basis. Any form of organic matter is suitable, but some may need composting first. If in any doubt about a material, try it out initially on a small area of land.

Grass cuttings make excellent compost but, since they're short and wet, they tend to pack down and rot without air to a smelly mess. They must be mixed with coarser material.

Well-made garden compost is brown and crumbly, smells of the forest floor in autumn and is almost good enough to eat. It's made from just about any material that'll rot down.

Weeds are ideal to mix with grass cuttings but you should not use any that are seeding and should avoid those with indestructible roots like couch grass or dock.

If you can't find enough weeds, keep a bag of fresh horse manure by the side of the heap to mix with your grass cuttings to make sure they're well aerated.

Kitchen scraps are fine, but avoid cooked food which attracts rats – unless you have a container which is definitely rodent-proof.

From the house, use old woollen or cotton clothing, newspapers shredded and pre-soaked in water, old income-tax bills – indeed, anything and everything that will rot down.

Making garden compost

The cheapest and, after animal manure, certainly the best soil conditioner of all is garden compost. It's nature's method of recycling and we should follow suit religiously. The only problem with compost is getting enough material to use, because there's certainly never enough in the garden to fulfil all your needs. If you're keen, and certainly if you're organic, you'll have to import some. The greengrocer always has lots of it, especially at the weekend; the local cricket or tennis club might have grass cuttings; and the council may well be pleased to let you cart away leaves, etc. Always have two heaps going, one to be filling while the other's rotting down. See p. 50 for how to make your own compost containers. The nutrient value of garden compost is very variable, but you can be sure that it contains a full complement of trace elements.

1 Start with a layer of coarse material and pile on about the same amount of grass cuttings if you have them. Mix together.

2 Carry on in the same way until the bin is full. Sprinkle on a 7.5cm (3in.) pot of calcified seaweed about every 30cm (1ft.).

3 After one to three months, depending on the weather and time of year, turn the compost: throw it out and back in again.

4 After a further two to three months, the compost can be used or stacked outside to clear the bin for making more.

Making leafmould

Leafmould is invaluable as a soil conditioner and as a constituent of potting composts. In fact it was used as the basic organic material in gardening until the advent of peat. It rots down in a slightly different way from other garden compost and takes slightly longer, so it's best composted separately. It takes at least a year, so you'll need two or even three containers. The local council is often a good source of leaves.

RIGHT Instead of being rotted down by bacteria, leaves are decomposed mainly by fungi. These don't require heat to do their work, so the leaves can be housed in a very simple wire-netting container. Put them in and tread them down as you fill. They may need a little water in dry weather but generally they can be left to their own devices. The nutrient value of leafmould is negligible and therefore extra nutrients will need to be added to any compost mix in which it's used. When sieved it makes an excellent constituent of potting composts.

Leaves can also be rotted down in black polythene bags with a few holes punched in the sides.

How to make and use a hot-bed

Victorian gardeners were pretty resourceful people. Even though they had access to very cheap coal, they would never waste the free energy that was available in horse manure. In most areas it's possible to buy it quite cheaply, so we can emulate those old gardeners. If you have access to sufficient horse manure and you have room in your garden, it's a good idea to make a hot-bed for raising early vegetables. Buy the manure fresh in the early spring and heap it up. It'll generate a considerable amount of heat that can be used to grow a crop of early vegetables without the expense of oil or electricity. After the vegetables have been harvested, the manure can be used on the garden in the autumn. And, by using it twice, you halve the cost of the manure.

1 Ideally, the heap should be enclosed in a wooden container where it'll generate more heat and conserve it better too. Note that the sides are removable. However, you could just heap up the manure, making a pile not less than 1m (3ft) square.

2 Cover the top of the heap with 23cm (9in.) of compost consisting of soil, garden compost (or spent mushroom compost) and coarse grit in the ratio 6:3:2. Sprinkle a light dressing of general fertiliser on top.

3 Put a coldframe on top and plant or sow. You could use early varieties of lettuce, radish, carrot, turnip, beetroot, cabbage, cauliflower and spinach. Water in well and leave the lid open just a crack. Ventilate during hot days.

4 At the end of the season, shovel out the manure and use it on the garden.

Secrets of success

Sowing or planting should be delayed until the bed has started to heat up. The old Victorian gardeners would push a stick into the heap and if, when pulled out, it felt hot, the bed was ready for planting. During the rotting process the heap will sink, so it may be necessary to remove some of the boards.

Growing a green manure crop

Green manuring is something farmers have been doing for centuries and it can also be invaluable for gardeners. It does have the disadvantage that a manure crop takes up space which will produce only an improvement in fertility, but where space is available for a while the advantages are great.

Both summer and winter green manures can be grown. When the crop is dug in, it adds bulky organic matter to the soil with all the benefits of manure or compost. The roots of the crop will help break up heavy soil and improve drainage, and winter crops in particular will retain plant nutrients that would otherwise drain away. Some plants will also add extra nitrogen to the soil through bacteria working in nodules in their roots.

In fact the winter crop is by far the more valuable for gardeners and no new vegetable patch should be allowed to have bare soil in the winter – much better to keep it covered with green manure. In summer it's possible to grow some fast-maturing crops, like mustard, underneath taller plants – brassicas or sweet corn, for example. The longer-lasting summer green manure crops are not worthwhile growing unless you have space to allow for a part of the plot to be given over to one instead of growing productive or decorative plants.

1 Green manure must be treated like any other crop and given the best conditions possible, so cultivate to produce a fine, level surface and use a general fertiliser before sowing. Smaller seed can be scattered over the top of the soil and simply raked in. Large seeds like broad beans can be dibbled in.

2 The crop should be dug in well before the stems become hard and woody. Skim it off with a sharp spade and allow it to wilt. Then dig in the manure, putting it no more than about 15cm (6in.) deep to ensure that the organisms that rot it down have enough air and warmth.

Secrets of success

The cheapest and one of the most effective ways to produce a green manure crop is to collect your own broad bean seed by allowing some pods from your spring and summer crop to ripen. They can be sown in August or September.

RIGHT **Grazing rye** An excellent plant for heavy soils since the powerful and extensive root system greatly improves the structure. It's winter-hardy but doesn't make nitrogen. Sow from late August to late November and dig in in the spring before flowering.

RIGHT **Mustard** This will be ready to dig in after about three to eight weeks, making it an ideal quick summer manure crop. Reaching about 60cm (2ft), it can be sown under taller crops. It doesn't make nitrogen and could be damaged by frost in winter. Sow between March and mid-September and dig in just before flowering.

Worms

Charles Darwin reckoned that the humble earthworm was the most important animal in the history of the world. It cultivates the soil, improving drainage and pulling organic matter down to the lower levels. As it digests organic matter, it coats soil particles with a glutinous material that forms a perfect crumb structure and also contains growth-promoting substances. So earthworms should be cherished in the garden and certainly never killed off.

Encourage them by providing plenty of bulky organic matter in the form of manure, compost or one of the alternatives. Avoid discouraging them by over-use of chemical fertilisers, soil insecticides and weedkillers. They can be looked upon as the outward signs of a healthy soil since, if you can see plenty of worms, you can be sure there are also plenty of micro-organisms you can't see.

ABOVE Earthworms are terrific workers of the soil, and if you dig up one with every spadeful you know it's healthy and alive.

MAKING A WORMERY

1 BELOW It's possible to get worms of a different type to work digesting compost materials to form a highly fertile additive for sowing and potting composts and to promote the growth of young seedlings outside. These are called brandlings or manure worms and are generally smaller and redder than ordinary earthworms or, in the case of some species, striped.

2 RIGHT A special container is needed to make a 'worm farm'. There are manufactured models available, or you can make your own. For this you will need a small dustbin with a few holes drilled in the bottom. Drill a few in the lid, too, for ventilation and stand the bin on a couple of bricks to help the drainage.

3 Put a 5cm (2in.) layer of rotted compost or manure in the bottom of the container, introduce the worms and cover with another similar layer. This just gets them settled in.

4 Add a shallow layer of compost materials. It's not a good idea to put in too much at a time, so never let the layer of new material exceed about 15cm (6in.) in depth. Mix it with the existing material and wait until the worms have digested most of this before adding more.

5 When the bin is full, remove the worms by sieving the compost. Replace a little of the sifted material together with the coarse stuff you've sieved out, plus, of course, the worms to form the starter for the next lot of compost.

6 The worms will work only at temperatures above about 15°C (59°F), so the bin should be brought into the greenhouse or the garage for the winter.

7 Use the finished compost mixed with potting and sowing composts at a ratio of about 1:3. It can also be sprinkled down sowing drills outside.

Mulching

Mulching is the covering of soil between plants, either with loose material like bark or gravel or with sheet material like paper or polythene. Its main purpose is to prevent the evaporation of water from the soil surface and to inhibit the growth of weeds. Organic mulches will also eventually be incorporated into the soil where they'll be turned into humus.

Mulching around plants is sometimes recommended as a control for slugs too. It's true that some materials can discourage these pests a little, but the effects of most are limited. Indeed, mulches can sometimes have the reverse effect, serving as a warm, moist hide-away for slugs, so some control methods may be necessary (see pp. 333, 347).

Remember that, as well as preventing evaporation, mulches also reduce the amount of rainwater reaching the soil. You must therefore always ensure that the soil has been well soaked before you put down the mulch.

Conifer bark and cocoa-shell In the ornamental borders, loose materials are much to be preferred. Conifer bark and cocoa-shell, a waste product from the chocolate industry, are freely available though somewhat expensive, but both make very effective weed inhibitors. A 5cm (2in.) layer will suppress all but the most persistent weeds. Annual weeds seem not to like either product as a seed bed.

Gravel An attractive mulching material, especially suitable for plants like alpines and those more exotic plants that prefer very well-drained conditions. It conserves water very well but provides a near-perfect seed bed, so some weeding of annual weeds may be necessary. Bear in mind, though, that in certain areas you may wish to encourage self-sown seedlings of cultivated plants, in which case gravel may be preferred and a little extra weeding considered a price well worth paying.

BELOW **Garden compost, manure and grass cuttings** All of these are effective weed inhibitors and they will also help to conserve water if put on thickly enough. With these materials a 10–15cm (4–6in.) layer is to be preferred. Unfortunately, all these materials can also import seeds, especially from annual weeds, so you may find that an initial weeding is necessary. Eventually they will all rot down and add valuable humus to the soil.

LEFT **Garden shreddings** One of the cheapest mulches available can be home-made with the help of a shredder. This machine will cut all your prunings, etc., into small pieces which, when composted for only a short time, make a very attractive and effective mulch. I always mix mine with all the old potting compost collected from the greenhouse, pile it up for about two months and then spread it between plants.

RIGHT **Sheet plastic** Several sheet-plastic materials are suitable as mulches but are mostly used between rows of vegetables. Where weeding is difficult, such as between rows of runner beans, woven black plastic is ideal and this can also be used in the usual way between rows of other types of vegetables. Although it is expensive, it can be used time and again. It's not really useable in the borders.

LEFT **Black polythene** Much cheaper and plants can be grown through it very effectively. However, some slug control may be necessary (see pp. 333, 347). Watering can sometimes be a problem, so it's a good idea to incorporate some kind of seep-hose under the sheeting before planting permanent crops.

RIGHT **Newspaper** The cheapest alternative. A layer three or four sheets thick can be laid between rows and covered with a thin layer of soil to hold it down and to improve its appearance. Surprisingly, the newspaper remains intact right through the season, after which it can be dug into the soil and will rot down to good effect.

pH soil testing

Before deciding which plants to grow, find out whether your garden soil is acid or alkaline (see p. 15). There's a wide range of plants for each condition but, while lime-lovers will generally survive on soil that's a little acid, the reverse is generally not true. Though it's easiest to grow plants that suit the prevailing conditions, you can alter the soil's acidity by the regular application of either acid or alkaline materials. This is particularly so in the vegetable garden where most crops will not do well on acid soil, making regular liming necessary.

1 Testing the soil is not difficult. Cheap and efficient soil testers are available at garden centres and they require no previous knowledge of chemistry. Start by collecting a soil sample from various places in the garden, taking the soil from about 7.5cm (3in.) below the surface.

2 Allow the sample to dry slowly and then put it into the test tube provided. Some kits already have the necessary reagent in the tube and require only the addition of water – ideally distilled. With other kits, the reagent needs to be added separately.

3 Shake the tube and allow the mixture to settle. Then compare the colour of the liquid with the colour chart supplied to give a very accurate reading of the soil pH.

4 Alternatively, there are electric meters available which are much easier to use. All you need do is to push the rod into the soil at intervals over the garden. In my experience, though, meters are less accurate than even the cheapest chemical kits.

BELOW **Raising soil pH** Where the test shows the soil to be acid, the pH can be raised by liming. The lime generally sold at garden centres is either ground limestone or hydrated lime. Hydrated lime is about twice as effective as garden lime. Alternatively, use magnesian limestone, sometimes known as 'Dolomite lime'. This is more expensive but its effects last longer and it also adds valuable magnesium to the soil. Calcified seaweed is also an excellent material in that it adds trace elements and magnesium, and it lasts longer, but it's quite expensive. The soil-test kit should indicate how much lime is needed to raise the pH the necessary amount. Bear in mind that the effect may not be immediate and that you will probably need to repeat the treatment annually. When applying lime, always wear gloves, goggles and a face mask. Don't apply it at the same time as manuring, since the resulting chemical reaction will release ammonia and the nitrogen content of the manure will be lost. The general rule is to apply manure in the autumn and lime in the spring.

Lowering soil pH Making a limy soil more acid is not easy. It's not enough just to dig a hole and fill it with an acid material: the surrounding limy water will quickly drain in and the material will become alkaline again, rapidly affecting acid-loving plants growing in it. A raised bed is necessary to prevent water draining in. In an effort to dispense with peat in my garden, for ecological reasons, I have successfully used cocoa-shell mixed with soil. The amount required will depend on your soil, so you'll have to incorporate it and do another test about a month later. Add more cocoa-shell to the surface and remember to top up annually to maintain the acidity.

Fertilisers

Gardeners take more from their soil than nature ever intended, so if your plot is to continue to be successful, you must put something back. That means either very large and regular inputs of animal manures or, more commonly, fertiliser.

It's important to understand the distinction between manures and fertilisers. Manures are bulky materials such as garden compost or the waste of animals plus their straw bedding. Manures do contain some nutrients but, unless you can put on very large quantities, not enough. So though manures have a vital part to play in maintaining soil fertility, they should be looked upon solely as soil conditioners.

Fertilisers, on the other hand, contain plant foods in concentrated form. Whereas you would measure manure use in kilograms per square metre, you'd measure fertiliser in only grams. Organic fertilisers are safer to use than non-organic ones but all should be put on strictly according to the instructions on the packet. Using too much could upset the delicate balance of the soil and scorch young roots as well – and it's considerably more expensive.

Organic fertilisers have two advantages. They do no harm to soil organisms and there is no need to be highly precise when using them. They can therefore simply be sprinkled on by hand, though it's best to err on the mean side.

LEFT There is evidence that artificial fertilisers do some damage to soil organisms and they certainly repress the nitrogen-making activities of bacteria. Since they're quite concentrated, they must be kept off the leaves of plants and must be applied with some precision. One way is to weigh out a handful first to get a rough idea of how much you're putting on when spreading by hand.

LEFT With most modern chemical fertilisers, however, this is not really precise enough and, though the manufacturers allow some margin of error, it's safer to take more trouble. A much more accurate way is to weigh out various quantities, put them into a plastic cup and mark the side. Then you can simply mark out an area on the ground and sprinkle the required amount into it from the cup.

ABOVE Plants can take up fertiliser only when it's in solution, so there's little point in using it when the soil's bone-dry. Wait until there's some moisture and then lightly hoe it in.

Lawn fertiliser can be applied by hand but, naturally, there's no way of keeping it off the leaves of the grass. It's vital to apply the right amount and if the feed also contains a weed-killer you'll need to take even more trouble. A special lawn distributor is the best and safest way to do it. Water in afterwards with a sprinkler if it doesn't rain.

If you do accidentally spill too much fertiliser on to plant leaves, and particularly on to the lawn, brush it off immediately and wash the area down with a hose; otherwise bad scorching is inevitable whether you're using an organic or a chemical fertiliser.

Blood, fish and bone meal
A popular organic fertiliser that contains all three major nutrients with the potash and phosphate being released slowly and the nitrogen fairly fast. Regular applications will maintain nutrient levels. Nutrient content: nitrogen 3.5 per cent; phosphorus 8 per cent; potassium 0.5 per cent.

Tomato fertiliser Another specialised compound which can be used for all fruiting vegetables. Use it as a base dressing before planting and top up during the season or liquid feed. Nutrient content: nitrogen 4 per cent; phosphorus 4.5 per cent; potassium 8 per cent.

Superphosphate An artificial straight fertiliser supplying only phosphorus. Use it to correct deficiencies. Nutrient content: phosphorus 17.5 per cent.

Sulphate of potash An artificial straight fertiliser supplying only potassium. Use it to correct deficiencies. Nutrient content: potassium 50 per cent.

Sulphate of ammonia A popular nitrogen straight fertiliser for giving a quick boost to growth. Use it only in the growing season. Nutrient content: nitrogen 21 per cent.

Lawn fertiliser Summer and autumn types are available, but if you use the summer one twice during the season there's no need for the autumn feed. Apply with care to avoid scorching. Nutrient content: nitrogen 14 per cent; phosphorus 4 per cent; potassium 4 per cent.

Controlled-release fertiliser
This enables the gardener to feed just once or twice in a season. A compound fertiliser is pelleted and then coated with resin. As the resin slowly dissolves, it releases the feed over a long period. The thickness of the coating will alter the release rate, so the gardener can choose a feed that lasts perhaps three months up to six months. Other types release their nutrients as temperatures increase.

Chicken manure concentrate Another organic compound fertiliser available as a powder or in the more convenient pelleted form which also gives it something of a slow-release action. Nutrient content: nitrogen 6 per cent; phosphorus 5 per cent; potassium 3 per cent.

Fertilisers

Whether organic or artificial, fertilisers are available as so-called 'straights' or 'compounds'. Straights supply only one of the three major elements required by plants (see p. 16) and are generally used either to correct a deficiency or to encourage one particular function of plant growth. A little extra nitrogen encourages leaf and stem growth, potash helps flower and fruit formation and phosphate gives a boost to roots. Generally, though, compound fertilisers, containing all three major elements, are sufficient. There are many straight fertilisers available and even more proprietary brands of compounds all claiming miracle results! I have included here those organic products that I favour and the most popular artificial types. When you're buying a compound fertiliser, look on the bag for the three numbers that will tell you its content. For example, 7.5.7 means that it contains 7 parts of nitrogen, 5 of phosphate and 7 of potash.

Hoof and horn An organic straight made from the hooves and horns of cattle. The material is sterilised, so it's perfectly safe. It has a slow-release action so must be used at least two weeks before its effect is needed. Nutrient content: nitrogen 13 per cent.

Rose fertiliser One of several specialised compound fertilisers, this can be used to feed all flowering plants and fruit trees and bushes in spring and summer. Nutrient content: nitrogen 5 per cent; phosphorus 7 per cent; potassium 10 per cent.

Dried blood A faster-acting organic fertiliser for supplying a quick boost to growth. Nutrient content: nitrogen 12–14 per cent.

Growmore The most popular artificial compound fertiliser. It has a rapid effect and is used most often on vegetables. It's also useful as a lawn fertiliser, slower-acting but much cheaper than most branded products. It comes in pelleted form. Nutrient content: nitrogen 7 per cent; phosphorus 7 per cent; potassium 7 per cent.

Bone meal Made from animal bones and quite safe if the packet states that it has been steamed. As with all fertilisers, it's still advisable to wear gloves and wash your hands after use. It's used in autumn and winter when planting, to give a boost to root growth. Again, it has a slow-release action. Nutrient content: nitrogen 3 per cent; phosphorus 22 per cent.

Rock potash Potassium is often short in organic fertilisers so this straight is invaluable. It's not easily dissolved, so its action is slow, but it lasts a long time in the soil. Use it if a potassium deficiency is diagnosed (see p. 16). Nutrient content: potassium 10.5 per cent.

Fertilisers

LIQUID FERTILISERS

Liquid fertilisers have the advantage over solids that they're instantly available to plants, but the disadvantage that they don't remain in the soil very long. So they're generally used on a regular basis, either to provide nutrients for demanding plants like tomatoes or cucumbers (when the compost they're growing in has been depleted) or to correct deficiencies. Just as with solid fertilisers, there are formulations for various purposes which contain nutrients in exactly the same proportions as the solids. So a general liquid fertiliser would be marked something like 'N7.P7.K7' on the bottle and a rose fertiliser '5N.7P.10K'.

BELOW AND RIGHT Home-made liquid fertiliser Country gardeners have, for generations, collected animal manures to make their own very effective, organic, liquid fertiliser. Any animal waste can be used but sheep muck is to be preferred. Simply put it into a hessian sack and suspend it in a barrel of water. For most applications the resulting fertiliser can be used neat, but dilute it to half-strength for seedlings and for foliar sprays. It contains about 0.8 per cent nitrogen, 0.5 per cent phosphorus, 0.4 per cent potassium and a full range of trace elements.

ABOVE Application with a watering can Most liquid fertilisers are applied in this way. If you buy manufactured liquids, don't be tempted to use more than the makers recommend, just for luck, especially if you're watering young seedlings. It's quite possible to scorch them, even with liquid feeds. For the same reason it's not a good idea to feed dry soil or compost. Give it a watering with clear water first and let it drain before feeding.

ABOVE Foliar feeding The fastest way to get a response to feeding is to foliar feed with liquid fertiliser using a sprayer. Plants can take up nutrients through both sides of the leaves, so this is a good way to correct deficiencies: the results are as instantaneous as they can ever be in plants. Never foliar feed when the sun is on the leaves since this could lead to severe scorching. If you suspect a trace element deficiency but are not quite sure which one it is, the best bet is to foliar feed with liquid seaweed which contains them all.

Application with a hose-end applicator A convenient method of feeding garden plants, but more fertiliser is used this way. All you have to do is to fit the filled applicator to the hose and turn on the water supply. Dilution is automatic. Most applicators can be refilled without your having to buy the fitting again.

Drainage

Very heavy clay soil with a clay subsoil can be a real problem. Because the soil particles are very small, water remains in the top layers of the soil, which becomes muddy and unworkable in winter and sets solid in summer. Artificial drainage with land drains would solve the problem and that's what the farmer would use. But he'd have a system of ditches to take the excess water away. It's all very well advising an elaborate herringbone system of drains, but only if you're lucky enough to have a ditch to run them into. Even a soakaway will take only a certain amount before it's full and you're back to square one.

There are alternatives, but if you have a convenient exit point or can persuade the local authority to allow you to run your land drains into their storm drains, a piped drainage system is certainly the best.

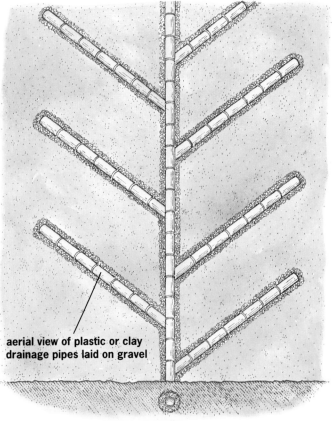

aerial view of plastic or clay drainage pipes laid on gravel

ditch

LEFT AND ABOVE **Land drains**
These are set out in a herringbone fashion to run eventually into a main drain and thence into the ditch. You can do the job with old clay drainage pipes but it's more common, cheaper and easier these days to use perforated plastic pipe. This is available from agricultural merchants. The side 'arms' of the system must slope gradually towards the centre and the main drain must slope towards the outlet. Line the trenches with gravel and dig in the drains, which should be positioned at the lowest depth of your topsoil. Cover the drains with more gravel, or if using plastic pipe with a special fabric supplied with it, to stop fine soil blocking them. Then replace the soil in the trench.

LEFT AND RIGHT **Help from plants**
Just growing plants on heavy soil will improve it. The penetration of roots creates channels for water to drain away and the plants add organic matter too. Trees like willows (left) and poplars which thrive in wet areas will remove an enormous amount of water from the soil and smaller shrubs and herbaceous plants will do so in proportion to their size. Naturally it's necessary to plant subjects that thrive in moist conditions and shade, like these acers, hostas and pulmonarias (right).

BELOW **Grit**
Digging in a quantity of coarse grit will make an immediate and permanent improvement in the drainage of heavy clay soil. Ensure that the grit is at least 3mm (⅛in.) in diameter and don't use sand which could make matters worse. The amount you need will depend upon the extent of the problem; but, as a guide, I have used about a barrowload to 3sq.m (3sq.yds) on my own heavy clay.

BELOW **Raised borders**
Raising soil by incorporating organic matter improves the drainage of the top few centimetres. This does, of course, make for a wetter lawn, but that's generally not a problem. However, if you do decide on this measure, it's worthwhile preparing the drainage of the lawn itself first.

Raised beds
In the vegetable garden there's no doubt at all that the problem of heavy soil is greatly alleviated by growing in 120cm- (4ft)-wide raised beds. Drainage is improved, the soil thus becomes warmer and compaction is reduced or eliminated because all the work is done from the side paths.

RIGHT **The well-drained lawn**
If a lawn lies wet it never really produces good grass, so it's worth preparing the ground well before sowing. Break up the soil two spades deep if you can, working a quantity of grit into the lower levels. Then put down a layer of coarse gravel or ashes about 10cm (4in.) thick. Cover with 15cm (6in.) of good topsoil and sow into that. A section cut through this lawn shows the various layers. Try not to cut or even walk on the lawn too much when it's wet.

Protecting plants against frost

Different plants can stand varying degrees of frost. Those from cold countries are naturally adapted to low temperatures and will be completely hardy. Others from warmer climes where frost is never experienced will succumb to the first cold spell of the season, and there are various degrees in between. The problem for gardeners is knowing where they can draw the line in their particular area and which plants they can safely leave outside all winter. That information comes only with experience. However, there are a number of ways in which plants can be helped in hard winters and, indeed, with the right equipment you can grow plants from just about anywhere in the world, wherever you may live.

RIGHT **Small cloches** Covering plants with glass or plastic cloches will protect them from a few degrees of frost. The problem with small cloches like these is that they tend to heat up greatly during sunny days, even in the winter, and then, of course, to cool again at night, and this large temperature fluctuation can be damaging to plants. So constant attention to ventilation is necessary. There's a much bigger buffer against temperature fluctuation with large continuous cloches (see p. 52).

BELOW **Coldframes** These give better protection than cloches but because they're not portable, they're not quite so versatile. Plants have to be potted and brought to the frames for winter protection. When severe frost threatens, it's advisable to cover the frames with sacking. Alternatively frames can be heated very effectively and cheaply, and they are then excellent for protecting valued tender plants and for raising tender seedlings in spring too.

BELOW **Greenhouse** This is the ultimate frost protection and, because it can be heated to whatever temperature your plants require, you could grow anything, however exotic. The limitation, of course, is your budget, since the cost of power of any kind is very high.

Polythene screen Some otherwise hardy plants can be damaged at certain times by frost. Pears and peaches, for example, are very vulnerable in colder districts when they're in flower. If you grow these (or any slightly tender ornamental plants) against a wall or fence, they can be protected to some extent with a simple polythene screen. Fix a sheet of strong polythene to two poles and, when frost threatens, simply unroll the sheet to cover the vulnerable plants, leaning the poles against the wall or fence. In the morning, the screen can be easily packed away. Don't be tempted to leave it there or pollinating insects won't be able to reach the flowers. Naturally, that would have the same effect as frost damage.

Fine netting A surprising amount of protection can be supplied by covering plants with fine netting when frost is threatened. Old net curtains are ideal, or you could use spun-polypropylene 'floating cloche' material (see p. 52).

Secrets of success

Plants are much more vulnerable to cold weather if drainage is bad. So, if you want to risk growing tender plants in areas considered a bit too cold for them, raise the borders by digging in lots of coarse grit and mulch around the plants with grit too. A situation near a south-facing wall will also help. Put the tenderest plants nearest the wall to take advantage of the heat collected by the brick or stone during the day and released at night. The orange-flowered tender perennial enjoying such a position below is *Mimulus aurantiacus*.

Cultivation methods

SINGLE AND DOUBLE DIGGING

Generally soil needs to be dug to only one spade's depth, but there are exceptions. If you buy a newly built house, you may find that the builders have run over the surrounding ground with heavy machines for months during building and then bulldozed a few inches of soil over the top to hide a multitude of sins. This leaves you with a very hard layer below the surface which plant roots will not be able to penetrate and which will inhibit drainage. It will have to be broken up. Even on land that was farmed, there's sometimes a hard layer at the maximum depth of the plough and there are soils which naturally compact below the surface. Normally double digging (going down two spades deep) is necessary only once.

The important thing to remember is not to bring up a lot of inert subsoil to the surface. Notice, too, that the organic matter is not put just at the bottom of the trenches as is sometimes recommended. It's much better to distribute it through all layers of the topsoil. It's also important to measure the width of the trenches. If you refill with exactly the same amount of soil you took out, you'll keep the digging level.

ABOVE **Single digging**
When single digging to one full depth of the spade, throw the soil forwards to form a neat trench behind. Note that the organic matter is put on the slope of the soil you have thrown forwards so that it becomes mixed through all levels.

RIGHT **Double digging**

1 Start double digging by taking out a trench exactly 60cm (2ft) wide and one spade deep. Remove the soil and cart it to the other end of the plot to refill the final trench. Fork over the bottom of the trench simply to break up the subsoil. Don't turn it over but just work the fork backwards and forwards in the soil to break it up.

2 Put in a layer of manure, compost or one of the alternatives (see p. 68) and mark out the next trench, again to exactly 60cm (2ft) wide, using a marking cane. Half-refill the first trench by throwing soil forwards from the second. Then put in another layer of organic matter and completely refill the trench. If you can spare it, cover the surface with more organic matter. Continue to work down the plot in the same way, refilling the final trench with the soil you dug from the first.

Secrets of success

Barrowing soil and manure on soft or wet land is hard work. Make it easier with a roll-up path formed by joining 30cm- (1ft)-long bits of scrap wood with nylon twine stapled at each end. After use the path can be rolled up for storage.

ALTERNATIVES TO HAND DIGGING

Hand digging large areas of land can be considered enjoyable exercise or an arduous chore, depending on your point of view and your physical fitness. It has to be admitted that it's time-consuming, so busy gardeners might also seek other ways of cultivating their plots. There are two methods that might appeal. Cultivating with a mechanical rotavator makes light and easy work of large areas in a short time, while for gardeners who, for one reason or another, may not be able to cope with hard physical exercise, the no-dig method is very attractive.

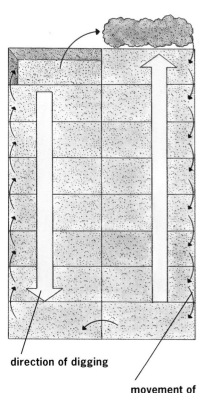

3 ABOVE AND BELOW A large plot can be divided in half. Then the soil from the first trench is simply shipped to the other side of the plot. Work down it, trench by trench, and when you reach the end, turn round and work down the second half.

soil from first trench

direction of digging

movement of soil into trenches

Rotavators
Rotavators are not expensive to hire by the day and will cultivate a great deal in that time. They have the disadvantage that they won't go very deep: about 23cm (9in.) is the normal maximum. And, of course, they won't weed like a hand digger would. In fact, if the soil is infested with weeds with running roots, they'll make a good job of taking root cuttings and spreading the problem even further. They are extremely useful for making a fine seed bed and for the first cultivation of areas to be grassed. Machines driven through the wheels, like this one, are easier to control and probably do a better job than those powered by the rotors (see p. 44).

The no-dig method
The no-dig method requires quite large inputs of organic matter, which is spread over the top of the soil each year. It's best to avoid compaction, so vegetables are most successful on 120cm- (4ft)-wide beds with the work being done from the path. Each season a layer of about 10cm (4in.) of organic matter is spread over the surface. Naturally all non-diggers should make as much compost as possible and I supplement mine with spent mushroom compost which is readily available and grows vegetables well.

The crops are sown or planted into the top layer of compost (see left) where they establish quickly. Their roots will grow down and penetrate the soil eventually. There is a certain amount of cultivation of the soil beneath, of course, when the vegetables are dug up, so it's a good plan to rotate crops year by year to ensure that all the area is disturbed from time to time.

Watering

Watering in some areas seems to get more difficult every year and could become worse if predictions of global warming are to be believed. So we gardeners must try to save water as much as possible and avoid using it on the garden where we can. This means relying on plenty of organic matter and mulches to conserve moisture and recycling water whenever feasible. Certainly we should use the water from baths and washing up, but this is safe for plants only if detergents have not been added. Water from the washing machine, for example, should not be used. Try to water in the evening when evaporation will be negligible, giving the plants a chance to absorb moisture before too much is lost the following morning.

Whenever plants are transplanted, it's important to 'puddle' them in well. Plenty of water will wash the soil round the roots and will also provide a reservoir which should last the plants until they're established.

Secrets of success

In the greenhouse or on the windowsill, if plants are in full sun, a drop of water resting on a leaf can act like a magnifying glass, causing severe damage. So try to water plants in this position very early in the morning or avoid wetting the leaves. In my experience plants growing outdoors in sunshine do not seem to suffer ill effects if water falls on their leaves.

Rainwater should be stored in a water butt wherever possible. Remember that this water is generally slightly acid, so it's ideal for use on acid-loving plants in particular.

BELOW It's virtually impossible to put enough water on a lawn with a watering can and it takes ages by hand, even with a hose, so a special lawn sprinkler is essential.

LEFT A very efficient method of watering is provided by a seep-hose. This is porous piping which seeps water throughout its length, putting it exactly where it's required. It is ideal down rows of vegetables and soft fruit.

Always water *before* sowing seeds (see p. 97). Watering afterwards can cause some soils to form a hard crust on the surface which can be difficult for young seedlings to break through.

In the greenhouse one of the cheapest and most efficient methods of semi-automatic watering is with a capillary mat. This is soaked once a day, providing a reservoir for the plants.

CHAPTER 4
PROPAGATION

Gardening is like no other leisure activity because we gardeners actually create hundreds, perhaps thousands, of new lives each season. That's utterly fascinating. It's not the power of 'playing God'; it's the wonder of being able really to get to grips with nature. And, in some cases, we actually manipulate the natural processes to get them to work for us. If you think gardening's boring, you've clearly never felt the thrill of seeing your own strong young seedlings push through the compost or known the sheer exhilaration of watching roots grow out from the tip of one of your cuttings. If you haven't done it, don't just take my word for how great it is: do it yourself and you'll certainly agree with me.

I've long been fascinated by the techniques of propagation, so I've made a point of studying the methods of commercial growers and I've converted them to a smaller scale for use by gardeners. Because growers have to find the simplest and most efficient method, all the techniques I've copied are pretty easy to use and cost next to nothing. You can sow seeds in a Chinese takeaway tray and you can strike cuttings under a plastic lemonade bottle. And nine times out of ten you'll be just as successful as the commercial growers with their sophisticated approach.

Gardeners can adapt the nurseryman's methods to produce more plants for themselves.

Sowing in open ground

The cheapest and usually the most successful way to raise plants in the garden is from seed. Most vegetables are started this way and many annual and perennial flowers could be and should be if you have the room and particularly if your budget's tight.

Nature has equipped seeds with everything they need to get through the soil. All you need to do is to give them the best conditions you can and they'll invariably do the rest. After that, of course, they'll need a little help from their friends.

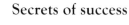

LEFT The cheapest way to fill your borders with flowers for the whole summer is to grow hardy annuals from seed sown directly into the ground. In front is dimorphotheca backed by echium and red linum.

1 ABOVE Unless you have soil that has been well worked in the past and is therefore weed-free, it's often best to reduce competition from weeds by starting with a 'stale' seed bed. This is a very old gardening trick that's still valid today. Cultivate the soil two to three weeks before you actually need to sow and then leave it for a while, allowing the weed seeds present to germinate. Then, before they themselves have a chance to seed, hoe them off. Finally prepare the seed bed and sow. Once you have eliminated that first flush of weeds your seedlings will get a good head start and should germinate in weed-free soil.

Secrets of success

Most unused seeds will last until the next season if they're stored properly. It's essential to keep them dry and cool, so put the packet into an airtight container – a plastic film container is ideal. Mark them clearly and put them in a cool spot. A drawer in a cool spare room would be suitable, or even the fridge – but *not* the freezer.

2 LEFT Seed beds need to be firm in order to ensure that the seeds are in intimate contact with the soil without large air spaces around them to dry them out. So, when the soil is dry enough on the top not to stick to your boots, tread it down. On heavy soils this needs to be only a light treading, while light soils need more compaction.

6 LEFT Sow the seed thinly. Remember that most of the seeds you sow will generally come up and the seedlings will then have to be thinned. So, for most seeds, it's wasteful to sow too thickly. Some expert gardeners can sow straight from the packet with accuracy, but I find it easier to take a pinch of seed between thumb and forefinger.

3 RIGHT Rake the soil surface to level it and to form the fine, crumbly structure that's often referred to as a 'fine tilth'. On heavy soils you may need to incorporate some good compost or other organic matter in order to create a really fine surface.

7 RIGHT Cover the seeds with soil by drawing the back of the rake down the centre of the drill and then tap it down with the back of the rake to make sure seeds and soil are in intimate contact.

4 LEFT Stretch a garden line in the place you want to sow and take out a very shallow drill either with the corner of a hoe or with a pointed stick. Most germination failures result from sowing too deeply, so make sure that the drill is no deeper than necessary.

BELOW Hardy annual flowers and vegetables grown in the ornamental borders are often sown in patches. First mark out the patch with a stick and draw shallow drills within the area. Cover by simply brushing over the top with your hand.

5 RIGHT Remember that in dry weather water should be applied down the drill before and not after sowing. If the soil is a little too wet and sowing can't be delayed, draw the drill slightly deeper than required and sprinkle some dry compost down it to return it to the correct depth.

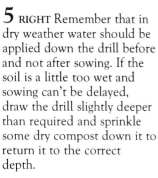

Thinning and transplanting in open ground

Once seedlings have germinated, they receive their first shock. The secret of success when growing from seed is to get plants going well in the first place and then to keep them growing steadily. Naturally the trauma of being uprooted and rehoused is going to cause some check to growth, so you'll need to make it as easy for the plants as possible. The smaller they are, the more easily they'll re-establish, therefore transplant as soon as the seedlings are big enough to handle comfortably.

The effect of creating a check to growth because of clumsy transplanting or of allowing the seedlings to grow too big is often seen in the vegetable plot. Some plants will run to seed prematurely, while cauliflowers in particular produce minute curds long before the plants are big enough to carry anything of a respectable size. I have also found that great care is needed to ensure that the seed leaves themselves are not damaged since this leads to much reduced and slower growth. It goes without saying that the tiny roots should be preserved as near intact as possible and never allowed to dry out.

1 Before either thinning or lifting and transplanting seedlings, it's wise to water well down the rows. Ideally do this an hour or two before starting work to give the plants a chance to become fully charged with water.

2 If you're just thinning, select the plant you wish to retain, put a couple of fingers either side of it to steady the soil round its roots and remove the surrounding unwanted seedlings. Never leave discarded seedlings on the ground since this can attract pests and diseases.

3 If you intend to replant some of the seedlings, they're best lifted carefully with a trowel or a hand fork to retain as much root as possible. Always handle them carefully by the leaves.

4 The vulnerable parts of the seedlings now are the tiny root hairs which you won't be able to see. They're extremely sensitive to drying out, so keep them covered and away from sunlight and drying winds.

5 Small plants can be replanted in soft soil with your fingers, though in stony ground or where there might be pieces of glass around it's best to use a trowel. Firm in with your fingers, avoiding pressing the neck of the plant. In most cases the seedling is replanted at exactly the depth it grew before. Planting too deeply could lead to rotting of the lower leaves, while shallow planting could result in the plants being lifted or blown out of the ground.

6 Tougher plants like cabbages or wallflowers are much more accommodating and can be planted with a dibber. Firm the soil around them by pushing the dibber into the ground a short distance away from the root.

Secrets of success

Dutch nurserymen ensure that the roots of transplants stay moist by making a hole in the soil, filling it with water and using this to coat the roots in mud. However, this method should not be used as a substitute for covering the roots.

7 Finally, 'puddle' the plants in with plenty of water and then leave them to their own devices for a while. Normally no more water should be needed until they start to perk up and grow away again.

8 Try not to transplant in very hot sunshine. If you can't avoid this, however, it's wise to shade the seedlings in their new position with newspaper or a piece of plastic greenhouse shade netting. The seedlings should root very quickly, after which the shading can be removed.

Sowing in the greenhouse or the house

When seeds are sown under cover in the greenhouse or in the house, it should be possible to provide perfect conditions to enable successful germination. Indeed, with some of the more difficult subjects, it's essential to do so. Often there's enough information on the back of the seed packet and these instructions should be followed carefully. Temperatures are especially important. Most seeds in the greenhouse will be sown in soilless composts. I use coconut fibre which I find better than peat for germination.

Sowing in a seed tray

1 Slightly overfill the seed tray with compost and firm it a little. Beware of overfirming soilless composts: pushing your fingers in at the corners and the sides of the seed tray and a couple of times in the middle is enough. Then level the compost with the top of the seed tray by pushing the edge of your firming board backwards and forwards in a sawing motion from one end of the tray to the other. Making your own firming board to fit a standard seed tray exactly will save hours.

2 Always water before sowing. Watering afterwards tends to push the seeds into patches and can even wash them right out of the tray. Sow seed accurately and thinly either in the same way as recommended for sowing outside (see p. 96) or by putting the seed into the palm of your hand, bending up your fingers to make a channel and tapping the side of your hand so that the seed falls on to the compost at the required rate.

3 Most (though not all) seed should be covered with a very light layer of compost sieved over the top. But make sure you don't bury the seed too deeply. There's no need for more water.

4 Cover the seed tray with a piece of opaque polythene to keep the moisture in and the light out and place it where the appropriate temperature can be achieved. You may need to boost the heat even in a heated greenhouse (or on a windowsill) with an electric propagator. Alternatively, place the tray in the airing cupboard. Generally the shelf just above the water tank will be too hot, so put it a couple of shelves higher. Note the polythene bag to keep the laundry clean!

Sowing in a pot

If only small amounts of seed are required, sowing in a pot is preferred: proceed as for sowing in a seed tray. Check to see if the seeds need light to germinate and, if they do, cover them not with compost but with vermiculite, which will allow light through. In this case the pots should be covered with clear rather than opaque polythene and they should *not* go into the airing cupboard. Supply gentle heat from beneath by putting them just above (but not on) a radiator or in a propagator.

Secrets of success

Some more difficult seeds, like impatiens, need light to germinate and also must have moisture around them at all times. The most successful way I've found is to sow them in rows in a seed tray and to cover them with a thin layer of vermiculite.

SOWING IN MODULES

A modern method of sowing much in favour with commercial growers is also available to amateurs and is extremely useful for certain subjects, particularly those that dislike root disturbance. Instead of being sown in

trays or pots the seeds are put into plastic or polystyrene modules with several separate cells per tray. So seedlings can remain in the cells without disturbance until planting out. This saves damaging the roots when transplanting, making for strong, earlier plants, and it saves all the work of pricking out.

1 Soilless composts are preferable for modules. Overfill the cells and then strike the compost off level with a flat board. Most modules are supplied complete with a special tool for firming. If this is not available, simply tap the tray once or twice on the bench. Remember that soilless composts should not be overfirmed.

3 Modules can't be used on slatted staging since the compost would dry out much too fast. They must be put on to capillary matting which is kept wet. When the plants are ready for planting out, they can be pushed out of the modules *en bloc* with the same tool used for firming the compost.

2 Large seeds can be sown individually, one per cell, and small ones sown sparingly in groups. With most plants no thinning will be necessary provided they're thinly sown. After sowing, stabilise the seeds by covering with a pinch of silver sand.

Modules are good for multiple sowing vegetables like onions and leeks with about six seeds per cell. They are not thinned but planted out at slightly wider spacings than normal. They simply push each other out of the way and grow into perfect-sized vegetables with little or no distortion.

Pricking out in the greenhouse or on the windowsill

Once seedlings have germinated they need a lot of loving care. Now they're at their most vulnerable stage, so they must be given as near optimum conditions as possible. In the heated greenhouse that's not difficult, but if you're trying to raise good plants in the house they'll need all the help they can get. Giving them enough light is the most difficult job and it's also important to avoid shocks of any kind which could cause a check to growth. This includes attention to correct watering, avoiding too much sunshine and keeping root disturbance to a minimum.

1 RIGHT Inspect newly sown seeds every day, especially those that are covered with opaque polythene or are in the airing cupboard. As soon as the first seedling germinates, bring the container into the light.

2 The healthiest, strongest seedlings are short and bushy, so make sure that they get maximum light. Early in the year the best place is as near the glass as possible but avoiding direct strong sunlight. Unfortunately, however big and sunny your windows may seem, they're not really a substitute for the greenhouse since the light comes only from one direction.

3 If you are limited to only a windowsill, you can improve light conditions by cutting the front out of a strong cardboard box, painting it white to reflect all available light and putting the seedlings inside. Remember that after dark the windowsill can become the coldest place in the room, so if frost threatens at night, move the seedlings away from the window into a warmer part of the room.

7 RIGHT Some seedlings, like lobelia and begonias, are too small to be handled so they're transferred in small clumps rather than individually. A plant label makes the ideal tool. The clumps grow on as one plant quite happily and need no further spacing.

8 LEFT After completely filling the container, water well, preferably with tepid water, and replace the container in a light spot. You will probably need to water the seedlings every day using a can with a very fine rose, but make sure that you don't overdo it.

4 ABOVE While good light is necessary, direct strong sunlight can scorch young seedlings, especially if they have drops of water on their leaves. So if there's a danger of strong sun shining directly on them, cover them with newspaper.

5 RIGHT When seedlings are large enough to handle, they should be transferred to another container at wider spacings. This is known as 'pricking out'. Always handle the seedlings by the leaves to avoid damaging the stems and use a stick to lift them out of the compost.

6 LEFT Transfer the seedlings to fresh compost, spacing them out to about 3–4cm (1–1½in.) between the plants, depending on their size. Plant them so that the seed leaves are at compost level. Firm by pressing near (but not on) the roots with the stick, pushing it right down to the bottom of the planting hole to ensure that the roots don't hang in an air pocket.

9 ABOVE Before they're planted out in the garden, young plants must first be acclimatised to the lower temperatures in a process known as 'hardening off'. Put them first in a closed coldframe and then gradually ventilate more each day until it remains open all day, but close it every night. Then repeat the process at night, opening a little more each night until the frame is fully open. However, you should keep an eye open for frost and, if it's threatened, close the frame completely.

Sowing tree and alpine seeds

Most hardy tree seeds and all alpines are germinated in the same way: in order to trigger the germination mechanism, a period of cold is necessary. In nature this ensures that the seeds germinate in the spring after the worst of the winter weather and can then be assured of better things. They therefore have a whole season to get established before the cold winter weather sets in again. I like to leave the process to nature, though it is possible to artificially 'fool' seeds into thinking they've been through a winter. The best results will always be obtained from fresh seeds, so those collected from your own garden and sown immediately are preferable.

SUITABLE TREE SEEDS FOR THE 'COLD' TREATMENT (NATURAL OR ARTIFICIAL)				
Most Acers	Alnus	Crataegus	Fagus	Laburnum
Aesculus	Betula	Davidia	Fraxinus	Liquidambar
Ailanthus	Carpinus	Eucalyptus	Juglans	Quercus

1 Nearly all alpines need very well drained conditions and, since the seedlings will be sitting outside in the wettest part of the year, tree seeds will benefit from the same mix. I use equal parts of soil, coarse grit and coconut-fibre compost. There's no need for added fertiliser.

Once tree seedlings are large enough they are best transplanted to the open ground to grow on before being moved to their final positions.

2 Firm the compost and sow the seeds thinly on the surface. If they're big enough, like these pulsatilla seeds, they can be placed individually. Big seeds with hard shells can be soaked in water first. To ensure a good cold spell, the best time for sowing is winter.

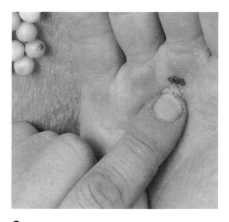

It's possible to induce germination with many species by putting the seeds into the refrigerator. Mix them with moist compost, place them in a plastic bag, seal and leave them in the salad compartment for the required period. Unfortunately optimum cold spells vary considerably, but generally about six to eight weeks is enough.

3 Seeds that are contained in berries must have the outer pulp removed before they'll germinate. Sometimes this is done by leaving the berries in sand for a winter, but I have had good results from simply squashing the seeds out and cleaning them up on a piece of absorbent paper.

4 Cover the seeds with a shallow layer of the same coarse grit used in the compost. There's no need to worry too much about the depth of covering. The grit will stabilise the seeds and prevent mosses and liverworts growing on top of the compost. Water afterwards.

6 Leave the pots for some time to allow as many seeds as possible to germinate. Sometimes this could be up to about three years, though most will show through during the first spring. But it's not a job for the impatient gardener! When the seedlings are big enough to handle they can be transplanted to individual pots.

5 Put the seeds into a coldframe which should be covered but well ventilated. If you don't have a frame, cover the seeds with a piece of glass to prevent birds or mice getting at them and put them in a shady spot outside.

Collecting and sowing your own seed

Many plants can be produced very cheaply if they are grown from seed you have collected from your own garden. You'll find too that societies and garden clubs often run seed-exchange schemes, issuing a list each year from which members can build up a varied and interesting collection of plants inexpensively. It's good to participate, not only by accepting seed but also by providing some that you've collected yourself.

1 Timing is vital when collecting seed – too early and they won't germinate, too late and the plant will disperse them automatically. So once the plants have finished flowering and have started to turn brown, like this *Campanula latifolia*, keep a close eye on them and collect the flower heads as soon as the first ripened capsules disperse their seeds.

SUITABLE PERENNIALS FOR SEED COLLECTION

Acanthus	Incarvillea
Achillea (but not hybrids)	Kniphofia
	Lathyrus
Agapanthus	Liatris
Alchemilla	Limonium
Alstroemeria	Linaria
Anaphalis	Liriope
Anchusa	Lychnis
Aquilegia	Malva
Astrantia	Meconopsis
Campanula	Oenothera
Catananche	Omphalodes
Centaurea	Paeonia
Cimicifuga	Papaver
Coreopsis	Phlomis
Delphinium	Physalis
Dictamnus	Polemonium
Dierama	Primula
Digitalis	Prunella
Echinacea	Rodgersia
Echinops	Rudbeckia
Erigeron	Salvia
Euphorbia	Sidalcea
Festuca	Sisyrinchium
Filipendula	Stipa
Gaillardia	Tellima
Gentiana (some)	Teucrium
Geranium	Thalictrum
Geum	Tiarella
Helleborus	Trollius
Hesperis	Veratrum
Heuchera	Viola

2 If you're too busy to check them regularly, wait till the flower heads turn brown and tie a paper (not plastic) bag over them so that the seeds aren't lost.

3 Choose a dry day to collect the seed heads and make sure that there's no residual moisture on them. Put them in a dry place in the sun for final drying.

4 When the heads are completely dry, much of the seed will simply shake out. If crushing is necessary, you'll find that you have chaff mixed with the seed; remove it with the point of a knife.

5 BELOW Alternatively, if you have a flour sieve of the right size, you should be able to separate the rubbish more easily. It's important to do it because the chaff may carry fungus diseases.

6 Finally either sow the seeds directly or, if they're species that are best germinated in the winter or spring, store them in envelopes in a dry, cool but frost-free place in the house.

Secret of success

Not all plants will come true to type from seed and with some you'll be wasting your time. The F1 hybrids, for example, are very unlikely to produce any plants of garden merit from their seeds, so it's not worth your while bothering.

The types of plant that are pollinated by insects in the field will generally come true, though there will often be very slight variations. This actually adds to the interest. To be on the safe side, collect from species and the older, well-established hybrids like *Rudbeckia fulgida* 'Goldsturm' (below).

Taking cuttings

HERBACEOUS PERENNIAL CUTTINGS

During the growing season many herbaceous perennials can be increased from soft cuttings. In the spring basal cuttings are best and are especially useful for plants like lupins and delphiniums that you have raised from seed. If you find a particularly good colour from a batch of seedlings, the only way to be sure of reproducing it exactly is by vegetative means. During the late spring and throughout the summer, soft tip cuttings will generally root very easily. No special or expensive equipment is necessary.

Basal cuttings

1 Basal cuttings are taken in the spring from new shoots that arise right at the bottom of the plant. Scrape away a little soil and cut the shoot as close to the crown of the plant as possible.

2 Now simply put it into a pot of moist compost and cover with a polythene bag. Place in a shady, warm spot. A coldframe will suffice but there the cutting will take a little longer to root.

Irishman's cuttings

Irishman's cuttings prove that the Irish are much more canny than most of us. They're simply basal cuttings taken with a small amount of root, a method which more or less guarantees success.

Stem cuttings

1 Stem cuttings are taken later in the year, generally from about June onwards. Remove a strong, non-flowering growth about 10cm (4in.) long from the tip of a shoot.

2 Take off the lower leaves, trim just below a leaf joint and dip the cutting into hormone rooting liquid or powder.

3 Dibble into a pot of compost, water and cover with thin polythene. Put the pot in a coldframe or in a sheltered spot outside.

SUITABLE PLANTS FOR BASAL CUTTINGS

Achillea	Gypsophila
Anaphalis	Hesperis
Anthemis	Lupinus
Campanula	Lychnis
Chrysanthemum	Malva
Delphinium	Polygonum
Dicentra	

SUITABLE PLANTS FOR STEM CUTTINGS

Acaena	Gypsophila
Ajuga	Helenium
Artemisia	Helichrysum
Ballota	Lysimachia
Centaurea	Penstemon
Dianthus	Phlomis
Diascia	Sedum
Euphorbia	Teucrium

TENDER PERENNIAL CUTTINGS

Most tender perennials – for example, geraniums, fuchsias and argyranthemums – can be propagated by softwood cuttings in late summer in exactly the way recommended for herbaceous plants (see p. 108). This is probably the best way to overwinter these plants and there's the bonus that the cuttings will provide further material in the following spring. There are some, however, like dahlias, that are best treated differently.

1 Plants with tuberous roots like dahlias, cosmos and perennial salvias should be lifted immediately after they've been touched by the first frost. Drain them of water by cutting the foliage back and turning the clumps upside down for a few hours. Chrysanthemums and argyranthemums can be lifted and shaken clean of soil; draining is unnecessary.

2 Then put them into boxes of garden compost or soil so that the crown of the plant is just above the surface. Store them over winter in a cool but frost-free place, keeping the soil around them almost (but not quite) bone dry.

3 In the early spring they should be brought into a position where they'll get full light, watered and regularly sprayed with water to encourage the production of strong young cuttings.

4 When the cuttings are 7.5–10cm (3–4in.) long, detach them near the base and trim in the normal way, removing the lower leaves and trimming just below a leaf joint.

5 Submerse them in fungicide, dip the tips into hormone rooting liquid or powder and dibble them into a pot or box of coconut-fibre compost.

6 Ideally these cuttings should be given a little bottom heat. They may need an occasional spray with water to keep them turgid. Once rooted, they can be potted and grown on in a cool greenhouse or on the windowsill until they're hardened off ready for planting out in early summer.

Taking cuttings

SOFTWOOD CUTTINGS OF SHRUBS

Probably the most successful way of propagating shrubs is by softwood cuttings. I've tried hundreds of different subjects with varying degrees of success but generally with a high strike rate. My advice would be to try the method with any shrub you wish to increase but, if you want one new plant, take ten cuttings. They can be taken at any time during the summer when soft growth is available but are most successful in late spring or early summer. Rooting time varies considerably from about three weeks to six months, so leave the cuttings in their pots until they show signs of perking up. However, they should be checked from time to time and any that show signs of rotting should be removed. At the same time water with a fungicide solution if the compost is dry.

1 ABOVE Select strong, young shoots that have grown this year and cut off 7.5cm (3in.) of the shoot tip, cutting just above a bud. Put the cutting into a polythene bag straight away and keep it out of the sun until you get back to where it will be prepared.

2 BELOW Using a very sharp knife, remove the lower leaves. If they're left on they'll rot and could spread disease to the stem too.

4 LEFT To make quite sure that the cutting is fully protected against fungus attack, submerse it completely in a solution of copper fungicide to coat it thoroughly. Shake off the excess.

5 RIGHT Dip the lower end of the cutting into hormone rooting liquid or powder. Liquid is more effective since it rapidly moves through the plant tissue, but you can enhance the effect of powder by dissolving it in a little methylated spirit.

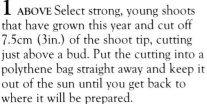

3 ABOVE Trim the cutting just below a leaf joint. With large-leaved plants it may be necessary to cut the top leaves in half to reduce water loss.

6 LEFT Dibble the cutting into compost. I have found coconut-fibre (coir) composts to be ideal on their own, though some gardeners prefer to mix in sharp sand or vermiculite in a 50:50 ratio. Water in with fungicide solution.

7 RIGHT Cover with very thin polythene so that it touches the cuttings lightly. It should be tucked underneath to make a hermetic seal. Don't support the polythene above the cuttings or moisture will condense on it, leaving the actual cuttings dry.

8 ABOVE Finally, put the pot into a shaded coldframe. Ideally you should vary the shade to give more on very sunny days, though one layer of plastic shading material is a satisfactory compromise.

9 LEFT If you have made the cheap coldframe (see page 57), the shading can be a piece of greenhouse shade netting.

Taking cuttings

HALF-RIPE CUTTINGS OF SHRUBS

If you failed with softwood cuttings of shrubs in the early summer, you get a second chance in late summer with half-ripe wood. This consists of young shoots made in the current season that have just started to go woody at the base. I've found that certain shrubs, like berberis, have proved quite difficult from softwood cuttings but have succeeded this way. They often take longer than softwood cuttings but should be rooted by late spring.

1 Remove the cutting by pulling it away from the main stem. This will also remove a small piece of bark, so take the cutting from where the scar won't disfigure the plant.

2 Trim the end of the cutting by removing most of the tongue of bark with a very sharp knife, leaving just a small piece attached. This prevents any problem of rotting.

3 Dip the whole cutting into a solution of fungicide and the tip into hormone rooting liquid or powder. Then put the cuttings into pots as you would softwood cuttings (see p. 111) or dibble them into sand covered with a shaded cloche. Water them in with the same fungicide in which they were dipped. It's important to check from time to time that the cuttings are not drying out. Should they look as if they might, use the fungicide to water them.

SUITABLE PLANTS FOR THIS TREATMENT	
Azalea (evergreen)	*Itea*
Berberis	*Kolkwitzia*
Buddleia	*Lavatera*
Buxus	*Lavandula*
Calluna	*Phlomis*
Ceanothus (deciduous)	*Philadelphus*
Choysia	*Photinia*
Cistus	*Potentilla*
Cytisus	*Pyracantha*
Daboecia	*Rhododendron*
Erica	*Ruta*
Escallonia	*Santolina*
Euonymus	*Senecio*
Genista	*Ulex*
Hebe	*Viburnum*
Hypericum	*Weigela*

4 LEFT Some cuttings will root quite quickly and you'll be able to feel the resistance of the roots when you give them a gentle tug. However, they can stay where they are until the following spring when they can be potted up or planted out into a nursery bed in a corner of the garden.

Making a home nursery

Propagating plants is one of those activities that tends to get a firm grip of you and refuse to let go. Once you're successful with your first cuttings, you'll certainly want to go on to tackle other more difficult areas. It's a fascinating way to build up the plant collection in your garden and, if you can beg cuttings from friends, it's cheap as well as far more interesting.

It's also a great way to make friends, because you should cultivate the habit of exchanging plants for cuttings. Once you start propagating you'll always find you have many more plants than you could possibly use in your own garden, so you'll need to give some of them away in any case. There are few greater pleasures.

If you do become a keen propagator, you'll find it worthwhile to set aside a small area of ground especially for your 'home nursery'. Here you can improve the soil for cuttings and make sure that young root systems have every chance of growing and thriving.

For most purposes it's best to select a site that's slightly shaded, though you may want to sow seeds in a sunnier spot. If you decide to keep it all together, go for a sunnier spot and provide shade artificially where it's needed. Ideally, edge the area with boards and raise the soil by incorporating a quantity of garden compost and coarse grit to make a well-drained yet water-resistant growing medium.

Where you wish to root cuttings directly into the soil, add a covering of about 2.5cm (1in.) of sharp sand to make an ideal rooting medium. By rooting directly into the soil you'll provide a buffer which will give you much better control over watering than you would get in pots or seed trays.

A few shaded propagator tops and perhaps the odd plastic bottle where you need only a few cuttings, plus the apple-box cold frame (see p. 57), are all the equipment you'll need to raise most cuttings of shrubs, herbaceous plants and alpines.

Mind you, the awful truth is that, once you get into full production here, you'll not be satisfied until you buy yourself a greenhouse. But that's another story.

Gardeners can, very cheaply, copy exactly what the nurseryman would do but on a much smaller scale.

Taking cuttings

HARDWOOD CUTTINGS OF SHRUBS

Just about the easiest way to propagate some trees, shrubs and fruit bushes is by hardwood cuttings. You need no special equipment or skill. Indeed, some subjects, like willows and dogwoods, will almost certainly root if you just break off a shoot and stick it in the ground. Timing, however, is important. There's a much better chance of success if the cuttings are put in while the soil is still warm. There's also an increase in rooting activity in the autumn when deciduous trees have just lost their leaves, so that's the time to do it.

SUITABLE PLANTS FOR THIS TREATMENT

Berberis	*Kerria*	*Salix*
Buddleia	*Leycesteria*	*Sambucus*
Buxus	*Ligustrum*	*Spiraea*
Cornus	*Lonicera* (non-climbing)	*Symphoricarpus*
Cotoneaster	*Olearia*	*Tamarix*
Escallonia	*Philadelphus*	*Viburnum* (deciduous)
Forsythia	*Ribes*	*Weigela*
Garrya	*Rosa*	

1 A few species will root readily wherever the cutting is taken, but there's no doubt that all have a greater ability to make roots at the base of the shoot where it joins the stem. Look for shoots that have grown during the current season and are about pencil thickness or more. Cut them off so that you leave just a small stub on the parent plant.

2 Trim the bottom of the cutting just below a leaf joint, and the top just above one. Ideally the shoot should be about 20–23cm (8–9in.) long with all the soft growth at the top removed. Cuttings from evergreen plants should have all the leaves except for the top three or four removed.

3 Dip the bottom of the cutting into hormone rooting liquid. If you have the hormone in powder form, you can make it more effective by diluting it with a little methylated spirits first.

4 Make a slit trench in a corner of the garden by simply pushing the spade in to its full depth and pulling it slightly backwards. Ideally the back of the trench should be upright.

5 Fill the trench to about a third of its depth with *sharp* sand (never use soft builder's sand). This will help to take excess water away from the base of the cuttings and will improve aeration.

6 Put the cuttings in about 7.5–15cm (3–6in.) apart, depending on the plant's vigour. The bases of the cuttings should rest on the sand and their tops should be about 7.5cm (3in.) above ground.

7 Refill the trench with soil and firm in the cuttings with your boot.

8 It'll take approximately a year for most cuttings to make sufficient root to enable them to be transplanted. The following autumn, therefore, gently lift those plants that show signs of growth and line them out into nursery rows in a corner of the garden. Most of them will be of a size suitable for planting in the borders by the autumn of the next year.

Secrets of success

Gooseberries go well from hardwood cuttings. Because they're grown on a straight stem and have a tendency to make suckers from below ground, the custom was to remove all leaves and shoots from the bottom of the cutting before putting it in the ground. It has been discovered, however, that rooting is more successful if those shoots are left on, so after rooting and before transplanting carefully lift the cuttings and remove any suckers at source.

Taking cuttings

LEAF-BUD, LEAF AND EYE CUTTINGS

There are some very specialised forms of propagation that are fun to try and often quite successful with certain species. In the greenhouse some plants can be increased by cuttings from their leaf-stalks, from the veins in the leaves and from single buds – a method also worth trying with a few hardy species too.

Leaf-bud cuttings

1 LEFT Plants with larger leaves, like rubber plants (*Ficus*), are propagated with leaf-bud cuttings. Cut off a small portion of stem with a bud and a leaf. If the leaf is large, it can be rolled up and held with an elastic band to reduce water loss. Insert it in compost so that the bud is just above compost level.

2 Once the leaf stem has rooted, a tiny shoot will grow from the base. Leave the original leaf on until it begins to wither.

Secrets of success

Some plants, especially those with soft stems, can be rooted in water. Fill a jar with water and cover it with baking foil. Poke the cutting through the foil and into the water. Put it in gentle warmth and replace the water if it becomes discoloured. The disadvantage with this method is that the roots are brittle and difficult to move into compost.

Eye cuttings

Eye cuttings are used extensively for propagating vines and are very successful. Here a piece of stem about 5cm (2in.) long containing a bud is used, so several cuttings can be taken from one stem. Remove the bark from the back of the cutting and press it into the compost. It helps rooting if a little silver sand is first sprinkled over the top of the compost.

HOUSEPLANTS SUITABLE FOR LEAF CUTTINGS

Aeonium
Begonia
Crassula
Echeveria
Gloxinia
Peperomia
Saintpaulia
Sanseveria
Sedum
Streptocarpus

HOUSEPLANTS SUITABLE FOR LEAF-BUD CUTTINGS

Cissus
Ficus
Rhoicissus

SHRUBS SUITABLE FOR LEAF-BUD CUTTINGS

Camellia
Mahonia
Rhododendron

Leaf cuttings

1 The leaves of plants like streptocarpus can be used for propagation. First remove a leaf from the parent plant.

2 Cut right across the leaf at regular intervals and put the pieces into the compost on their sides, making sure that the end which was nearest to the plant goes downwards.

3 After six to eight weeks small plantlets will develop from the side of the cutting in the compost.

LEFT The leaves of some begonias can be cut into small squares and laid flat on compost where they'll eventually root. It's important to hold the pieces flat with wire hairpins.

RIGHT A method of increasing African violets (*Saintpaulia*) and gloxinias is to induce roots from the leaf-stalks. Cut each leaf-stalk with a sharp knife or razor blade to leave it about 2.5cm (1in.) long. Insert two leaves back to back in a pot of compost where they'll eventually form roots and produce small plantlets.

Taking cuttings

ROOT CUTTINGS

Taking cuttings from the roots is a very successful way of increasing many plants that are difficult by other means. Perhaps because the parents have to be dug up to get at the roots, this method is not as popular as others, but it really is worth trying. The parent plant can always be successfully replanted afterwards.

It's essential to take cuttings from young plants that are growing vigorously. Those from older plants stand much less chance of success. The time to take root cuttings is in the dormant season with the very best time, in my opinion, being early winter. The technique varies a little, depending on the thickness of the roots.

1 Dig up the plant, keeping as much of the root system intact as possible. It may be necessary to wash the soil from the roots.

2 In the case of fleshy-rooted plants, remove the roots from the parent with a clean cut straight across near the crown of the plant. Cut into sections about 5cm (2in.) long, making the lower cuts at an angle to ensure that you know which way up to put the cuttings. Remove any fibrous side roots.

3 Put the pieces into a polythene bag containing some fungicide powder and shake them about to cover them. Then insert them into coconut-fibre compost with the sloping-cut end downwards and the top just below the surface.

SUITABLE PLANTS FOR THIS TREATMENT

Acanthus	*Lythrum*
Ailanthus	*Nepeta*
Anchusa	*Papaver orientale*
Anemone hybrida	*Phlox*
Brunnera	*Primula denticulata*
Catananche	*Rhus*
Clerodendrum	*Robinia*
Crambe	*Romneya*
Dicentra	
Dictamnus	
Echinacea	
Eryngium	
Limonium	

4 LEFT In the case of thin-rooted plants, remove the roots from the parent as above but cut them into sections about 7.5cm (3in.) long. Again cover them with fungicide, but this time lay the cuttings horizontally on the compost and just cover them.

5 The cuttings need no heat and can be rooted successfully in a coldframe or greenhouse. Cover the frame with sacking only if very severe frost is forecast. The cuttings should be showing signs of shooting the following spring when they can be potted up or lined out in rows in a corner of the garden. However, with all cuttings it's wise to wait until they're at least big enough to see comfortably before you plant them out or they're likely to get swamped by other plants or even by weeds.

INTERNODAL CUTTINGS

Clematis is pretty peculiar in that the cuttings are taken in a slightly different way from those of other plants: you cut between the leaf joints instead of just underneath. These are called 'internodal cuttings'.

I have had most success with this method in summer, and have found it an easier and more satisfactory method than layering (see p. 120), with the cuttings rooting in about six to eight weeks.

1 Remove a section of stem from a vigorous plant and trim between the leaf joints to leave about 5cm (2in.) below the pair of leaves. Trim the top of the cutting immediately above the leaves.

2 Immerse the cutting in a solution of fungicide, dip the end in rooting powder and then put it into coconut-fibre compost so that the buds in the leaf joints rest on or just below the surface.

3 Cover the pot with very thin polythene and tuck it underneath to form a hermetic seal. Put the pot into a shaded coldframe.

4 When the leaves perk up and the cuttings have formed roots, they can be potted individually and grown on to a good size before being planted in their permanent quarters.

Layering

One of the surest ways to propagate plants is by inducing roots without actually cutting the shoots off the plant. This process is called 'layering' and, because the shoots have a source of food and water from the parent while they're forming roots, they have every chance of survival.

1 Select a branch that will reach the ground and wound the underneath of the stem to induce rooting. This can be done by cutting a slit in the bark or by removing a small section entirely. Alternatively, with some plants, like this rhododendron, a sharp twist will damage the tissue enough to make it form roots.

If it's impossible to reach the ground with the stem you wish to layer, it can be sunk into a pot of compost. It may be necessary to cut a nick in the side of the pot.

2 Dig a hole near the plant at the point where the wounded shoot touches the ground and, if necessary, prepare the soil with a little compost and sharp sand. Push the shoot into the hole. To hold the branch down, peg it with a forked stick and then cover it with soil.

3 It's a good idea to put a large stone over the top both to hold the layer in place and to conserve moisture. It could take a long time for the layer to root – even up to two years. When it does, it can be detached and replanted.

With plants that have supple stems like climbers, several layers can be made from the same shoot. This is called 'serpentine layering'. Prepare the soil and lay the shoot on the surface. Hold it down at each leaf joint with a wire staple and roots should form at each point.

AIR LAYERING

Upright-growing plants with stiff stems can't be bent down to the ground but in many cases can still be layered if the compost is taken to the layer rather than the other way around. It's a technique often used for house plants, but some hardy plants will also respond. It's certainly worth trying, preferably in the early spring.

<table>
<tr><td colspan="3">**SUITABLE PLANTS FOR THIS TREATMENT**</td></tr>
<tr><td>Akebia</td><td>Corylopsis</td><td>Osmanthus</td></tr>
<tr><td>Azalea</td><td>Cotinus</td><td>Parrotia</td></tr>
<tr><td>Azara</td><td>Fothergilla</td><td>Pieris</td></tr>
<tr><td>Blackberry</td><td>Hamamelis</td><td>Rubus</td></tr>
<tr><td>Camellia</td><td>Hedera</td><td>Sunberry</td></tr>
<tr><td>Campsis</td><td>Hydrangea</td><td>Syringa</td></tr>
<tr><td>Celastrus</td><td>Jasminum</td><td>Tayberry</td></tr>
<tr><td>Clematis</td><td>Kalmia</td><td>Vitis</td></tr>
<tr><td>Cornus</td><td>Magnolia</td><td>Wisteria</td></tr>
</table>

1 Start by making a cut in the stem just below a leaf joint and passing vertically through it up the stem.

2 Sprinkle a little hormone rooting powder on the cut and keep it open with either a matchstick or a small wad of moist sphagnum moss.

3 Wrap moist moss around the joint and then wrap the whole thing with a piece of clear polythene tied top and bottom.

4 After a while roots will form and you should be able to see them through the polythene. If you can't, unwrap the sheeting from time to time to check.

5 When the shoot has rooted you can detach it from the parent simply by cutting below the rooted section using secateurs.

6 Then pot the detached plant in the normal way. Note that the new plant will have all the vigour of youth, so you may need to repot it fairly soon.

Division of herbaceous perennials and alpines

The easiest and most convenient way to increase many herbaceous perennials and alpines is by division. Most of those that form mats or clumps will actually benefit from being split up from time to time – generally at about three-to-four-year intervals. The centre of the plant becomes old and tired and often dies out completely, leaving vigorous areas of growth on the outside of the clump with an ugly bare patch in the middle. Regular division will avoid this and give the plant new vigour and energy.

1 Division is best done either in the autumn, while the soil is still warm, or during the spring, just as the plants begin to grow. Lift the whole clump with a fork or spade and put it on to a piece of polythene on the lawn.

2 Some plants can be divided by forcing the clump apart with two forks pushed in back to back and pulled apart.

3 More often, division is a simple matter of cutting off vigorous young growths from the outside of the clump. The old centre is discarded.

4 Plants with thick, fleshy roots like hostas need to be sawn into pieces. Do this in the spring when it's possible to make sure that each piece cut off has a new shoot. An old bread knife is ideal for the job.

5 If you're replanting in the same place, revitalise the soil with manure or compost and a little bone meal for autumn planting or general fertiliser in the spring.

6 Plant the new plants in groups, firming in with your hands, and water well afterwards. They will very soon fill the same space occupied by the old clump and you'll still have plants to spare, enabling you quickly to build a fine herbaceous border.

Alpines

Alpines such as saxifrage can be divided in much the same way, though the plants are generally on a smaller scale and can simply be pulled apart.

Some alpines, like the houseleeks, form offsets which can be lifted carefully with a trowel and replanted.

Plants with rhizomes

1 Plants with rhizomes, like the bearded irises, are treated somewhat differently. They're lifted after flowering in the summer and young rhizomes are cut from the old plant.

2 Cut the leaves in half to prevent wind-rocking and replant so that the top of the rhizome is above soil level.

SUITABLE PLANTS FOR DIVISION

				Geranium	Iris	Phlomis	Rodgersia	Stachys
				Geum	Lamium	Phlox	Rudbeckia	Stipa
Acaena	Aster	Centaurea	Doronicum	Helleborus	Liatris	Polygonatum	Saponaria	Tellima
Achillea	Astilbe	Chrysanthemum	Echinacea	Helenium	Liriope	Polygonum	Saxifraga	Tiarella
Alchemilla	Astrantia	Coreopsis	Echinops	Hemerocallis	Lysimachia	Potentilla	Schizostylis	Tradescantia
Anaphalis	Bergenia	Crocosmia	Epimedium	Hesperis	Miscanthus	Primula	Sedum	Trollius
Aquilegia	Brunnera	Delphinium	Erigeron	Heuchera	Molinia	Pulmonaria	Sidalcea	Veronica
Armeria	Campanula	Dicentra	Filipendula	Hosta	Papaver	Rheum	Solidago	Waldsteinia

Budding

Budding is a technique used to propagate roses, fruit and many ornamental trees. It involves removing a bud from the variety you want and transferring it to a special rootstock. The reason for doing this is to control the vigour of the variety; weak rose varieties, for example, are budded on to a strong-growing relative of the wild rose to increase their vigour. The job must be done in the early summer when the plant is actively growing so that the bark comes away easily from the stem. It requires some skill: don't expect to get it right first time, but persevere because it's very rewarding.

Getting hold of rootstocks is probably the most difficult bit. For roses, you'll generally find that professional growers will sell you a few stocks.

Most bush roses, like this 'Mountbatten', are budded on to *Rosa laxa*, a relative of our own wild rose.

BUDDING ROSES

1 Cut a fresh, strong, young shoot and remove the thorns and leaves, leaving only a small part of the leaf stalk.

2 The bud is between the leaf stalk and the stem. Cut just below it, and draw the knife upwards.

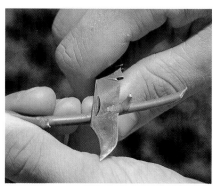

3 There will be a small sliver of wood behind the bud and this should be carefully removed.

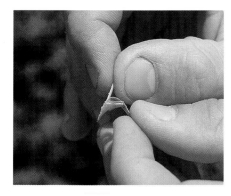

4 Now prepare the rootstock by cutting a T-shaped slit in the bark.

5 Lift the edges slightly away from the stem. They should come away easily.

6 Now push the bud into the T-slit so that the bark holds it in position.

7 LEFT Cut off the top of the shield flush with the top arm of the T.

8 Hold the bud in place using a special rubber tie. While you're buying the rootstocks, beg a handful of these from the grower. Three weeks to a month later, the bud should begin to grow out. Allow the plant to grow on until the early spring of the following year, and then cut off the top of the stock to leave the variety. By the autumn it will have produced a respectable plant which can then be planted out in its permanent position.

CHIP-BUDDING

Fruit and ornamental trees are also budded, sometimes to increase vigour and often, in the case of fruit trees, for example, to reduce it to keep the trees small. A slightly different technique, known as 'chip-budding', is used. The technique is not difficult to master and has a high success rate. Again, getting hold of rootstocks is difficult, so you will need to find a specialist catalogue or cultivate a friendly nurseryman.

1 RIGHT The bud is removed from the variety in much the same way as recommended for roses except that it's not necessary to remove the sliver of wood.

2 Now prepare the rootstock. Make a cross nick into the bark and slice off a piece of bark down to the nick.

3 Then it's simply a case of replacing the slice of bark you've removed with the bud, holding the bottom behind the nick in the bark.

4 Finally tie it in, preferably with a special tie begged from the nurseryman or with tape or string. Then continue as recommended for roses.

Grafting

Grafting is really another form of budding, but this time using lengths of shoot instead of just the bud. It's a method used widely with some fruit trees and many ornamental trees and shrubs. Naturally you can't graft any plant on to any rootstock. They have to be compatible, so choose the same genus or find out what has proved successful. Rhododendron varieties, for example, are generally grafted on to *Rhododendron ponticum*, but the pineapple broom (*Cytisus battandieri*) is grafted on to laburnum.

The best time to graft is just as growth begins in the spring, but the shoots of the variety (known as 'scions') are collected in December or January and stored by half-burying in soil outside until use. Look for strong, young growth of the previous season and remove the soft tips before storing.

An important principle to note is that the section of both scion and rootstock that will eventually fuse is situated just below the bark. It's called the 'cambium layer' and it's essential that the cambium of the scion is in direct contact with the cambium of the rootstock. So to give yourself a double chance of success by getting the cambium on *both* sides of the stem to fuse, the scion and the rootstock must be of the same diameter.

The pineapple broom is grafted on to a laburnum rootstock.

'SPLICE' GRAFTING

1 The easiest and most popular graft is the 'splice' graft. Start by making a long, sloping cut in the rootstock.

2 Select a scion of the same width and prepare it in the same way, making sure that the cut is straight and even. You'll need plenty of practice, so be prepared to fail a few times at first.

3 Put the scion on to the stock so that the two cambium layers coincide. Provided that the stock and scion are the same width this will happen automatically of course.

4 The graft can be tied together with string or raffia and then coated with a grafting wax to keep out water. However, I have been more successful with plastic waterproof tape which is much easier to use.

'FRAMEWORK' GRAFTING

It's possible to change the variety of a fruit tree, for example, or to add another variety, by a modified form of 'framework' grafting. If you decide to change the variety completely, much of the existing wood should be removed: take off all the side branches and leave just the main framework. Leave just a few smaller branches situated just below the grafting points or, alternatively, leave a couple of main branches which can later be removed. Their function is simply to draw up water and nutrients and to keep the tree alive while the grafts are taking. They're known as 'sap-drawers'.

My recommendation would be to try out the method on a few branches first, before cutting the tree right back.

Saw back to a convenient length the branches you intend grafting, bearing in mind that small cuts heal faster than large ones, so it's as well to cut back two smaller branches just above a fork than to cut below it. The preparation should be done during dormancy and the scions should also be cut and stored as described opposite. The grafting is done in late April when the bark will part easily from the branch.

1 RIGHT Remove most of the side shoots except for the few sap-drawers and cut back the branches to leave just the main framework of the tree.

2 Tidy up the sawn ends of the branches so that they're clean and smooth and then cut a slit in the bark. Open up the slit slightly with your knife.

3 Prepare the scion in the way suggested for 'splice' grafting but without making the tongue.

4 Slide the scion downwards into the slit in the bark which will hold it quite firmly while you're tying it in. Repeat the process with two to four scions, depending on the size of the branch.

5 Finally tie the branch tightly to keep the scions from moving and seal with grafting wax or waterproof tape.

CHAPTER 5
GARDEN PLANNING

THE BEAUTY OF gardening as an art is that each and every one of us can do it. You don't need to be able to draw or to work a sculptor's chisel, you don't have to be born with musical talent or the touch to coax magic from the potter's wheel. You need only to be able to wield a spade and to tip a watering can to create the natural beauty that plants bring to your life. But the art of the garden is a strictly personal thing.

It may be that you're transported with delight at the sight of massed ranks of bedding plants, you may drool over pastel shades and single-colour borders, or you may prefer the formality of grass and box hedging. It doesn't matter. The fact that we are all capable of gardening diminishes it as an art not one whit, and the fact that what you may like your neighbour may detest is quite irrelevant. If it delights your eye and lifts your spirit, you have achieved a masterpiece.

So far be it from me to diminish your own, unique talent by presuming to tell you what's good for you. But we all have to learn the basic rules. Even Van Gogh was taught to use a palette knife and Rodin to wield a mallet, and garden design has its dos and don'ts too.

I therefore ask you to consider the basic rules in this chapter – and then to let your imagination run riot!

You can be assured that, after a year or two, the planting will transform even the most modest scheme.

Starting to plan your garden

The very first and most important rule of garden design is: 'Take your time'. Ideally, if you can bear to wait, you could, in the first year, fill your plot with a mixture of grass, perhaps a few hardy annuals raised cheaply from seed to give a bit of colour and strong-growing vegetables like potatoes to break up the ground. Then you'll have a breathing space and the opportunity to gather inspiration.

In that first season read as much as you can, especially about plants, and get out and about to friends' gardens, to flower shows and gardens open to the public. Certainly most are likely to be much bigger and grander than your own, but you'll still come back with a host of

ideas. Take a notebook and preferably a camera as well, because there's too much to learn to keep in your head.

Even then, take time to map out your plans on paper and be prepared to change your mind – a lot. Walk around the plot, viewing it from every angle, until you know it backwards and are sure of exactly what you want.

It's a good idea to make a list of necessities, like a place to put the dustbin, the clothes line or the children's swing, and then to indulge yourself in another list of desirables. In my experience, the second list is always miles too long, but make it anyway and cut it down as space dictates.

The short, wide garden This can be made to look longer by swinging the main axis so that your eye is drawn from corner to corner instead of straight to the back fence only a few yards away. This is done by arranging a viewing point in one corner and then shaping and planting the borders so that your natural impulse is to look to the other corner. An eye-catching statue or a striking plant in that corner will help to catch your attention. With a bit of thought you can arrange several vistas to be viewed in the same way from other vantage points.

BELOW **The long, thin garden** Unless you're blessed with a very large plot, most designs are influenced more than anything by the constraints. A long, thin garden will certainly tax your imagination.

It's a good idea to divide such a plot into a series of 'rooms', but it's a mistake simply to cut it across from side to side. That's restrictive and boring.

The simplest way to divide it interestingly is to wind a path through it in an S-shape, using plants to block the view from one end to the other.

Alternatively, you could divide it with open trellis planted with climbers. That way you'll give the impression of reducing the length but, because you can catch glimpses of the rest of the garden through the spaces, you avoid the claustrophobic effect of a solid division.

ABOVE **The garden with a view** The small garden with a fine view can 'borrow' the surrounding countryside to make it appear that the garden is part of it. This is done by hiding the fence with planting to give the impression that it merges with the background. You may want to lower the fence to increase the view.

Conversely, if you have an ugly view or if your garden is overlooked by other houses, you can regain your privacy by screening with trees, while still leaving 'windows' here and there to allow a glimpse of any more attractive scenery that may also be seen. You may need to do some judicious pruning from time to time.

Measuring the garden and drawing a plan

It's best to design your new garden on paper. If you make it piecemeal, you invariably end up with a hotch-potch that lacks co-ordination and looks like – well, a hotch-potch. Of course, you can still retain a certain amount of flexibility, even when you've arrived at your final plan. You'll often find, for example, that what looks like a good shape on paper can be improved when it's transferred to the ground. The reason is that when you draw the plan you'll be looking straight down on it, whereas when you're in the garden your eyeline is much more horizontal so you may need to make some minor adjustments. However, at least the drawing will give you a good, cohesive working plan and a base from which you can start.

1 BELOW Measure the shape and dimensions of the garden by 'triangulation'. Take a fixed point – the house is most convenient – and measure from one corner (A) to one corner of the garden (C). Then measure from the other corner of the house (B) to the same point (C). Repeat for the other corners of the garden and for any fixed objects, like trees, you may wish to keep. Note all these measurements down on a rough plan.

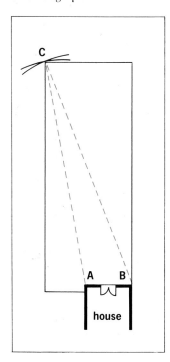

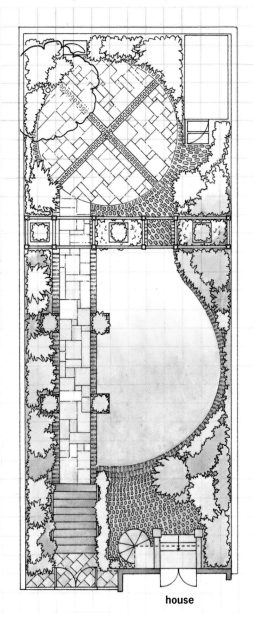

house

2 LEFT Transfer the measurements to squared paper pinned to a piece of board. The measurements must first be reduced down to a convenient scale to suit the size of your garden and your piece of paper: something like 1cm to 30cm (or perhaps 1in. to 2ft). Draw in the house first. That's easy because you can be sure that what look like right angles actually are. Then mark an arc of the appropriate diameter from point (A) and another from point (B). Where they cross will be point (C), which is the position of one corner of the garden. Repeat for the other corners of the garden and for the fixed objects, if any, that you have decided to keep.

With the shape of the plot laid out and the permanent features drawn in, all you have to do now is to visualise your ideal garden. Something like this takes a lot of visualising, but with the help of your list of requirements try to draw in the shape of beds and borders, then features like a pool, a patio or a play area for the children. Of course, you'll make many mistakes and you'll change your mind endlessly – even the professionals do that. But you'll only be making your mistakes on paper.

OPPOSITE BELOW The great art of landscape designing is to be able to see in your mind's eye what the garden will look like when you have finished all your improvements. A site like this offers little inspiration . . .

. . . But after the design has been implemented (ABOVE), it has been transformed into a garden that will grow in beauty year after year. This isn't easy and you probably won't get it right first time, but the great thing about gardens is that you always have another chance. Eventually, you're sure to win.

Basic rules

If you travel on a train almost anywhere where people live, you get a marvellous insight into garden design. Often you can sit back and look at a wonderful diversity of back gardens flashing by. And the most exciting part is that, even though the houses may be identical and the gardens of equal size and shape, there are *never* two the same. Like fingerprints, gardens are unique.

The following four designs for the small plot of a semi-detached house are certainly not intended to be copied. I use them simply to illustrate a few basic design rules. Look at them as a guide, but then let your own imagination rip! You'll get a much more satisfying result.

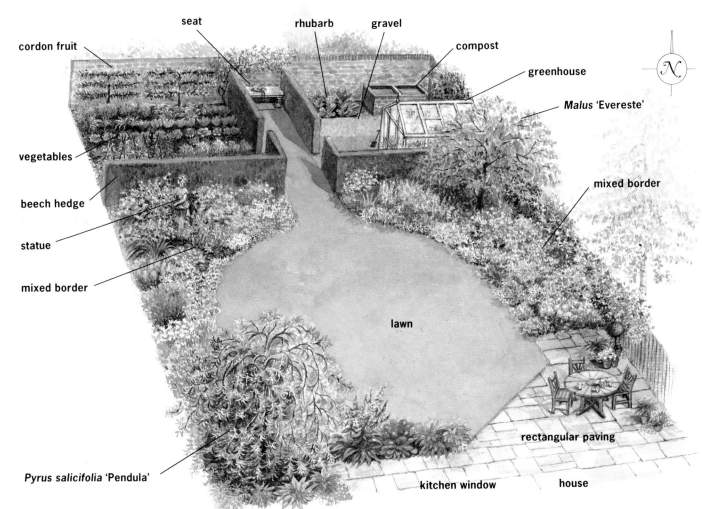

1 The first design is very simple and aimed really at the busy gardener. It should take no more than three or four hours a week to maintain.

The sitting-out area in all the gardens has been sited in the corner near the house for two reasons. First, the patio doors are at that side, so it's easy to step straight out with food or drinks. But notice, too, that the triangular shape of the paved area makes a more useable space in which to put a table and chairs than would a thin strip along the back of the house, even though it takes no more room.

Because it's small, the axis of the garden runs from corner to corner with the eye being drawn from the paved area to the statue. But a view has also been established from the kitchen window since it's from here that much garden viewing is done. The grass and borders are curved in informal shapes. Note that the curves are long and gentle, giving a more relaxed look and, incidentally, making mowing much easier and quicker than sharp curves and awkward corners. And easy mowing always makes for better-quality grass.

2 This is a very formal garden. The axis runs straight down the middle from top to bottom and the shapes are all more or less symmetrical. The lawn, for example, is circular except for the piece 'bitten' out of one side. The extension path at the top leads the eye to a feature seat, backed by a striking, columnar copper beech. To avoid breaking up the shapes, the access path runs along one side.

The paved area again uses the corner near the patio doors with a formal, raised pool to add interest. But to avoid making the garden a source of worry, note that no pool, however safe you may think you've made it, is a good idea if you have small children. It's important to note the narrow border around the raised pool. Without it, cutting the edge of the grass against the wall would be impossible with the mower and very time-consuming with a strimmer or hand shears.

I have used an octagonal greenhouse in this design to save space. It's excellent for a small garden since it's easy to fit in anywhere and looks very attractive too.

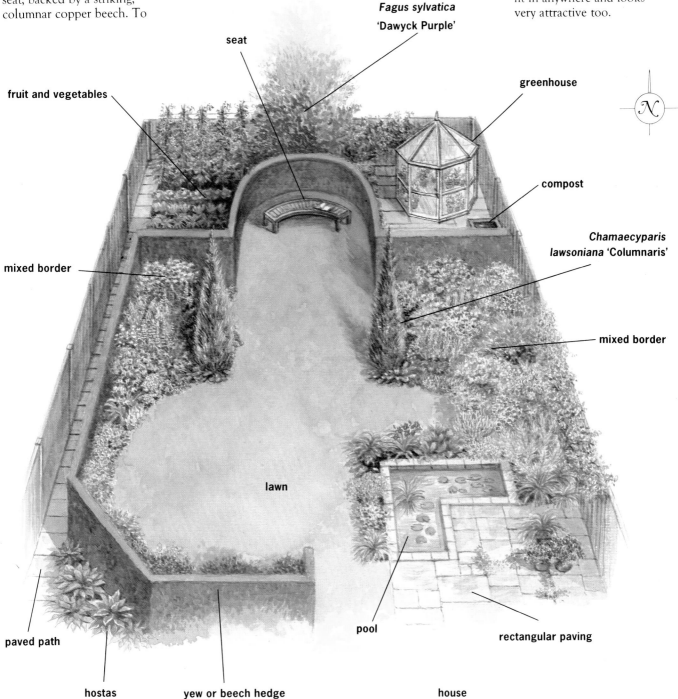

seat

Fagus sylvatica 'Dawyck Purple'

greenhouse

fruit and vegetables

compost

Chamaecyparis lawsoniana 'Columnaris'

mixed border

mixed border

lawn

paved path

hostas

yew or beech hedge

pool

house

rectangular paving

Basic rules

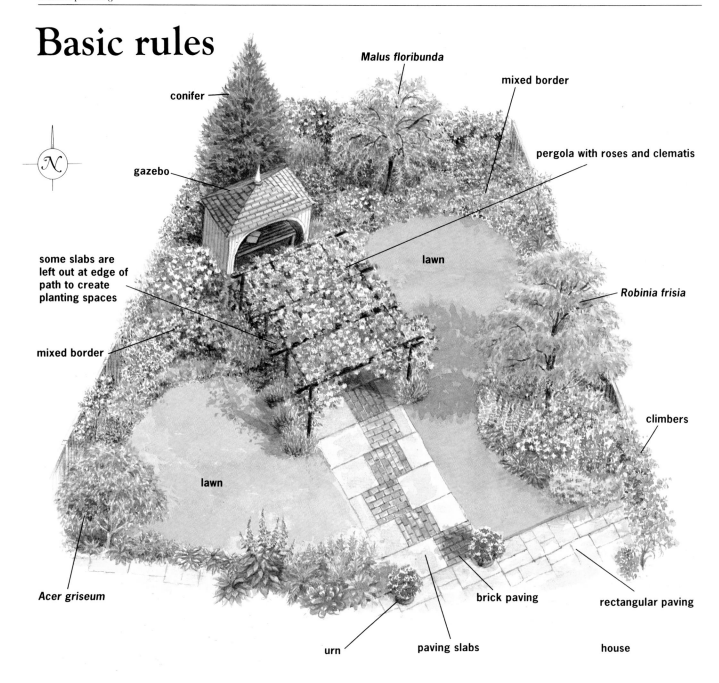

Malus floribunda

mixed border

conifer

pergola with roses and clematis

gazebo

lawn

some slabs are left out at edge of path to create planting spaces

Robinia frisia

mixed border

climbers

lawn

Acer griseum

brick paving

rectangular paving

urn

paving slabs

house

3 This garden is a mixture of the formal and informal. Again the triangular-shaped patio is in the corner near the patio doors and again the axis has been swung round to the diagonal. But here the main feature is a wide path leading to a gazebo.

Paths create a peculiar problem in small gardens. They take up a lot of space that any gardener worth his or her salt would rather use for growing plants. Yet narrow paths tend to look mean and cramped and actually reduce the apparent width of the garden. So I've compromised. The main part of the path is made with paving slabs in a dead straight, formal way, but inside these brick paving has been used to make a winding path down the middle. Then plants in the borders are allowed to spill over on to the paving, with some slabs here and there actually left out to make more planting room while still retaining the illusion of a continuous straight edge.

This is very much a plant-lover's garden, so the lawns have been kept small and informal, purely for access and to make an attractive foreground for the planting. In a small garden like this overplanting should be the order of the day if anything, so that not a centimetre of soil can be seen. It entails quite a lot of maintenance because plants need to be restrained all the time.

4 Another enthusiast's garden, but this time it's completely romantic. The design and planting are intended to attract wildlife and to provide a natural setting for native and 'cottage-garden' plants.

Here the path is narrow, but that's acceptable if it winds between and around features and the planting is over-abundant. The main feature is the pool which is informal and incorporates a bog garden.

I have included a small patch of fine grass to provide somewhere to sit, but it's bordered by longer grass planted with wildflowers. That area is cut no more than twice a year.

It's not absolutely necessary to fill the garden with wildflowers or 'weeds' to attract insects, birds and small animals, so the borders can still be 'gardened' in the normal way, using cultivated plants that will also act as a lure to wildlife.

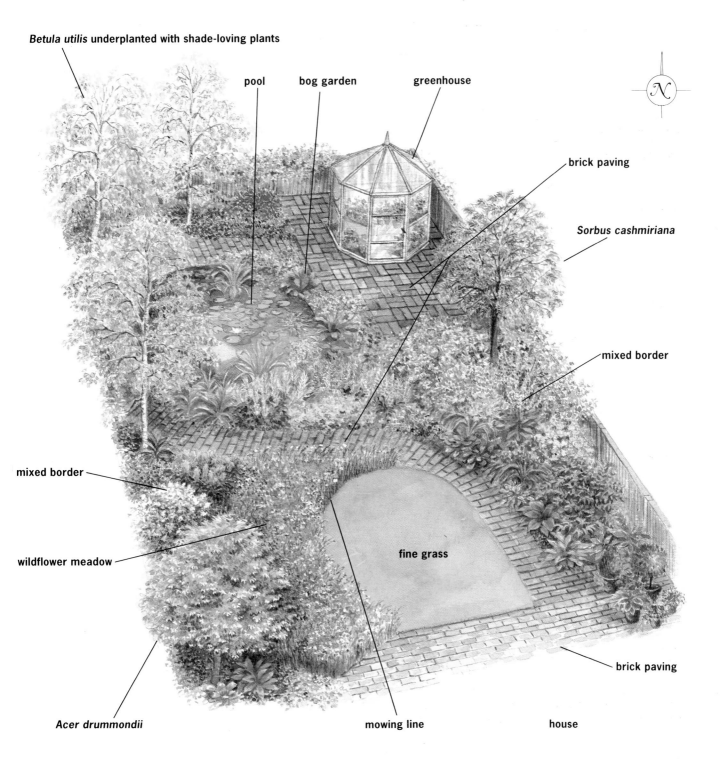

Betula utilis underplanted with shade-loving plants

pool

bog garden

greenhouse

brick paving

Sorbus cashmiriana

mixed border

mixed border

wildflower meadow

fine grass

brick paving

Acer drummondii

mowing line

house

137

Marking out the plan on the ground

Setting out the drawing on the ground demands a fair amount of accuracy, so don't be satisfied with a school ruler and a few bits of hairy string tied to sticks. Make proper lines with nylon string and, if necessary, hire a surveyor's tape, a long spirit level and a straightedge. If you expect to do a lot of construction work, it'll certainly be worth your while buying all this equipment.

But always remember the first rule of landscaping: 'If it looks right, it *is* right.' So be prepared, when setting out, to be a bit flexible. When you've set something out, walk around it, viewing it from all sides, and change it if it looks unbalanced or off line.

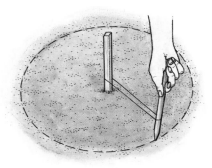

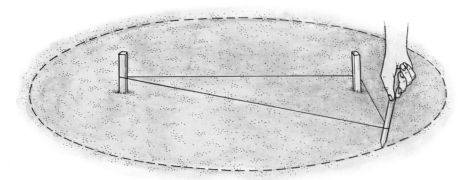

Marking a circle This is fairly obvious. Put a stout stick in the ground, measure a loop of twine to the exact radius of the circle, put another stick in the loop and scratch a mark in the soil.

Marking an oval Much the same as marking a circle except that two sticks are employed.

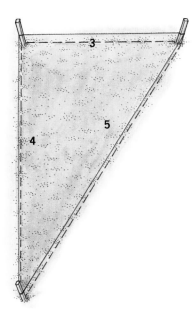

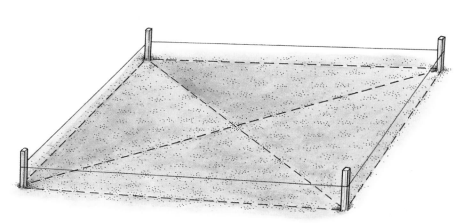

Checking a rectangle When you've laid out a rectangle, check that the angles are exact right angles by measuring all sides and then from corner to corner. Both corner measurements should, of course, be the same.

Marking a right angle Use a triangle, either of string on posts or specially made of wood, making the sides respectively 3, 4 and 5 units. So the shortest side may be 3m (10ft) long and the longest 5m (16½ft) with the angle between the shorter sides being 90 degrees.

Secrets of success

A clearer way of marking lines on the ground, particularly ideal for indicating planting lines, is to substitute the marking stick with a bottle filled with dry sand.

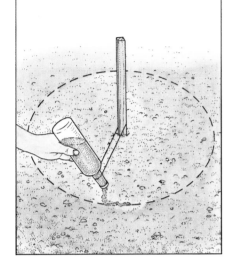

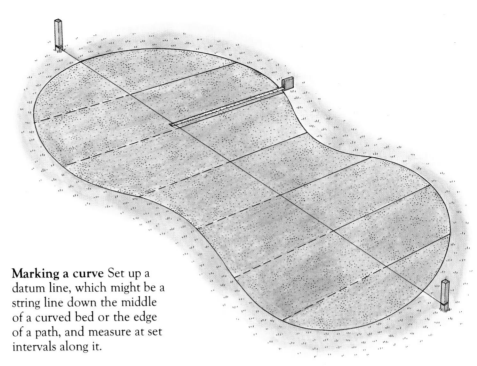

Marking a curve Set up a datum line, which might be a string line down the middle of a curved bed or the edge of a path, and measure at set intervals along it.

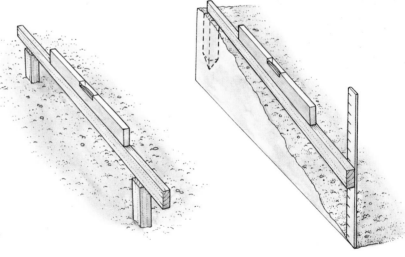

Marking a slope To ensure that a slope is even throughout its whole length, use pegs, a straightedge and a spirit level. Put in the first peg (A) at the required level and set the second peg (B), using a block of wood on top. Remove the wood and set the third peg (C), again using the block. When the wood is removed, the three pegs will represent an even slope.

Levelling For anything that demands a degree of accuracy, like paving or concreting, this must always be done with pegs. Cut good pegs that are square on top and level them using a straightedge and spirit level.

Measuring a gradient You will need to do this before putting in steps, for example. Put a straightedge on a peg at the top of the slope, level it with a spirit level and measure the height above ground at a fixed point. You may prefer to put in a peg or, alternatively, get help to hold the straightedge steady while you measure.

CHAPTER 6

HARD
LANDSCAPING

IF YOU'RE STARTING a new garden, you'll have plenty of
'hard landscaping' to do. Paving, walling, fencing and
concreting are all pretty messy jobs involving trampling
of soil and potential damage to grass and plants. So it's
obviously best to try to get them done first. In existing
gardens, where it's not possible, make sure that you
have a ready supply of wide boards to minimise damage.
You can hire scaffold planks quite cheaply.

Remember too the message that was dinned into me
for the whole of my first five years of gardening – to
clean up as you go. If you keep the site clean and tidy all
the time, you'll save yourself hours of work in the end
and you'll enjoy the work that much more.

Finally, don't skimp or cut corners. If you decide to
save on time or costs by reducing the thickness of the
concrete under your paving, for example, you're certain
to regret it. It'll sink all over the place within a very
short time and you'll be faced with taking it up and
starting again. It's always best to do the job properly,
even if that means waiting a while to save the money.

Bear in mind that, properly done, your hard
landscaping will be a source of pleasure to you for years
and that you'll easily recoup the cost of each
improvement you do when you sell the house.

Every garden needs an area of hard material, perhaps to sit
out on or as a path. With care it can be made very attractive.

Concrete and concreting

In new gardens you'll need to use concrete whenever a solid, permanent job is required. You can also use it for decorative hard areas since it can look very attractive with a variety of finishes. Concrete is made with a mixture of ballast (sand and gravel mixed), cement and water. The normal ratio is 6–8 parts ballast to 1 part cement, with the stronger mix being used where the concrete will be seen. If you really can't face mixing it or if you have a large area to do, buy ready-mixed concrete.

Mortar is used for wall building and to set paving slabs. It's made with soft sand, special masonry cement (which is more flexible than ordinary concreting cement) and water. If you use ordinary cement, there's a danger that, if the walling moves fractionally as it normally will when temperatures vary, the bricks or stone may crack. The normal ratio is 3 parts sand to 1 part cement. For both concrete and mortar it's *vital* to use fresh cement.

1 When mixing most concrete, measure by the shovelful since accuracy is not necessary. Spread the ballast out in a wide, flat heap and cover with the cement. For concrete that will be used as a finish, all mixes must be the same colour, so measure with a bucket.

3 Mix the materials together dry first, turning the heap into the middle and then moving it to one side and back again to ensure a really good mix. As a base for paving, a dry mix like this is sufficient, but for any other work you'll need to mix it with water at this stage.

5 For bigger jobs you can save an enormous amount of time by hiring a cement mixer. Again, measure rough concrete by the shovelful, but where it'll be seen use a bucket to measure more accurately.

2 When mixing mortar for walling, uniformity of colouring is also important, so again use a bucket for accurate measurement. As well as using special masonry cement for this job, you'll need cement plasticiser, though if it's only a small job you can put a few squirts of washing-up liquid into the water to make the mortar more plastic.

4 Make a hole in the middle of the heap and pour in water, but don't overdo it. Then push the mixture from the sides into the middle, avoiding overflows. If the mixture is too dry to work comfortably, it's easy to add a little more water, but until you're used to how much you need it's best to add it cautiously at first.

6 Most concrete will need shuttering. This is made with 7.5×2.5cm (3×1in.) timber which is sufficient for most jobs. Ensure that there are enough pegs to keep the shuttering firm under the weight of the concrete. Level it with a spirit level.

7 If the soil has been newly disturbed and is likely to sink, as it would, for example, right next to a new house where the trenches for the footings have been recently refilled, it's wise to dig out more deeply and put in at least 15cm (6in.) of hardcore. Do the same for driveways where the concrete has to take the weight of a vehicle.

8 Pour in the concrete and tamp down and level it by banging the surface with a board laid across the shuttering. This will leave a ribbed and therefore non-slip surface.

9 If you want a smoother surface, still tamp down and level with the board but then finish off with a float.

Secrets of success

The hardest part of pushing a wheelbarrow full of cement is turning it round, so make sure that the barrow faces in the direction you're going *before* you fill it up. The same principle applies with any material, of course, but you'll notice it more with concrete!

10 For a more attractive finish, you could divide the area into large 'slabs' with wooden shuttering as shown. The concrete could also be coloured with a powder which is added while mixing. Here, of course, it's essential to be very accurate when more than one mix is needed. A patio like this is very much cheaper than paving and, provided you make sure that the concrete is far enough below the damp-proof course of the house (see p. 144), it could still be used as the base for paving when the budget allows.

Paving

There's no doubt that rectangular paving has, over recent years, become by far the most popular way to make hard surfaces and with good reason. If you use artificial stone, it's relatively cheap, fairly easy to lay and certainly the best finish for modern buildings. The once-popular crazy paving should be strictly reserved for older, rural houses.

There are many types and patterns of slabs available, mostly made of concrete or reconstituted stone to give a very fair imitation of the real thing. Bear in mind, however, that highly coloured paving is inappropriate for most gardens except in hot climates where it looks a little less incongruous. The colour of all slabs tends to fade slightly in any case after a few years. One other point to bear in mind when ordering is that reconstituted stone is easier to cut by hand than concrete, though neither is difficult if you use an angle grinder.

Slabs are available in a variety of sizes and can be attractively mixed to give a random effect. When ordering make sure that you order equal *areas* of each size rather than equal *numbers* or you'll finish up with too many of the larger sizes.

1 Start by setting a number of level pegs across the area you wish to pave. The tops of the pegs should correspond with the required finish level of the paving. Ensure that it's at least two courses of bricks lower than the damp-proof course of the house and that it slopes gently away from it.

2 LEFT Dig out the soil to allow for the thickness of the paving, plus 2.5cm (1in.) of mortar to set it on, plus 7.5cm (3in.) of concrete foundation. On hard soil that's unlikely to sink and where 4cm (1½in.) slabs are being used, you'd need to dig out 14cm (5½in.). On soft soil an extra layer of hardcore is advisable.

3 RIGHT Use an 8 to 1 mix of concrete and mix it dry. Spread it out over the surface and tread it down hard. Rising dampness and subsequent rain will soon harden it up.

4 LEFT Each slab is laid on five points of mortar, one at each corner and one in the middle. Make sure that this mortar is mixed fairly dry to prevent it slumping under the weight of the slab.

5 RIGHT Put the slab on top of the mortar and line it up accurately with the house wall or the fence. Then tap it down using a straightedge on to the nearest peg to ensure that it's level.

6 LEFT Check the level both ways using other pegs, making sure that the straightedge sits flush with the top of the slab. If the slabs are contoured, a little guesswork is needed, but the uneven surface means that absolute accuracy is not quite so important.

7 ABOVE Lay the second and subsequent slabs in the same way, butting them up tight. There's no need to point in between: the small cracks left will allow drainage.

8 ABOVE Inevitably, some cutting will be necessary. If the slabs are stone or reconstituted stone, they'll cut with a hammer and bolster. Mark the cutting line and then gently tap both sides until the slab falls apart along it.

Crazy paving This is laid in much the same way as ordinary paving except that each piece is set on a solid bed of mortar. Fit the pieces together, leaving about 1.3–2.5cm (½–1in.) between them for pointing in later. For extra strength this is generally done with sharp rather than soft sand. Mix it at 3 to 1 like the mortar, keeping it fairly dry so as not to stain the paving.

9 LEFT The easiest way is to hire an angle grinder with a stone disc which will cut both stone and concrete. It's *essential* to wear gloves and goggles for this job so, if you don't own them, get them from the hire shop with the grinder.

10 RIGHT Make sure that no one walks on the newly laid paving for at least twenty-four hours. After that you can sweep it down and spend an hour or two admiring it!

Walling

Winston Churchill found the building of brick walls in his garden to be a fine therapy. It's certainly fun and not as difficult as it looks.

Brick or stone walling is an excellent way to add interest to the garden by changing the levels and it's a convenient way to terrace existing slopes. Of course, it's a skill that takes time and practice to acquire, but most gardeners who are reasonably handy will be able to cope with walls up to three or four courses high.

BELOW A well-planted wall makes an outstanding feature.

1 Dig the foundations 15cm (6in.) deep and twice the width of the wall. This will suffice for walls up to 1m (3ft) high. Level with pegs to the top of the foundation.

2 Fill with concrete and tamp down. Note that the foundation finishes a little below the grass level to hide the concrete.

3 RIGHT Set the bricks or stones at the ends of the run, putting them on a 1.3cm (½in.) bed of mortar (for mixing see p. 142) and tapping down. Check that they're level both ways with a spirit level, which should be used frequently. Note that if the wall continues at right angles to the first run, you should set both runs simultaneously in order to make a 'bond' later.

4 RIGHT Wrap a builder's line around a couple of stones and set it so that it runs exactly along the front top edge of the stones. You will almost certainly have to tap the first two stones into position again to line them up exactly. The line will show the correct height as well as the right line of the wall.

5 LEFT If the wall does incorporate a corner, adjust it to an exact right angle using a set square and then set another builder's line in the same way as the first. A bad angle will forever offend the eye, so take special care to get it right.

BELOW If you feel you can't face building walls in this way, it's possible to buy walling where the stones have been more or less pre-set into blocks. They're then fixed together with special cement like tile cement to make a fairly convincing job. Another alternative is reconstituted stone walling.

Secrets of success

If you're building a retaining wall, either to hold back soil on a slope or to make a raised bed for planting, it's important to incorporate 'weep holes' in the first course to allow water to get out. You can simply leave a half-stone out about every 1m (3ft), but the wall will look much more attractive if a clay drainage pipe is mortared in.

6 Lay the rest of the first course using the line as a guide. When you lay bricks, you use slightly wetter mortar than you would with stone, since the surface is smoother and excess mortar easily cleans off and it's easy to put a wedge of mortar on the end of each brick as you lay it. Stone with a rougher face needs drier mortar which won't stick, so you'll have to point in the cracks after laying each course.

7 When you lay the second course, you'll need to cut the first stone in half to ensure that the joints don't coincide. This creates a firm bond. Alternatively, if the wall incorporates a corner, start there and lay alternate stones side-on and then end-on to make the bond. Check regularly both ways with the spirit level to ensure that the wall is level and perpendicular.

8 When the mortar's dry but before it sets hard, rake out the joints, using a piece of wood, to make an attractive effect. Then, when it's finally dry and hard, you may need to go over the stone with a wire brush to take off any crumbs of mortar that may be sticking to it. Never forget this final job when you finish for the day.

9 The top of the wall needs finishing both for effect and to prevent frost damage. A wider coping is used, overlapping the front of the wall by about 2.5cm (1in.). Generally these are available in the same material as the walling.

Steps

Steps make an attractive feature in a garden and, of course, provide access from one level to another. When designing them, keep in mind two factors. First, narrow steps look mean and skimped while wide ones have an expansive, noble air, so make them as wide as space permits; and second, make sure that the height of the risers is about right. If the risers are too high, they can be difficult for the old and very young to negotiate, while if they're too low, they form 'trips' and can be dangerous. About 12–15cm (5–6in.) is an ideal height.

1 First measure the slope using a straightedge and spirit level (see p. 38) and then measure the length of the proposed set of steps. From this you'll be able to calculate the height of the risers and the width of the treads.

2 Always start building at the bottom of the slope and set the first slabs level with the lawn or path.

3 Dig a footing behind the slabs and concrete it so that the concrete finishes about 6mm (¼in.) below the paving.

4 Set in a row of stones (the risers) as for walling (see p. 146) and fill in with concrete behind. Make sure the risers are 2.5cm (1in.) narrower than the slabs that will go on top so that they'll protrude by that amount. Rake out the joints between the stones.

5 Set slabs on top of the risers to make the treads in the way recommended for installing coping stones on walls (see p. 147). The next step is then made in exactly the same way as the first.

Informal steps These can be made with wood, and old railway sleepers are ideal. Hold them with stakes driven in behind and nailed to the sleepers. The 'treads' are made with an infilling of bark chips.

Look upon a slope in the garden as a distinct advantage and use steps as a feature in themselves.

Paths

Many gardens need some kind of path for access, perhaps to the back gate, the washing line or the greenhouse. In small gardens, paths pose a problem because they take up valuable space which could be used for growing plants. However, there's no reason at all why the paths themselves should not become an interesting feature, and indeed they can also be used to grow plants. In the same way as with steps, ensure that a path is in proportion with the rest of the garden and avoid making it too narrow.

LAYING A STEPPING-STONE PATH

BELOW A stepping-stone path can be planted with low-growing, spreading plants. You need to watch where you walk to avoid damage, but the attractive display is worth the extra time.

1 Wooden edgings are needed first and these are put in as described for concrete shuttering (see p. 142). Set the edgings to form a path 15cm (6in.) wider than the slabs you intend to use. If you need to curve the path, make a series of saw cuts about half-way through the shuttering on the inside of the curve so that bending is easier.

2 Dig out the soil between the edgings and use it to make a compost of equal parts of soil, coarse grit and sieved garden compost or coir. Spread, tread it firmly and rake it level.

3 The paving slabs should be placed on the levelled compost. Use a 7.5cm (3in.) piece of wood to ensure that the slabs are in the middle and have a uniform gap between them.

4 Tap the slabs down so that they're level with the top of the edging. They will subsequently sink a little but this doesn't matter. They're easy to lift and relevel if necessary, though the roots of the plants will quickly stabilise them.

5 Put a layer of coarse grit between the slabs and then plant with alpines and other spreading plants which will soon grow to soften the hard lines of the edges.

LAYING A GRAVEL PATH

1 To make a gravel path, you'll need to put in wooden edging in the same way as for a stepping-stone path. Then dig out the soil, if necessary, to allow a 7.5cm (3in.) layer of material to be put in. Put down a layer of consolidating material like hoggin as a base, making sure that it slopes from the centre to the edges to take away excess water.

2 Hoggin is sand and gravel with a high clay content, so it rolls down quite hard with a hand roller. For pedestrian use this is all that's needed. You may need to wet the hoggin slightly as you go.

3 Cover with a 5cm (2in.) layer of gravel and roll a second time to incorporate some of the gravel into the top layers of the hoggin. Again, wetting may be necessary.

Paths

LAYING A BRICK PATH

Brick paths look warm and attractive and the bricks can be used in all kinds of patterns to create interesting effects. They're not difficult to lay but it's essential to use the right materials. Bricks made for building walls will generally not do since they'll flake and crack in freezing weather. There are plenty of brick paviors made specifically for the job, so it's best to stick to those.

Brick paths can be laid in a variety of patterns. They suit old and new houses alike.

The mellow colours of red brick provide a fine foreground for borders and a serviceable, non-slip surface too.

1 Some kind of edging is necessary and the cheapest and most convenient is timber, as recommended for stepping-stone paths (see p. 150). First set out some bricks to roughly the width you require the path to be, leaving about 6mm (¼in.) between each brick. Then measure the width of the bricks to ascertain the required distance between the edging boards. This will save a lot of cutting.

2 It's essential to have a solid base, so, unless the soil underneath is rock-hard and unlikely to sink, it's best to dig out 15cm (6in.) deep and put in 7.5cm (3in.) of dry concrete as recommended for paving (see p. 144).

3 Fill between the boards with sharp sand and tread it down firmly with your heels. Then level with a notched board. The notches are cut 4cm (1½in.) deep, which will leave the bricks just the right distance above the boards.

5 Brush dry sharp sand down between the bricks to prevent them tilting sideways. The finer this sand is, the better, though I've found ordinary sharp sand to be effective.

6 The bricks are beaten down using a strong, wide board like a length of scaffold board. Use a fence post to ram them down but make sure you wear gloves to avoid splinters. The bricks will go just level with the edgings. Then brush more sand over the whole path to refill the cracks.

4 Now set out the bricks to the required pattern on the sand bed. Again, leave a gap of about 6mm (¼in.) between the bricks. If you work off a board, you can put all the bricks down first before consolidating.

You can cover quite large areas with brick paving, though if it has to support cars and delivery lorries, the base will have to be stronger, probably reinforced with a layer of hardcore, and the bricks will need to be vibrated down with a special machine. It's best to leave this job to a professional.

Fencing

There's no doubt that the quickest means of defining the boundary of your garden, which at the same time provides privacy, is a fence. Unfortunately, a tall wooden fence in a small garden does give a somewhat 'boxed-in' feeling, but a covering of green can very quickly be achieved with climbers, making a real three-dimensional garden very fast.

There are several different types of fence, the most popular being the panel variety which is not too difficult to build yourself. Whichever you choose, the most

important point is to make sure that the posts you use are *pressure*-treated with preservative, which should guarantee them more or less for life. If the fencing manufacturer can't supply them, buy the posts from a timber merchant who'll be able to get them treated.

Putting up fencing is definitely a job for two pairs of hands, so don't attempt it on your own. And don't try to put all the posts in first and then fit the panels to them: the *only* way to do it is to fix the panels to the posts as you go along.

PUTTING UP A PANEL FENCE

1 Posts should be of 7.5 × 7.5cm (3 × 3in.) timber and 60cm (2ft) longer than the height of the fence. Mark the boundary with a line, dig the first hole and concrete in the first post so that the top is 15cm (6in.) higher than the panel. This leaves 45cm (1½ft) in the ground. Check the post both ways with a spirit level to ensure that it's perfectly upright.

2 RIGHT If you concrete in the posts, make sure that you bevel the top of the concrete so that water runs off it away from the post. Another popular way of fixing posts is with metal spikes that are driven into the ground. The post fits into a socket in the top of the spike. These are ideal for fencing up to 90cm (3ft) in height but will not satisfactorily support a tall panel in strong winds.

3 LEFT Measure for the second post, using a panel capping strip to provide an accurate marker. Dig the hole about 45cm (1½ft) deep. Remember that all the holes should be on your side of the line.

4 RIGHT Offer up the first panel to the first post, resting it on a brick or block of wood to ensure that it's about 7.5cm (3in.) off the ground. Fix it either with nails driven through the edges of the panel or, much better, with special metal fixing brackets.

5 The top of the first post should be 7.5cm (3in.) above the top of the panel. To make sure that all the panels are the same, cut a piece of wood as a marker which you can carry in your pocket and use to check each post before concreting it in.

6 Check that the panel is dead level and that the top of the second post is the right distance above the top of the panel and then fix the post to the panel. Concrete in and check again to ensure that it's upright both ways.

7 BELOW After fixing the first panel, support it with a spare fence post or a board with a nail in the end and hooked over the top. This will hold the panel firm until the concrete sets, so check again with the spirit level that it's upright, just to be on the safe side.

8 BELOW Now the next panel can be nailed on and the fence progresses in exactly the same way to the last panel. This one, of course, won't fit exactly, so it'll have to be cut. Concrete the last post in first to give you the exact measurements.

9 RIGHT Mark where the panel should be cut and then remove the end struts. Nail them on in the correct place and then cut off the excess.

10 RIGHT Once the concrete has set hard, the struts can be removed and the final job is to fix a post cap to the top of each post with a couple of nails.

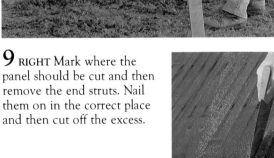

FENCING

STEPPED FENCING

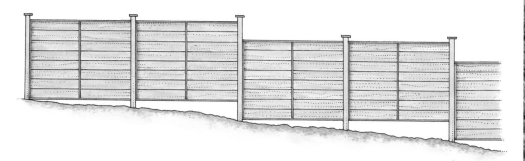

If you're erecting panel fencing on a slope, it has to be stepped. When ordering the fencing, note that some of the posts will need to be longer. If you need a progression of steps, try to make them at equal intervals or the fence will look messy.

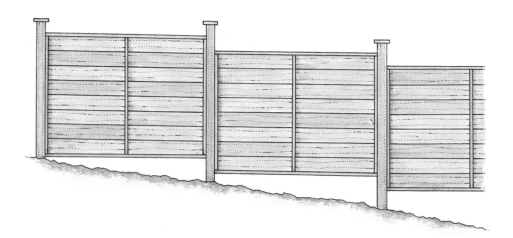

Secrets of success

A very cheap yet attractive fence can be made with secondhand floorboards. They're nailed to 7.5 × 4cm (3 × 1½in.) floor joists which are bolted through the posts. Leave a small gap between the boards to allow wind to filter through, so presenting less of a solid barrier.

ALTERNATIVE FENCING

LEFT **Post-and-rail fencing** This makes a good boundary marker, perhaps for a front garden, but of course gives little privacy. The posts are installed in the same way as for panel fencing, though here they can all be put in first. Then the boards are nailed, screwed or jointed on the fronts of the posts.

Square trellis panels Now used widely for fencing, these make an ideal support for climbing plants. They're especially useful as screens within the garden since they can be arranged to provide a broken view through it to create intimacy without claustrophobia. The panels are available in a wide range of patterns and finishes.

BELOW **Wattle fencing** Ideal for rural gardens and especially good as a temporary barrier where hedging is being grown. Make sure, though, that the panels are at least 30cm (1ft) away from the hedging plants to allow them to grow. The panels are simply wired on to stout posts which are driven into the ground. The panels will last about ten to fifteen years.

Pergolas

For any garden big enough to take it (and most are), a pergola is a feature worth considering. Even bare it'll provide instant height and interesting patterns of shade and light. But covered with climbing plants it really comes into its own. Pergolas can be used for any sort of climbers from roses to wisteria and, in fact, in small gardens it's best to mix the planting to provide a show of colour all season long. On my own pergola I've used laburnum, wisteria and honeysuckle, plus climbing and rambling roses with clematis growing through them, to provide a mass of colour right through the season.

RIGHT Timber is the easiest material to use and relatively inexpensive. For a large structure somewhat heavier timber is necessary to give solidity and proportion, but do-it-yourself kits are available in a variety of designs and sizes. They're not difficult to erect. Alternatively, buy pressure-treated timber and make your own.

BUILDING AND PLANTING A PERGOLA

1 Measure the positions for the holes very carefully, using the cross-members as a guide. This is especially important if you're using a kit, because if a post is slightly out of line it will have to slope slightly to fit the notch in the cross-beam and that will constantly offend your eye. If you're constructing your own pergola, use 7.5 × 7.5cm (3 × 3in.) fencing posts for the uprights, making them long enough to leave 2.1m (7ft) out of the ground. Check with a spirit level that they're upright both ways.

2 Fix the side rails which are made from 4 × 7.5cm (1½ × 3in.) timber. With some kits they simply slot into the top of the posts, but if you're making your own from scratch, either bolt them through or screw them on using coach screws. It goes without saying that the fixing must be very secure for safety's sake.

3 With some kits the cross-rails are also cut to slot into the side rails. You could do the same thing with the do-it-yourself job if you're handy with a saw and a chisel, but the alternative is to screw them on to the top of the side-rails using a metal angle bracket. Note that the ends of the cross-rails are shaped to make a more attractive finish.

4 The climbers are planted into prepared soil at the bottom of each post and then simply tied to the posts with soft string. Since the aim is rapid growth it's best to dig deeply and to improve the soil with compost or manure plus fertiliser.

ABOVE Traditionally, pergolas were built of brick or stone and very impressive they were too. Few gardens have the room for a magnificent structure like this, but there are other options, perhaps not quite so grand but certainly cheaper! In large gardens you can also afford to make one really spectacular show per year with perhaps wisteria or laburnum. In a smaller garden, however, it's best to get a succession with several different climbers.

As the climbers grow, make sure that they're twisted around the posts, which will restrict the flow of sap and encourage flowering.

Arbours and arches

A decorative arch, like a pergola, will add instant height and makes an attractive division between parts of the garden. Again, it provides another place to grow a variety of climbing plants. Archways are easy to build, though there are also several types available ready-made.

An arbour in its simplest form is not difficult to make yourself. After all, it's really no more than an arch, closed on three sides with trellis. You can, of course, put a solid roof on the top, though that's not by any means necessary. Clothed with climbing plants, it makes an attractive place to sit, so it's good to use perfumed climbers like roses and honeysuckle in this situation.

Metal arches are also readily available and they make an excellent support for trained fruit trees. Alternatively, they can, of course, be used for ornamental plants or, provided you avoid rampant growers, for a mixture of the two.

A wooden garden arch makes a fine feature and it's not difficult to imagine how, with the addition of a bit of trellis to close in the open sides, it could easily be converted into a small arbour.

My own carpentry skill is hardly world-class, yet I managed to build this arbour quite easily using ready-cut timber from a pergola kit, plus four 2.1m (7ft) fencing posts and three 1.8m (6ft) trellis panels. It makes a very pleasant place to sit and enjoy the garden.

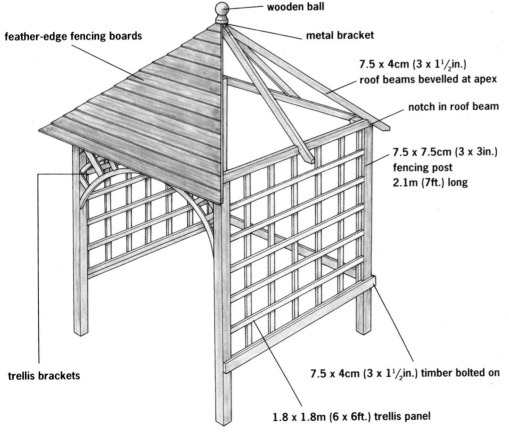

feather-edge fencing boards

wooden ball

metal bracket

7.5 x 4cm (3 x 1½in.) roof beams bevelled at apex

notch in roof beam

7.5 x 7.5cm (3 x 3in.) fencing post 2.1m (7ft.) long

trellis brackets

7.5 x 4cm (3 x 1½in.) timber bolted on

1.8 x 1.8m (6 x 6ft.) trellis panel

The only part of this arbour that's not straightforward is the roof. The beams are made with timber from a pergola kit, but they do have to be bevelled at the apex. However, remember that the joints will be covered with boarding, so if they're not perfect it doesn't matter a bit. The feather-edge fencing boards used to cover the roof are a bit fiddly to cut and fit, but really not very difficult. All the materials, including the two trellis brackets at the front and the wooden ball on the roof, are available at the garden centre.

CHAPTER 7

LAWNS

GRASS IS A marvellously accommodating plant. What else can be walked on every day and pruned back hard every week and still come up smiling? Alas, such renowned good nature often militates against it, because we tend to forget that grass is a plant and needs just as much loving care as any other. This is particularly true when conditions are unfavourable and it has to struggle against drought or bad drainage or lack of light. And, my goodness, it'll repay you like no other plant if you do take care of it.

Most gardens in the northern hemisphere, except perhaps the very smallest, include a bit of grass because it makes such a good neutral foreground to ornamental borders. An expanse of green has a very restful effect on the eye and, of course, it's pretty useful too for access, for relaxing on and even for practising golf or croquet.

I hesitate to point out that a large area of grass can also reduce labour in the garden because I firmly believe that the 'labour' is the most enjoyable bit. But reducing the chores is sometimes necessary. If you can spend only a limited amount of time tending your garden, if you're not as young as you were, or if you simply prefer to concentrate on other aspects of gardening that you enjoy more, a well designed and mechanised lawn can be a real boon. And just think of all that compost the grass cuttings will produce!

Grass makes a superb foil for planting and is cool and restful to the eye.

Preparation for sowing or turfing

Making a new lawn deserves all the care and trouble you can give it. A great misconception is that turfed lawns need less preparation than those grown from seed, but if you're going to spend a fair amount of money on turf, it's crazy to waste it by poor preparation. Make the most thorough job of it you can by preparing for turf in just the same way as you would for seed.

1 RIGHT Generally, digging to one spade depth is enough. Alternatively, if the area is large, hire a rotavator. However, you should first dig down a couple of spades deep in a 'test area', and if you find a hard pan underneath, the whole site will have to be broken up by double digging (see p. 90). Very heavy soil should first be lightened with the addition of grit (see p. 64), while low-lying or badly drained soil will need the full treatment, incorporating a special drainage layer (see p. 86). Light soil will benefit from the addition of rotted manure or compost.

2 In order to ensure that the subsequent firming is even over the whole area, roughly level it with the back of a fork. If you need to fill large holes, tread each 7.5cm (3in.) layer firm as you go. This is a job to do when the soil is dry enough not to stick to your boots.

3 Consolidation is of paramount importance to prevent local sinkage. To make sure that every centimetre is evenly firmed, go over the whole area, treading it down with your weight on your heels, then apply a light dressing of fertiliser. During the growing season, and especially if you are going to sow rather than turf, use a general fertiliser with something like a 7.7.7 analysis (see p. 83) at about a handful per square metre or square yard. If you intend to lay turf in the dormant season, use bone meal only at about the same rate. The application rate is not critical, but err on the light side if anything.

4 Finally, rake the soil level. This is tricky and does take a bit of practice. Keep the head of the rake fairly horizontal and just in front of your feet, raking a small area at a time and removing large stones as you go. Step back from time to time, bend down and squint across the soil's surface. If you get your eye near to the ground you can see more clearly where the bumps lie. It's worth going over the soil at this stage to make quite sure that it's just as you want it. Remember that it's not the large undulations you need to worry about but the local hollows. It's these that will be missed by the mower, encouraging areas of coarse grass.

Making a lawn from seed

Making a lawn from seed is certainly cheaper than using turf and it always gives you the opportunity of choosing the grass varieties you want. Seed mixtures are available ready-mixed in various grades, but you should think carefully before choosing. There's no point in buying a very fine grade unless you can cut it at least twice a week, feed it, water it and walk on it very little and with care. If your children will play football on it or you can commit yourself only to minimum maintenance, it's best to buy a hard-wearing grade. It'll still give you a very good lawn. The best time to sow is late summer when you can expect some damp weather but the soil is still warm. Alternatively sow in mid-spring, but try to avoid dry spells. Sow at about 50g per sq.m (1½oz per sq.yd).

1 It's not really necessary to measure out the lawn into strips as is sometimes recommended. If you stand with your feet widely planted and lean forward as far as you can, you'll be covering about a square metre. Two handfuls of seed sprinkled over this area will be about the right amount. This is quite a high sowing rate, so accuracy isn't vital.

3 After sowing, try to protect the seed from birds as best you can, though you must expect to lose some. A few posts with flapping strips of plastic help a bit. Try to avoid watering until after germination as this tends to wash the seed into patches.

5 After another day or two, the grass can be cut with the mower blade set at its highest level so that it simply trims the top. Lower the blade on subsequent cuts until it's down to the required height. In the first year you shouldn't cut too closely. Don't worry if the grass looks thin to start with. It takes about six months or sometimes even more to fill in completely.

2 The best way to rake in the seed is with a springtine lawn rake. The aim should be to cover something like half the seed, and the springtine rake will do that without disturbing your carefully produced levels. Remove any large stones you might unearth.

4 When the grass is about 5cm (2in.) tall, the first job is to roll it to induce 'tillering'. This is like pinching out the top of a plant in that it activates growth buds at the base of the leaves, so thickening up the lawn.

Secrets of success

A very convenient hand sower can be made with two plastic flower pots. Use 23cm (9in.) pots and put one inside the other. By twisting the pots you can make the size of the holes larger or smaller to give the correct sowing rate when the pots are shaken over the soil. If you're concerned about close accuracy, weigh out 50g (1½oz) of seed before you start and spread it over a measured metre or yard just to see what it looks like.

Making a lawn from turf

Turf is considerably more expensive than seed but has the advantage of producing an instant visual effect. It is, however, two months or so before a turfed lawn can be used, but that's still much sooner than a new lawn grown from seed. It can also be laid at any time of year provided the ground isn't frozen and you're confident of being able to water continually if necessary.

When ordering, be careful to ensure the quality you'll get since it can vary considerably. If you intend to buy cheaper turf, which is basically a farm field that has been cut, rolled, weed-treated and fed for a season, it's best to try to see it first. Point out to the supplier that you will return poor quality turf and make sure you're there when it's delivered. Alternatively buy cultivated turf which has been sown with a special mixture and grown to produce a perfect, weed-free product. You can even choose the type of grasses, just as you would when buying seed. The disadvantage is that it costs twice as much. Specify a delivery date which will ensure that you can put it down immediately. Turf can't be left in the roll for more than a week in winter or two days in summer. The ground is prepared as for sowing (see p. 164).

1 Mark out the shape of the lawn and start by laying the edging turves. Stand back from time to time to check that the shape looks right and adjust it if not. Tap down the turves with the back of a rake.

2 Starting on the longest, straightest side, lay out the first row of turf. If no side is straight, lay out a straight line of turves slightly in from the edge and fill in the gap later.

3 Stand on a wide board (scaffold planks are ideal) and tap down the first row with the back of the rake. If the ground has been levelled well, you should need only to tap it in to ensure that the roots are in contact with the soil; but, of course, any local bumps should be beaten down level.

4 Working from the board, lay out the second row and pull it hard into the first row using the back of the rake. There's no need to worry about 'bonding' the turves like bricks as is sometimes recommended.

5 At the ends of the rows, lay the turf over the top of the edging turf and cut off the excess with an old knife to make a perfect fit. Continue laying in the same way, always working from the board.

6 Sometimes you'll come across a turf with a hole in it where perhaps there has been a large stone near the surface or the ground has been uneven. This can be filled by simply cutting off a patch from another turf and fitting it in.

7 ABOVE When all the turves are laid, you're bound to have some patching to do at the ends, which is again done by laying a turf over the edge and cutting off the excess.

8 RIGHT New turves contain a lot of thatch to help hold them together. This should be raked out after laying. In spring and summer it's also essential to water turf after laying and it may be necessary even in a dry winter. If you let them dry out before they're rooted, turves will shrink, leaving ugly gaps. Use a lawn sprinkler and apply the water little and often. Once they've rooted, watering can be reduced. Mow in the early stages as recommended for sown lawns (see p. 165).

Lawn maintenance

Regular maintenance really is the key to a good lawn. It's possible to turn a cow pasture into a bowling green simply by good maintenance – I've seen it done, albeit over several years. Alas, it's also possible to go the other way. So you must first decide on the time and money you have available for your lawn and that will very largely determine the quality of the seed or turf which you buy.

ABOVE Mowing
The more often you mow, the finer the lawn will become. This is because fine grasses thrive under heavy mowing while coarse varieties don't like it and will eventually die out. For a standard lawn, mow at least once a week while the grass is growing, except in very dry weather, but don't cut the grass too close. If you shave it, you tend to encourage bare patches which will later be colonised by moss. Lawns in shade should be left longer and cut less frequently than sunny ones. To avoid building up excess 'thatch' of dead grass and to prevent cuttings 'walking' into the house, it's best to remove them except in very dry weather when they act as a water-holding mulch. For choice of mower see p. 42.

LEFT Worm casts
These will be flattened by the mower to form perfect, super-fertile seed beds for weeds, so they're to be discouraged. However, worms are so valuable for their aeration and manuring functions below the lawn that they should never be destroyed. Instead, if you're troubled with casts, simply brush the lawn to spread them about before mowing.

LEFT AND BELOW Getting rid of weeds

You can reduce work by killing any weeds that may crop up in the lawn with a fertiliser/weedkiller mixture. Alternatively do it with a liquid lawn weedkiller watered or sprayed on separately. Either way, make sure that none goes on the borders where it'll kill broad-leaved plants.

If you're organically minded and don't want to use chemical herbicides, you can kill weeds by putting a tiny pinch of salt on the centre. Make sure, though, that none goes on the grass.

An alternative is to remove weeds bodily with a special tool which twists them out of the ground very effectively. It's ideal for even deep-rooted weeds like dandelions.

LEFT Feeding

Grass needs feeding only twice a year – in spring and mid-summer. If you do it then, autumn feeding is unnecessary. There are many solid and liquid fertilisers available, though a general fertiliser will also do. The best way to spread solid fertiliser is with a special distributor; apply liquid feeds with a watering can. Never exceed the maker's recommended distribution rates or you may scorch the grass.

If it hasn't rained two days after you spread solid fertiliser, you must water the lawn artificially or scorching may occur. For this and for regular watering during dry spells, a sprinkler is essential. Watering just the surface actually does more harm than good by bringing the roots to the surface where they'll be even more vulnerable to drying out.

Cutting the lawn edges

After mowing try to find time to cut the edges, which gives a really neat and well-groomed appearance. The normal and most therapeutic way is with a pair of long-handled shears. However, if you have a large run of lawn edges to cut, you can buy or hire electric or petrol-driven machines which will do the job very quickly but perhaps not quite so perfectly as shears.

Secrets of success

The mower tends to flatten some of the grass without cutting it, so it pays to mow in opposite directions each time. If you mow straight up and down it's difficult to remember exactly which way you went last time. So mow diagonally across the lawn from opposite corners on each occasion. Put a marker in the corner where you start every time to remind yourself to start from the opposite corner when you next mow.

Lawn maintenance

Apart from those jobs described on pp. 168–9 that are essential to the maintenance of the lawn, there are various other operations that will greatly improve the growth and therefore the look of the grass, and some repair jobs that may occur irregularly. A little extra attention will always pay dividends.

ABOVE AND BELOW
Removing the 'thatch'
After a while, constant use of the lawn and mowing in particular will encourage the formation of a mat of dead grass below the living shoots. This forms a close 'thatch' which reduces aeration and impedes the entry of water and nutrients. Remove it regularly by raking with a springtine rake at least twice a year in spring and autumn.

Raking is quite hard work, so you may prefer to buy or hire a special raking machine. Most are mains-electric powered and are very efficient.

ABOVE Top-dressing
In autumn the rooting area of the lawn can be improved and local hollows can be taken out by top-dressing. Mix up a compost consisting of 3 parts of good sieved soil, 2 parts of sharp sand and 1 part of sieved compost, leafmould or coir. Cut the grass first and then spread the compost evenly over the lawn with the back of a rake, making sure that it's not too deep or fine grasses could be smothered.

LEFT Improving poorly drained patches
If there are badly drained patches on the lawn where water lies after rain, they should be dealt with as follows. Use a garden fork, working it backwards and forwards to enlarge the holes which should be at about 15cm (6in.) intervals across the wet patch. Then immediately brush in sharp sand: if you don't do this, the soil tends to spread and the holes close again. In extreme cases you can use a hollowtine fork which removes cores of soil.

BELOW Dealing with patches of coarse grass

1 Sometimes patches of coarse grass can appear in an otherwise fine lawn. This could be the result of the mower riding over the area because it has sunk. If it has, cross-hatch the coarse grass with an old knife and pull it out, adding soil to raise the hollow.

Repairing damaged edges

1 If the edges of the lawn have been broken down, cut out a square of turf around the damaged area.

2 Turn the turf round to give a firm, straight edge but leaving the hole nearer the middle of the lawn. This can then be filled with soil and resown.

2 Then reseed with seed mixed in good garden soil. For fast results the area can be covered with a piece of clear polythene with a few holes punched in it and held down with small wire staples. Remove the polythene as soon as you see germinated grass.

Rectifying uneven areas
Remove bigger lumps or hollows by taking away or adding soil underneath the turf. Lift enough to cover the area plus a little around it, remove the lump or fill the hollow and then replace the turf.

Alternative lawns

While grass must be the most versatile and popular plant to use for lawns, it's by no means the only alternative. If you have a small garden and you don't expect to give the lawn a lot of wear, you could grow either a chamomile or a thyme lawn, both of which look very attractive and don't need cutting. However, the initial planting would be quite expensive unless you raised your own plants.

Alternatively you could do your bit for wildlife and sow a wildflower meadow of grass mixed with native flowers. This sort of area looks attractive and requires very little maintenance.

Wildflower meadow This is a very pleasant proposition since it's reasonably cheap, requires little maintenance and attracts many insects. There are several different mixtures available these days, so check with the seed catalogue to ensure that you buy the best one for your soil and situation. Preparation is the same as for a lawn except that no fertiliser should be added. Poor soil will suit native plants better. Sow in the autumn or early spring and cut the grass in April if it's established by then, or in October when the plants have seeded. In subsequent years you should mow only at these times, leaving the grass at least 5cm (2in.) long. You may also need to pull out the odd strongly growing 'weed'.

Chamomile lawn Chamomile, for years known as *Anthemis nobilis*, has, alas, changed its name to *Chamaemelum nobile*. Don't be put off; it's still the same plant and just as attractive as it was when used in medieval times. It forms a thick, bright green lawn which is very drought-resistant, remaining green when grass has browned in dry weather. It gives off a very pleasant perfume when the leaves are bruised but will not stand hard wear. Buy the non-flowering variety 'Treneague' and set the plants 10cm (4in.) apart in soil prepared as for lawns (see p. 164).

Secrets of success

An alternative way to establish wildflowers, especially if you inherit existing rough grass, is to put plants direct into the grass. A bulb planter is an ideal tool for the job. Make sure that the plants don't go short of water until they're established.

Thyme lawn Common thyme (*Thymus serpyllum*) also makes a green mat, gives off a pleasant perfume when crushed and has the added bonus of flowers in shades of pink, red or white. You could perhaps choose the varieties 'Albus' with white flowers, 'Coccineus' with red flowers or 'Lanuginosus' with lilac flowers. The plants should be planted 15cm (6in.) apart in spring. After flowering they should be clipped over with shears to prevent them becoming thin and straggly. Bear in mind that neither thyme nor chamomile lawns can stand the wear that grass will. Occasional walking on them is fine but playing football is not!

CHAPTER 8

ORNAMENTAL BORDERS

IT'S THE PLANTING, of course, that really makes a garden and the growing of plants that constitutes the biggest thrill in gardening. The initial planting and the subsequent adjustment to the borders gives everyone the opportunity of using the creative skills that all of us undoubtedly have to produce a *real* work of art. And the marvellous thing is that each and every one will be unique and individual.

Mind you, we all, without exception, feel daunted when we first tackle the overall planting of a garden. And that's just as it should be. It's a task that has a million permutations and complications and, like all the most worthwhile projects, it's not easy. You won't get it right first time, but here again nature has been good to us. Because if you get a plant in the wrong place it doesn't really matter: you move it.

The main thing is to have a go and to be self-critical. If you think you've made a mistake and that bright yellow berberis clashes with the pink rhododendron, admit it as soon as you can and do something about it. Provided you act fast enough, you'll be forgiven! And 'fast enough' in nature's timescale means within a year or so!

Plants will brighten up even the dullest place and a mixed border of shrubs, roses, herbaceous plants, bulbs and annuals will bring the garden alive all year round.

Planning borders

Gardeners will argue forever about the best way to plant borders. There's the 'co-ordinated' school which believes that colours must match like curtains and wallpaper and that contrasts offend the eye. Then there's the 'Sissinghurst' lot who feel that, because that famous English garden boasts a superb white border, every garden should have one – and another in reds and another in blues, and so on. There are the 'cottagers' who are content with nothing less than a garden full of hollyhocks and old roses; and the 'rebels' who don't mind what form their garden takes as long as it's like no one else's.

But don't knock it. Each of these styles has produced some marvellous, artistic and very satisfying examples, and each can teach us a lot. But where do you start?

Well, the very first thing, before you get carried away with artistic fervour, is to provide the plants with the conditions they need to grow well. Consult a good plant book and perhaps ask for advice from the nurseryman when you buy your plants. It's a good idea to see what kind of plants other people in your area grow, especially when you're deciding what's hardy enough and what will thrive on the local soil. If your neighbour grows tender rhododendrons, so can you.

Check plant heights and spreads, relative hardiness, preferred soil conditions and aspect. Only then can you start thinking about art, and that's when the fun begins.

Obviously the garden you finish up with will vary according to your own personal preferences, but it's still worthwhile seeking inspiration from others. Spend some time getting out and about to gardens open to the public and always take your notebook with you and a camera if you can. Make notes not only of plants that catch your eye, but also of associations with others. Gradually you'll build up a 'feel' for the job.

If you decide you'd like a 'co-ordinated' garden, it's a good idea to get hold of a chart of the colours of the spectrum. If you start with reds and pinks, blending them through the border with orange, then yellow, through green, blue and indigo to violet, you'll avoid clashes. Like as not you'll decide that you want to break up the smooth flow with a contrast here and there, but those plants can easily be added later.

Self-coloured borders are easy, of course, though you don't necessarily have to stick to just one colour. If you decide on white, for example, you could find great relief by using pale cream, green, pale blue and pale pink too.

If your garden's small, my own feeling is that the best treatment is to emulate the old cottagers of the past and put everything together in a glorious jumble. And I mean everything! There's no reason at all why you shouldn't grow cabbages with the cabbage roses and onions with the petunias; flowers, fruit and vegetables all together in the same border actually make a marvellous effect.

Above all, have a go! Remember that, if you decide you've made a mistake, there's no reason at all why your plants shouldn't be moved around later.

If time is short, borders using shrubs, conifers and bulbs are best. This border with its rhododendrons and camellias would suit only acid soil.

A copy of the famous white border at Sissinghurst. Here, nicotiana, roses and lilies back the silvery foliage of lamb's ears.

'Co-ordinated' colours from one side of the spectrum together. Here the pinks of alstroemeria and poppies blend with the reds of penstemon and dianthus.

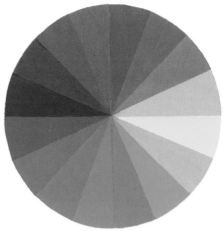

Colour wheel Colours of the spectrum merge gradually, so a softer effect is obtained if this colour sequence is followed. But the creation of a border is very much a matter of personal preference and some gardeners will want to provide a 'shock' by using contrasting colours in certain situations.

ABOVE The 'cottage-garden' style uses lots of pink roses unashamedly mixed with the yellows of achilleas and lady's mantle but remains very easy on the eye.

RIGHT If you live in a favoured area you can afford to rebel against all the so-called 'rules' of planting to great effect. Here, canna lilies, day-lilies and even palms give a flavour of the tropics.

Hedges

Before planting the borders, it's as well to give a thought to the backing. This will, in the majority of small gardens, also act as the boundary between you and your neighbour and as a means of providing privacy. Most small gardens will probably use a fence because it takes up less room, but if you have space for a hedge it'll provide a superb living background to the border and, depending on what you choose, will not be too long in creating a peep-proof screen. Hedges also provide a much more effective windbreak than solid barriers (see pp. 146 and 154).

LEFT Informal hedges
An informal hedge like this escallonia takes up a little more room than a formal one because, if allowed to grow fairly naturally, it'll provide the added bonus of attractive flowers. If space is limited, the hedge can be trimmed back after flowering. Several of the berberis species can be used, as well as fuchsias, griselinia and olearia. An informal hedge is really no more than a row of shrubs, so the choice is very wide.

Secrets of success

Because of their large leaf area, coniferous hedges lose water very quickly. These are often planted as a windbreak but will suffer themselves in the early years unless protected by a temporary screen of plastic windbreak. Support the material on strong stakes and leave it there, generally for one or two years, until the conifers have established.

Conifer hedges
Conifers make excellent, quick-growing hedges. They too need regular clipping and must not be allowed to grow too tall before topping. The quickest is Leyland's cypress (× *Cupressocyparis leylandii*), which makes a fine hedge when clipped regularly. Alternatively use the slightly slower *Thuja atrovirens* pictured here, which has a more glossy, emerald leaf. Yew makes a superb though quite slow hedge.

Formal hedges

Formal hedges are clipped regularly to maintain a bushy habit and a neat appearance. Beech is an excellent subject since it retains its old leaves during winter to make a fine, russet-coloured background to the garden. The old leaves are pushed off by the new ones in spring. Alternatives are hornbeam, laurel, holly, the small-leaved honeysuckle (*Lonicera nitida*), the purple-leaved plums (*Prunus × cistena* and *Prunus cerasifera* 'Nigra') and privet, though the last is definitely not for small gardens since it's a very greedy plant indeed.

Planting a hedge

1 It's essential to achieve fast growth from your hedge, so it's important to prepare the ground very well. Dig an area at least 1m (3ft) wide, breaking up the bottom of the trenches and incorporating manure, compost or one of the alternatives.

2 Stretch a line along the planting area and plant bare-rooted plants by putting in the spade, twisting and placing the plant in the opened slit. Pot-grown plants will need a hole dug for each one. Plant beech and privet 45cm (1½ft) apart and informal hedging and conifers 1m (3ft) apart. Note that the roots of plants awaiting planting are protected from drying wind.

3 After planting, some plants, like this *Prunus × cistena*, should be cut hard to within about 15cm (6in.) of the ground to induce bushy growth. Treat all the informal hedges mentioned, the two purple-leaved plums and privet in this way. Beech, holly and the conifers should not be tipped until they have reached 1m (3ft) higher than they're needed to allow bushy growth at the top (see p. 180). Feed every spring with rose fertiliser or an organic general feed.

Cutting hedges

There's a great danger that hedges can creep up on unsuspecting gardeners and grow too tall or too wide before they realise it. If this happens there's very little that can be done, so it's essential, especially with formal hedges, to trim them as soon as they reach the required size. Informal hedges are pruned like shrubs (see p. 196).

Conifer hedge A well-maintained hedge is a real joy, making the ideal background to the border and the perfect living barrier. Conifers are particularly suited to cutting in a formal shape. Note that the top is narrower than the bottom, allowing sun and air to reach all parts and so ensuring that the foliage remains healthy right down to the bottom.

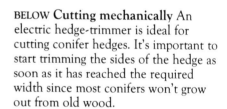

BELOW **Cutting mechanically** An electric hedge-trimmer is ideal for cutting conifer hedges. It's important to start trimming the sides of the hedge as soon as it has reached the required width since most conifers won't grow out from old wood.

Beech hedge Beech can also be trimmed formally, either narrower at the top or with dead-straight sides.

Cutting by hand It's not a great problem to trim by hand with shears and they probably give better control. With beech hedging, trim the sides when they have reached the required width but don't prune the top at all until it has grown as high as you want it.

Achieving the required height Conifers should be allowed to grow to about 1m (3ft) taller than the required height and should then be cut back to 15cm (6in.) below it. This allows new growth to form an even top to the hedge.

Getting the top straight For obvious reasons it's important to cut the top of the hedge dead straight, so it's not a job to be done in a hurry. While it's possible to rig up a string along the top as a guide, I've found that there's no substitute for a good eye. Fortunately, if you do make the mistake of cutting a bit too low, the hedge will soon regrow.

Cutting large-leaved hedges Hedges with large leaves, like laurel, look superb but have the slight disadvantage that they must be pruned with secateurs. Trimming with shears cuts the leaves in half, making the hedge look messy. Fortunately laurel needs trimming only once a year.

Low hedges Shrubs such as box, lavender and cotton lavender can be used in low hedges to make formal, geometric designs such as an Elizabethan knot garden. Trim them once a year in spring, using shears rather than an electric trimmer which tends to cause bruising and temporary browning of the leaves.

Topiary Box is also ideal for trimming to make small, formal topiary which looks very effective as single specimens. For larger effects use yew or privet.

Planting bare-rooted trees and shrubs

With one or two rare exceptions it's best to plant trees and shrubs in the autumn, and if you can find a nursery that grows them in the field and lifts them bare-rooted you'll generally get a better bargain. Garden-centre trees grown in containers are designed to fit into a car, so they're smaller, thinner and often more expensive. There are some, though, like the false acacia (*Robinia frisia*) and silver birch which are such poor transplanters that they're best bought pot-grown.

If, when bare-rooted plants arrive, the roots look dry, soak them in water for a couple of hours before planting. Always keep roots covered against drying sun or wind; and, of course, protect the plants from frost if you are unable to plant them straight away. If planting has to be delayed for long, it's best to 'heel in' the plants. Dig a trench, throwing the soil forwards, and put the roots into the trench with the stems lying on the soil you dug out. Cover the roots and gently tread the soil firm.

1 If you simply dig a hole in uncultivated soil, you turn it into a sump to drain all the water from the surrounding land. No plant would be happy in this situation, so when planting prepare as large an area as possible, digging to at least one spade deep and working in plenty of organic matter.

2 It's important to plant trees at the right level. With a bare-rooted tree you'll be able to see the soil mark on the stem where it grew in the nursery and that's the correct planting level. Lay your spade across the hole and measure the tree against it to check.

4 If the soil is heavy or poor, it's as well to add extra organic matter to the soil you've dug out, even though the whole site has been previously prepared. Also use a couple of handfuls of bone meal if planting in the autumn, or general fertiliser for spring planting. Refill the hole with a little soil and then grab the stem and shake it up and down a few times to work the soil around the roots. Gradually add more soil. This process is not necessary, of course, with container-grown plants.

3 Small seedling trees need no stake but larger trees must have some root anchorage. With bare-rooted trees the stake should go in first to avoid root damage. Note that it's short, and will come only about a third of the way up the stem, allowing it to move in the wind while holding the roots firm. The stake should be placed so that the prevailing wind pushes the tree away from it.

5 RIGHT When the hole is about half-full, firm the soil gently but firmly with your boot. Then completely refill and firm again. Tidy up the top with a fork to level off and make the site look neat.

Planting container-grown trees and shrubs

Planting trees and shrubs that have been grown in containers is much the same as for bare-rooted subjects, though there are one or two important variations. First, of course, the root system remains intact, so planting can take place at any time provided attention is paid to watering. In my view autumn is still the best time for most species because the soil is warm enough for root growth to start immediately and there's little chance of the weather turning dry until the spring.

6 Fix the tree to the stake with a proper plastic tree tie – never use plastic twine or wire, which will cut into the bark and could kill the tree. Fix the tie to the stake with a short nail. In later years it will be necessary to check that the tie is not too loose or too tight. After about three years it can be cut off.

7 Finally mulch with more organic matter to suppress weeds and retain water. Alternatively cut up an old compost bag and put that round the trunk, holding it down with a layer of soil or bark. All trees and shrubs will need constant attention to watering in the first couple of years and should be fed annually in spring.

1 If plants are planted in dry compost, it's very difficult to wet it again and the roots take a long time to emerge into the soil. So, whatever the weather, it's essential to give the compost a thorough soaking first.

2 You must forgive me for reminding you to remove the pot, but it's not unknown for a plant to be planted still in it! If the roots are running in a circle at the bottom of the pot they tend to continue doing so even after planting, and they should therefore be carefully teased out.

Planting shrubs grown as a stool

Some plants, like roses and flowering currants, are grown as a stool with the flowering shoots arising directly from the ground rather than on a leg. To encourage this stooling habit it's best to plant these a few centimetres deeper than they grew in the nursery: you'll normally be able to see a soil mark on the plant as an indication. The plants should always be pruned back quite hard after planting to induce some really strong growth in the first year, but make sure that you encourage them by feeding with a general fertiliser in the spring. Again, apart from pruning (see p. 196), annual mulching and watering, this is the only aftercare they need.

3 Planting is the same as for bare-rooted plants, but with container-grown trees it's best to drive in the stake *after* planting. Put it in at an angle to avoid damaging the root ball. Again, fix it with a plastic tie which should be nailed to the stake, and don't neglect the subsequent watering and feeding as recommended for bare-rooted plants.

Transplanting large shrubs

Most shrubs can be transplanted successfully even when they're quite large, but they do need great care. Transplanting will certainly set them back somewhat and it carries a certain degree of risk. So it's well worthwhile doing everything that will give them the best chance of survival and get them growing away again. This is a job best done in the autumn and it should not be attempted until there has been sufficient rain to soak the soil thoroughly. Note too that moving large plants, like this spotted laurel, is a job for two strong people.

3 RIGHT Cut through underneath the plant all round as far as you can get, cutting right through the roots underneath. With fibrous-rooted evergreens this is rarely a problem. You may need a hand here to pull the plant slightly backwards, but be very careful not to break the root ball.

4 BELOW When you have cut right through, tilt the plant backwards and work a sheet of hessian or polythene under the root ball as far as it will go.

1 Tie up the branches of the plant to be moved to give yourself room to work comfortably around it. You may also need temporarily to dig out some of the surrounding plants.

2 Dig a trench around the plant, leaving about 30cm (1ft) of soil between trench and plant. You'll need to dig down to the subsoil and a little way into it.

5 ABOVE Tip the plant forwards again and pull the sheet right through. Finally wrap it tightly round the root ball and tie it firmly. This is the trickiest part of the operation since it's vital to keep the root ball intact until the plant's in its new position.

6 RIGHT A large plant will be very awkward to handle, so the best way is to lash a stout stake to the stem just above the root ball and lift it out that way.

7 Have the new hole already prepared in the normal way with organic matter and fertiliser mixed into the soil you have dug out. Try to guess the correct depth first time. Put the plant in and refill, firming as you go.

8 Most large plants will need staking to prevent them rocking. Even slight movement in the soil will break young roots as they try to establish. The best way to maintain stability is with three stout ropes to pegs in the ground.

9 Finally water the plant in well to settle the compost around the roots and mulch with organic matter. Make sure that you attend to watering and feeding during the following season and possibly beyond.

Planting and care of herbaceous perennials

Herbaceous perennials provide a tremendous amount of colour in the garden very nearly throughout the year and they do it cheaply and with a good grace – most are very simple to grow. Because the majority die down as the cold season approaches, in small gardens it's a good idea to mix them with shrubs so that there's still winter interest. Bare-rooted plants should ideally be planted in early autumn, though any subjects that might suffer from frost damage are best left until the spring. In colder areas it's often wiser to let the nurseryman take the risk.

1 Prepare the borders in the way recommended for shrubs (see p. 182), digging as large an area as possible to at least one spade deep. Again, use bone meal for autumn planting and a general feed if you're planting in spring.

2 If plants arrive through the post, it's best to soak them in water for an hour or so before planting. As with shrubs, bare-rooted plants that can't be dealt with immediately should be heeled in (see p. 182).

3 Herbaceous plants are generally planted in groups to give a mass display. If you're planting a whole new area, start by setting the plants out on top of the soil and adjust the spacings as necessary.

4 Whether the plants are bare-rooted or container-grown, put them in with a trowel, setting them at about the level they grew in the nursery and firming with your fingers. They'll need watering afterwards too.

5 RIGHT There's a little more to do with herbaceous plants than with shrubs. Most will relish being split up every few years (see p. 122) and planted in revitalised soil, and they'll respond well to a feed of general fertiliser in early spring. Taller ones will need to be staked, the very tall ones like delphiniums with canes to which they should be tied as they grow. Don't leave it too late. After flowering, seed can be collected from most herbaceous plants (see p. 106). If you don't want to do that, cut the stems down after flowering and put them on the compost heap.

6 Lower-growing plants like the phloxes can be staked with a wire-mesh ring on wire legs. The support is placed over the plant in early spring and the shoots will soon grow through and completely hide the frame.

7 If you decide you've made a mistake with a herbaceous plant and wish to move it, you can do so at almost any time, even when the plant's in flower, though it's obviously advisable to avoid hot, sunny days. Give the plant a good watering first, dig it up with as much root as you can, move it to its new quarters and give it another good watering. It will wilt for a while but should soon pick up again and grow away.

RIGHT Properly planned and maintained, herbaceous plants, either in a border on their own or mixed with other plants, can provide a succession of flowers for most of the year.

Secrets of success

If the budget's tight, there's no need to plant in groups. If you have patience, one plant put in this spring will generally grow to make at least three next year. Even newly bought plants can often be divided straight away to produce two or three separate ones that will soon grow back to size. And remember that many are very easy to raise from seed sown outside with no extra equipment (see p. 96).

Raising annuals and biennials

If it's a mass of colour you're after, annuals and biennials are the plants to give it to you. Whether it's in tubs, troughs, windowboxes, hanging baskets or the border, there's no doubt that they provide the longest and brightest display possible. Of course, they have the disadvantage that they're only temporary residents. Annuals will die after one season, while biennials last just eighteen months from sowing to compost heap. But in the meantime they'll flower their hearts out.

The cheapest way to grow hardy annuals is to sow them direct into the borders, while the half-hardies have to be raised in heat or bought in as bedding plants. This makes the latter considerably more expensive and time-consuming; nonetheless they give a marvellous display all summer and are generally considered well worth the expense and effort.

Biennials are sown in the summer of one year and flower in the spring or summer of the following year. They're very easy to raise from seed but do take up a fair bit of space. If you have the room, you'll generally raise much better ones than those you buy from the garden centre and they'll cost you a lot less too.

RIGHT Annuals like nicotiana are invaluable as fillers to provide colour and interest between more permanent plants while they're still growing.

Sowing direct into the border

1 LEFT Fork over the soil and dig in a little garden compost. A light sprinkling of fertiliser is generally sufficient as too much will result in luxuriant growth but little flower.

2 RIGHT Hardy annuals can be sown *in situ* in early spring. Sow them in drifts marked out with sand or by scratching the outline in the soil. Sow in straight drills within the marked areas. If weeds germinate you'll know that the plants you want to keep will be in straight lines. Sow in rows 15–30cm (6–12in.) apart and thin to the same distances.

Sowing in modules in the cold frame

A good alternative is to use modules (see p. 317) to raise plants in the coldframe. Sow a tiny pinch of seed in each cell in early spring and put the modules on a sand bed in the coldframe. Don't thin the seedlings but plant out the whole clump when the plants are about 4cm (1½in.) high.

Biennials

Biennials are sown in a specially prepared seed bed in a corner of the garden in early summer. When they germinate it's best to transplant them about 15cm (6in.) apart to produce some really bushy plants. They'll flower in spring or summer, depending on the species, and should then be removed and discarded.

Dead-heading to prolong flowering

With all annuals, both hardy and half-hardy, flowering will be greatly extended if you can 'dead-head', pinching off the flowers after they've faded. This avoids the plants wasting energy in the production of seed. Other than weeding and watering, little else is required.

Half-hardy annuals

LEFT Half-hardy annuals can be raised in heat in the greenhouse or on the windowsill (see p. 100). Grow them on in seed trays or, for really good-quality plants, pot them into 7.5cm (3in.) pots and plant them out from those.

RIGHT Alternatively, to save the heat and time needed to raise from seed, most seedsmen offer half-hardy annuals as seedlings. These are generally very successful and, because the germination is done for you, they can be grown on in lower temperatures.

Hardy bulbs

The great value of hardy bulbs and corms is that they seem to take up no space at all. They can be planted in among herbaceous perennials and shrubs where, as long as they're fed, they'll provide little competition. Some, like the early spring crocuses and narcissi, will produce leaves and flowers before most of the herbaceous plants appear, while others, like the lilies, will grow up through lower-growing plants to make taller strata of colour. What's more, most of the hardy ones will remain, uncomplaining, for years, producing larger and larger clumps until, like herbaceous plants, they're best split up and replanted.

Plants like *Cyclamen hederifolium* are actually corms rather than bulbs. They make an attractive group which reappears and multiplies by self-sown seed each year.

BELOW **When to plant** Spring bulbs are planted from late summer to early winter, while summer, autumn and winter flowerers go in from late spring to late summer. It's important to plant at the correct depth, so check the optimum for each bulb. As a general rule bulbs should be covered with soil to about twice their own depth.

BELOW **'Naturalising' bulbs** Some bulbs can be 'naturalised' in grass where they can remain undisturbed. Choose early-flowering types unless the grass need not be mown until quite late, since bulb foliage should not be cut off until at least six weeks after flowering. The easiest way to plant is with a special bulb planter.

Planting in very heavy soil It helps to rest bulbs on a layer of sharp sand or grit if planting them in very heavy soil where the drainage is likely to be poor. A bulb's base plate is quite susceptible to rotting and this measure serves to prevent it actually sitting in water. And, as suggested for any other planting, prepare as large an area as possible to avoid turning the planting holes into drainage sumps.

Creating an informal effect in the mixed border Plant in drifts rather than in straight rows, and, so that you know exactly where to plant, set the bulbs out on the surface first. Bulbs like daffodils are best planted among herbaceous plants whose foliage will later hide the leaves of the bulbs which look untidy after flowering until they die right down. Naturally it's best to plant the herbaceous perennials first.

Bulbs to plant 'in the green' Some bulbs, like snowdrops and cyclamen, must be planted when they're very fresh or they won't suceed. With these it's wise to wait until after flowering and to buy and plant the bulbs freshly lifted and with their leaves still on. Some specialist nurserymen offer such plants in this condition, which they call 'in the green'. Alternatively you could plant pot-grown plants.

Secrets of success

In established gardens, unless the bulbs are well labelled, it's often hard to know at planting time where existing clumps are. In this case simply pot up the new bulbs and put the pots against a cool, shady wall; then plant out the new bulbs when the existing ones are showing. You can even wait until the potted bulbs are in flower to ensure that you get them in just the right spot.

Care after flowering Never cut off the leaves of bulbs after flowering until they're brown and withered, because they're required to build up the flowers for next year. If you need the space the bulbs are occupying, lift them and 'heel' them in in a corner of the garden where they can remain undisturbed until the foliage has completely died. Then lift them and store them until next planting time. After they have flowered, whether lifted or left, feed them with a general fertiliser.

Dividing congested clumps Old clumps of bulbs can become congested and then flower quality will be reduced. To avoid this, lift the clumps every five or six years, revitalise the soil and replant the largest bulbs at wider spacings. Smaller ones can be grown on in rows for a year or two and then replanted in another part of the garden.

Tender bulbs

Not all bulbs, of course, are hardy in all gardens, so – as with any other type of plant – you'll need to establish, either by gleaning some local knowledge or by trial and error, which will survive the winter in your own plot. Those that come from warmer countries and will not survive winter cold and wet can still be grown, but the technique is rather more complicated than that for hardy bulbs. It would be a great mistake, however, to be put off by a little extra work, as the tender bulbs are among the most exotically beautiful.

Some of them, like the clivias and eucomis, are on the borderline of hardiness and will be at home in some gardens but not in others quite close by. With these it's always wise to play safe and plant them in well-drained conditions at the base of a south-facing wall where they'll be more protected. The vast majority of these tender bulbs come from sunny countries and will do best in the brightest spot you have in the garden.

LEFT Tender corms like gladioli are often used for cut flowers, but planted in groups they make superb border plants too.

1 Most tender bulbs can be treated in much the same way, so I'm using gladioli as an example. Plant the corms on a layer of grit to avoid the danger of them sitting in water. In the borders they make a more dramatic impact if grown in clumps, so plant them in a circular area about 10cm (4in.) apart. Planting is normally done in spring.

2 A stake in the centre will be sufficient to hold all the stems as they grow. Alternatively they can be grown in rows in the vegetable garden and used for cut flowers.

3 After flowering allow the foliage to remain for as long as possible, but make sure that you lift the corms well before the first frost. Take care over this job since there will be plenty of small cormlets which, with a bit of patience, can be grown on to produce new plants in future years.

4 Allow the corms to dry in a sunny spot and then break off the remains of the stem and the old bulb at the bottom.

5 Remove the small cormlets as well if you intend to grow them on.

6 Clean up the corms, removing any soil and loose skin that may be clinging to them, and store them in paper bags or boxes in a dry, cool but frost-free spot until planting the following spring.

7 An alternative way to grow tender bulbs is to put them into pots or tubs where they can stay more or less permanently. At the onset of cold weather the tubs must be brought into a cool but frost-free greenhouse or shed where they should remain until all danger of frost has passed. This is a particularly useful way to grow more exotic plants like agapanthus if your garden is in a cold area. Of course, the pots can also be sunk into spaces in the borders to liven them up in the summer.

Pruning: general rules

If plants are simply allowed to grow naturally, of course they'll be quite happy and so, for a while, will you. Nature's design is pretty well perfect for plants that are growing in the wild. After all, they have no reason to present an attractive shape or to have their vigour controlled – very often quite the reverse. But in the confines of a garden, it's a different story.

The size and vigour of most plants, for example, can be controlled to some extent by regular cutting back. Their productive life can be considerably prolonged by judicious pruning coupled with feeding and their shape, while not important in the wild, can be improved to make them aesthetically more pleasing. Finally pruning can be used to increase flowering and fruiting and to remove disease. There are a few basic rules that apply to all woody plants.

RIGHT One aim of pruning is to let in light and air to all parts of the plant, thus improving vigour, leaf and stem growth, flowering and fruiting. You should therefore regularly remove completely all unnecessary growth. This includes branches that are dead or diseased, crossing each other or simply overcrowded, together with those that are growing in towards the middle of the plant. If you do the job regularly, you'll never be faced with the problem of butchering the plant by removing large branches.

BELOW When pruning always cut back to just above a healthy bud and bear in mind that the new shoot will grow out in the direction that the bud faces. If you leave a snag of growth above the bud, it's likely to die back to the bud, leaving a short stub of dead wood that's not only ugly but also prone to disease.

LEFT Generally the harder you prune, the more vigour the plant will put into producing robust, new growth. Therefore, if you're looking for strong branches, especially on young plants, it often pays to cut them back really hard. When you do this, though, make sure that you encourage new growth by feeding at the same time. Note too that there are some exceptions: not all plants will respond to hard pruning, so it's necessary to get to know the plant first.

BELOW With some plants the aim of pruning is to remove old wood to encourage the growth of vigorous new shoots, but other plants will not regrow if you cut out the old wood so remove only the current season's growth from those. Whichever way the pruning is done, you must be able to differentiate between old and new wood. The old is usually rougher, more fissured and darker in colour and the young is smoother and lighter. It's normally quite easy to trace down from the tip of the new growth to see where it began at the start of the current season.

Some plants, like lavender, rosemary and broom, will not grow out vigorously from old wood, yet if not pruned will become straggly and bare in the centre. These plants need to be trimmed back regularly with shears or secateurs immediately after flowering.

LEFT If you need to cut back a large branch, make the first cut underneath the branch and then saw from above. This prevents the weight of the branch pulling it down and tearing off a strip of bark. The latest research suggests that painting large cuts with a pruning compound could be counter-productive, so the branch is best left to heal naturally. The exception to this is for trees susceptible to silver leaf fungus such as Prunus, when painting wounds is still recommended.

BELOW The result of pruning is to produce vigorous new shoots from just below the pruning point. So in order to keep some plants small and bushy, pinch them back regularly as they grow. It's a particularly useful method for plants that produce their best foliage colour from young shoots.

Pruning deciduous shrubs

There are basically two methods of regularly pruning deciduous shrubs, depending on whether they flower on old or new wood. There are, of course, some shrubs, including most evergreens like rhododendrons and camellias, that require no pruning at all, but that doesn't mean that cutting back will actually harm them. Certainly you should remove dead or diseased wood or any branch that's causing problems by overcrowding or growing where it's not wanted.

Shrubs that flower on wood made the same season
These should be cut back hard in the early spring to leave no more than about 5cm (2in.) of the previous season's growth. The same method is used for shrubs grown for their coloured bark or for their young foliage. Examples are: *Buddleia, Caryopteris, Ceanothus, Cornus, Eucalyptus, Fuchsia, Leycesteria, Ligustrum, Salix, Sambucus, Santolina, Spiraea × bumalda.*

ABOVE If you have a mixture of shrubs in your garden, they're likely to want pruning at different times and in different ways.

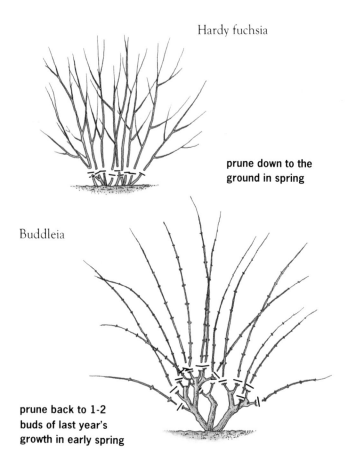

Hardy fuchsia

prune down to the ground in spring

Buddleia

prune back to 1-2 buds of last year's growth in early spring

Know your plant's flowering habits
A border planted with a diversity of shrubs will tax your memory and knowledge a little because it's important to know each plant's flowering habit before pruning. If you're likely to forget their names, it's worth labelling each plant permanently. Then it's easy to look up the pruning method.

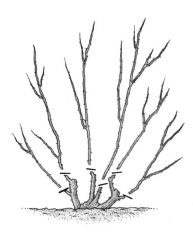

Bush roses

1 Prune each year in early spring. I prune hybrid tea and floribunda types in exactly the same way. Remove completely all weak shoots or those growing in towards the centre of the bush, together with dead or diseased branches.

2 Cut back the healthy shoots to a bud that faces outwards to retain an open-centred bush. Cut weaker shoots to leave about 2.5cm (1in.) of the previous season's growth and stronger ones to leave about 5–7.5cm (2–3in.). Remember always when pruning to cut just above a bud.

Shrub roses

These need little pruning. Simply cut out a proportion of the older wood right down to the base each winter to encourage new shoots. At the same time remove dead, diseased, crossing or overcrowded shoots.

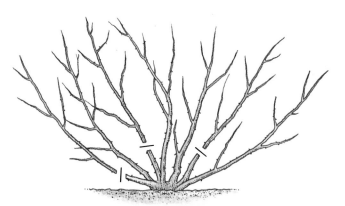

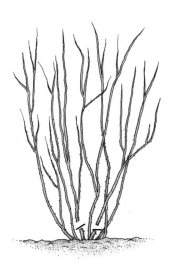

ABOVE **Shrubs that flower on wood made the previous year**
These must not be pruned in winter or spring or you'll be cutting off all the potential flowers. So prune them directly after flowering, cutting out the shoots that have flowered. Note that it's not necessary to cut them all back each year if you want to increase the size of the bush. Examples are: *Cytisus, Deutzia, Erica* (trim with shears), *Forsythia, Hydrangea* (prune in spring), *Jasminum, Kerria, Lavandula* (trim with shears), *Philadelphus, Weigela*.

Climbers

There are few more colourful climbers than clematis. This is 'Ville de Lyon'.

Climbing plants create the third dimension in the garden, adding instant height, clothing walls, fences and pergolas (see p. 158), or scrambling through trees and over shrubs. Most are not difficult to grow provided you make the right choice in the first place. Check before you buy that plants for use on a wall or fence will enjoy the aspect and that they will not become too vigorous.

RIGHT **Planting**
If you're growing a climber against a house wall, bear in mind that this is generally the driest part of the garden. Prepare the soil particularly well with organic matter and plant a little distance from the wall to avoid the very driest spot. Keep an eye on the plant in the early stages and water if necessary. Annual feeding with a general fertiliser is also essential.

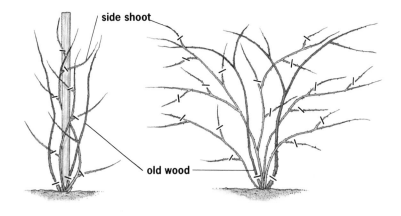

Tying in
The aim with permanent climbers on walls is to cover the space quickly, so allow them to develop a basic framework first. With climbing or rambling roses the main shoots are tied in to wires fixed to the wall (see p. 199). Note that the side shoots are tied down horizontally to encourage flowering.

Pruning climbing roses
Generally less vigorous than ramblers, most of these will flower right through the season, making a difference in the pruning methods. Prune them in the early spring, removing a proportion of the old wood and cutting back side shoots to two or three buds or tying them down horizontally.

Pruning rambling roses
Most ramblers give only one or perhaps two flushes of flower and should be pruned directly after flowering. Try to maintain a succession of new shoots by removing those that have flowered and tying in new ones. If the plant hasn't produced enough new shoots, leave on some of those that have flowered but cut their side shoots back to two or three buds.

Care of clematis

Some of the less vigorous clematis are ideal for growing through trees and shrubs to complement the existing flowers or to extend the season of colour. Note that clematis are planted with the top of the compost about 15cm (6in.) below soil level in case the plant is attacked by the disease clematis wilt. If this occurs and the plant wilts from the top, cut it back to soil level and it will reshoot with healthy growth from below ground.

If you choose varieties that flower late, they can be cut right down to ground level each year at the end of the summer. The old shoots can be taken out of the tree to give it room to grow until the new clematis growth again clothes it the following year. This hard-pruning treatment should be used for any clematis variety that flowers after mid-summer.

Varieties that flower early in the season before mid-summer should be pruned immediately after flowering. This consists of shortening side shoots to within a few buds of the main framework. Old plants can be reinvigorated by cutting back hard to ground level in early spring. This will induce strong growth and flowers lower down the plant but you'll lose that year's flowering.

BELOW **Fixing climbers to a wall**

The best way to fix climbers to a wall is to use galvanised wire, which is much less conspicuous than trellis. On old houses the wires can be fixed with special toughened vine eyes driven into the mortar, but on new houses, where the mortar is much harder, you'll have to drill and plug the wall to take a hook-eye.

For plants like roses, which are actually tied in, horizontal wires will suffice, but for self-clingers like clematis you'll need to provide vertical wires too, to form a mesh. These are made with thinner wire twisted round the horizontals. Without them the plants are likely to run horizontally.

Pruning other vigorous climbers

Some climbers, like the small-flowered clematis and wisteria, quickly become too big to prune with secateurs. The way I cope with these is to cut them back with shears where they're encroaching in places they're not wanted. This is done immediately after flowering.

Pruning wall shrubs

Plants such as pyracantha can, in general, be left unpruned except for the removal of shoots growing directly away from the wall and others in inconvenient positions.

The wildlife garden

With millions of hectares of gardens throughout the world, we gardeners are in charge of a vast alternative habitat for threatened species of plants and animals and we should be using it to the full. There are great pest-control advantages too, but for me all this is secondary to the sheer joy to be obtained from filling the garden with birds, bees, butterflies, moths, dragonflies and millions of other insects, together with friendly small mammals and reptiles. They bring your garden alive with extra colour and interest with very little effort on your part. Encouraging them is mostly a matter of *not* doing things like spraying with chemicals, or weeding over-meticulously, but there are positive steps you can take too. And you *don't* have to fill your plot with couch grass and stinging nettles!

A garden for wildlife needn't be unkempt and certainly not a nettle patch.

The pond Start by providing a source of water. All living things need to drink and a pond will attract them like a magnet. It also, of course, offers another type of habitat for aquatic plants and animals you would not otherwise be able to keep. Even a very small pond will do and it's not difficult or expensive to install (see pp. 206–9).

RIGHT **The log pile** A pile of logs in a corner of the garden can be made to look very attractive, perhaps clothed in ivy or planted with ferns. And it'll provide a home for attractive mosses, lichens and toadstools together with hundreds of beetles (which control many garden pests) and other insects as well as perhaps even a family of hedgehogs.

ABOVE **Attracting birds** Make your garden attractive to birds by providing them with trees in which to perch and nest and by growing food plants like those that produce edible seeds and berries. Encourage them to nest by siting special boxes well out of the reach of cats and inquisitive children. These are best put 2–3m (6½–10ft) high and either in permanent shade but out of the wind or in any direction facing between north and south-east to avoid scorching sun and the wetter winds.

RIGHT **Attracting butterflies** In a small garden it may be difficult to provide plants to encourage butterflies to breed. Native plants are ideal but these may be considered too much like weeds by gardeners and fairly large areas are naturally more successful. If your garden's large, you may well be able to find space for a corner in which to cultivate special butterfly breeding plants, but if not there is another way. Attract them in to feed by growing nectar-rich plants like the ice plant (*Sedum spectabile*) or the butterfly bush (*Buddleia davidii*).

RIGHT **Plants for bees and hoverflies** Other beneficial insects such as bees and hoverflies can be attracted by growing suitable plants. Bees will come for almost any plant that's in flower, while hoverflies prefer those with an open structure like the poached egg plant (*Limnanthes douglasii*) shown here or the dwarf convolvulus (*Convolvulus tricolor*). And always remember that chemical sprays will kill your friends as well as your enemies.

ABOVE **Bat boxes** Bats can also be encouraged by the provision of special boxes in which they'll roost during the day. They're much like bird boxes except that, instead of a hole, they have a narrow slit at the base for an entrance, and inside the back board is grooved so that the bats can cling to it.

The ornamental kitchen garden

One step on from the wildlife garden is the ornamental kitchen garden. By growing this way I believe that you can dispense with pesticides completely while still maintaining a beautiful, productive and pest- and disease-free plot.

The one abiding problem in agriculture is monoculture. It naturally follows that if you grow a large area of a single crop you'll always attract all the pests and diseases specific to it. Most pests are attracted by sight or by smell, so it's inevitable that a huge advertisement in the form of 50 hectares of a single species will have its effect. Diseases might arrive by chance but, given the close proximity of similar plants, any disease specific to that crop will spread like wildfire.

Farmers have been plagued with the problem since the demise of strip farming and, in more recent times, have been forced to fight it with chemicals. Surprisingly gardeners have adopted similar methods even though for us there's certainly no need.

In fact before the Victorians decided that vegetables and fruit were 'vulgar' and banished them to a special plot out of sight of the house, cottage gardeners grew everything together. Flowers, fruit, herbs and vegetables all complemented each other in the same borders, and chemicals were unheard of. The reasons are simple.

First of all, tucking a few cabbages away in among the marigolds actually camouflages them from pests which are attracted by sight or smell. Eager to get to the huge field of the things a kilometre or so away, the cabbage white butterflies fly over yours without so much as a second glance.

But the main reason is that growing a wide diversity of plants attracts an equal diversity of wildlife. Therefore, though your roses may draw greenfly, the marigolds nearby attract hoverflies whose larvae soon polish off the aphids. This way you build up a natural balance of wildlife so that no one species ever gains control and becomes an embarrassment. Of course, you do get a little damage and it's wise to protect some plants physically (see p. 345), but there are rarely, if ever, major attacks to worry about. I've been following this practice in my own ornamental kitchen garden at Barnsdale for several years now and I have actually never used a chemical spray there, so I know that it really does work and at the same time it produces a garden that looks *wonderful*!

Instead of growing in long rows, sow or plant vegetables in patches among the flowers.

Some vegetables, of course, are decorative in their own right, as the spiky, architectural foliage of the noble globe artichoke shows.

The principle of the ornamental kitchen garden involves turning each border into a 'deep bed' and working from the side paths. Inevitably this means more paths than normal, so it's essential to make them attractive and to soften them with lush planting. Brick paving is now widely available and easy to lay. It looks mellow and warm with generous planting either side. Make sure that you use special paviors (see p. 152) and not ordinary walling bricks, which will flake in the winter when water that has soaked in freezes.

Cottage borders mix all kinds of plants together and vegetables have their place. Grown in the mixed border, many of them will even outshine the flowers. By mixing flowers, fruit and vegetables together you get the best of all worlds – beautiful and productive borders, fruit and vegetables completely free from chemicals and a garden buzzing with wildlife.

Provided the fertility of the soil is kept very high with regular additions of compost and organic fertilisers, the garden will prove to be extremely productive even though close planting makes for extra competition.

CHAPTER 9

WATER GARDENS

EVER SINCE we've been making gardens, designers have been fascinated by water and it's not difficult to see why. From the dramatic fountains of the grand formal gardens to the tiny dewpond in a traditional cottage plot, water creates an interest that can't be rivalled.

With the help of a cheap electric pump it's quite easy to make a rippling stream or a tumbling waterfall, or you may prefer the quiet, reflective qualities of a sheet of calm, still water.

For the plantsman a garden pool provides another growing environment for a completely different range of plants both in the water and in the boggy soil around it. And the animal lover can go to town by stocking it with fish to give the garden yet another interest.

Time was when making a pool involved tons of concrete and the possibility of equal amounts of heartache if it wasn't installed with sufficient skill. Nowadays modern materials have made concrete unnecessary and construction simple and straightforward. A mini-Versailles in your own back yard is no longer beyond the realms of possibility.

The returns from a pool in terms of pleasure and interest greatly outweigh the small amount of time and expense involved in building it.

Types of pool

There's no doubt that *every* garden, however small and whatever the design, has room for a pool, but it's important that it fits in with the overall feel and layout of the rest of the garden. To shove a formal, rectangular shape into the middle of a woodland would obviously be as nonsensical as a stream and waterfall on a paved patio. Fortunately there's no limit to what can be done with water, and with a little thought it can be incorporated into any design.

First, though, I must issue the obligatory word of warning. You've heard it before but it's worth repeating. If you have small children, a pool simply isn't worthwhile. A toddler could drown in a few centimetres of water, and since the whole point of gardening is the enjoyment it brings, it defeats the object to build in any element of worry.

Consider initially whether your garden design would be suited by a formal or an informal feature. In small gardens a square or rectangular shape can really only be used if the rest of the design follows similar lines. However, a perfectly circular pool will fit in anywhere.

Avoid getting carried away and allowing the pool to dominate the whole garden. To have a comfortable feel, it needs an adequate setting. With an informal pool that will probably be a surround of plants or grass, or a mixture of the two. A formal design will require some kind of paved edge, either with slabs or wooden decking, and space to soften the whole effect with plants.

If you decide on a waterfall, you'll need to be even more careful. Nothing looks more unnatural than a heap of rocks surrounded by flat ground, so you'll want to blend the contours of the rest of the garden into the waterfall setting. Unless there are natural changes of level, therefore, you'll need to think about it right from the start, before any work is done on the garden at all.

For the greatest success with aquatic plants the pool should be sited in a sunny spot. It's also often recommended that you avoid trees which will deposit leaves in the pool to foul the water. In a small garden I don't think this is very realistic, so my advice would be not to worry too much but instead to net the pool in the autumn to catch most of the leaves. However, it's best to site any trees on the northern side of the pool to avoid shading it.

If you're using the pool to attract wildlife, it's important to position it where visitors will feel happy and confident. Birds and small mammals will prefer an

ABOVE **Informal pool** Very simple to make with a liner. The edges can be hidden under turf or a paved edge. I like to conceal the liner completely with a covering of soil, but even without it the plastic soon discolours to become quite unobtrusive.

RIGHT **Raised pool** This is easy to build and ideal for older or disabled gardeners. It can be faced inside with waterproof cement or the outer shell can be lined with a plastic or butyl liner. The top edge of the liner is incorporated into the mortar below the top coping. Alternatively a pre-formed rigid plastic shell can be used.

area of planting nearby, where they can hide while making sure that there's no danger from predators. Try also to arrange a seat close to but camouflaged from the pond so that you can spend some time watching them.

With a formal pool on the patio, it goes without saying that it's best to site it well out of the way of regular routes. You may be well aware of it, but visitors will not thank you for an unscheduled dip!

Barrel pool For tiny gardens a small pool can be very easily made with half a wooden barrel. It's best to sink it so that the top's level with the soil since this will keep the water cool and stop it going green. It also helps to put a layer of soil in the bottom. It's cooler and also a more natural habitat for plants and aquatic animals. Note the potted marginal plant which provides a step to enable any creatures that go into the pool to get out again.

Formal pool A small area of moving water is useful for softening the hard outlines of formal paved areas.

Making a pool with a liner

The easiest way to make a pool is with a liner, but it's a false economy either to buy a cheap one, which won't last for long, or to skimp on the job. Once the pool's installed you'll want it to remain undisturbed and without problems for a very long time. Believe me, there's nothing more frustrating and annoying than a leaking pool, and the time to solve that problem is *before* you build it. The best bet is a butyl rubber liner with a proper 'quilt' underneath it. My own method deviates from the norm in that I recommend covering the liner with a shallow layer of soil. This makes a better environment for wildlife and helps keep the water clear.

1 Mark out the hole with pegs round the perimeter. These should be levelled at the same time and set so that the tops correspond with the required finished level. Take care over the levelling so that the water will come exactly to the top of the liner all round.

2 Dig out the hole, making it at least 1m (3ft) deep at the lowest point. Note that it slopes up gradually on one side. You can leave shelves about 23cm (9in.) deep all round to take pots of marginal plants, but I prefer to refill with a little soil and plant into that.

3 To prevent sharp stones pushing up through the liner, cover the hole with a layer of sand, strong polythene sheet or, much better, with a special under-lining 'quilt'.

4 Lay the liner in the hole, folding and tucking it to make it as neat as possible.

5 Then cover the whole thing with about 7.5cm (3in.) of soil. Finally fill up with water. At first it'll look very muddy and cloudy, but it'll soon clear.

6 When the water's right at the top, you'll be able to see where to cut off the excess material. Leave about 15cm (6in.) all round, then cover this with soil and a strip of turf to finish it off. Alternatively sow it with grass seed.

ABOVE Once the pool has been planted it starts to come to life. It can take a while to build up a good balance of plant and animal life, but nature will sort that out for you. The pool is bound to attract plenty of wildlife with no further effort.

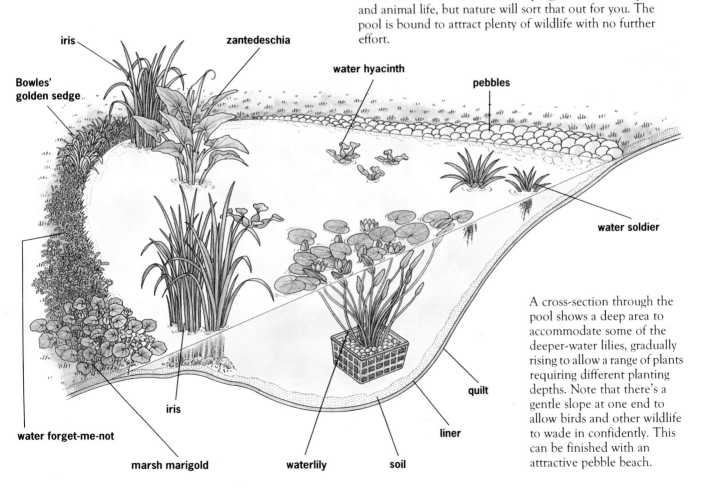

iris

zantedeschia

Bowles'
golden sedge

water hyacinth

pebbles

water soldier

water forget-me-not

iris

marsh marigold

waterlily

soil

liner

quilt

A cross-section through the pool shows a deep area to accommodate some of the deeper-water lilies, gradually rising to allow a range of plants requiring different planting depths. Note that there's a gentle slope at one end to allow birds and other wildlife to wade in confidently. This can be finished with an attractive pebble beach.

Making a bog garden

While building an informal pool, you could, if you have the room, take the opportunity to build a bog garden as well. This is an area lined with the same butyl liner and then refilled with soil which is kept moist at all times. In it you'll be able to grow yet another superb range of plants which demand wet soil. The water from the pool will feed the bog garden but, since this will increase the area of evaporation as well as providing more transpiration through plant leaves, you'll need to top up the pool more often.

1 Dig a second hole next to the pool with a wall of soil between the two. Note that the dividing wall is a few centimetres lower than the water level will be. This ensures that water from the pool feeds the bog garden.

2 Line the hole with a butyl liner and then refill with soil. If you have allowed for different depths here too, you'll be able to grow a wider range of plants.

The bog garden will provide a completely different habitat, enabling you to grow a diverse range of plants that would otherwise be impossible. It needs very little attention, though it's important to ensure that it's regularly topped up with water.

Making a pool with a pre-formed shell

1 Perhaps the simplest of all ways to make a pond is to buy a rigid, pre-formed shell. It's worth putting a little concrete underneath to ensure that it doesn't sink or tilt at a later stage.

2 As with all pools make quite sure that the shell's perfectly level so that the water reaches the top all round.

3 Then fill with water, at the same time refilling around it, ramming in soil to make a really firm job. Finally hide the edges with paving or turf.

There are many large-leaved plants that can be grown in the wet conditions of the bog garden, creating an exotic, almost tropical effect. Plants like *Gunnera manicata* make a dramatic show. They'll grow to about 3m (10ft) in deep soil but you can reduce their size by restricting the root run.

Plants such as the globe flowers (*Trollius* species) can be relied on to give a cheerful show of bright yellows and oranges over a long period. They're happier with a shallower root run.

Planting aquatics

Just as in the rest of the garden, it's the planting that really makes a pool come alive. But you'll need to choose the plants carefully. Avoid over-vigorous water lilies in a small pool and marginal plants like bulrushes which will soon become too dominant. Consult a good catalogue and you'll find hundreds of real mouth-waterers that are suitable for even the smallest pool.

One thing you'll certainly need is some oxygenating weed which helps keep the water clear and also some plants with large, floating leaves which will provide shade and restrict the growth of green algae – lilies are ideal. Spring is the best time to plant.

Water lilies

1 BELOW Even if you have soil in the bottom of the pool, lilies are best planted in special plastic baskets. Line the baskets with hessian to prevent the soil drifting out.

2 BELOW Put the plant in the basket and fill round with heavy garden soil or a special planting medium obtainable from a specialist centre.

3 LEFT Cover the surface of the soil with gravel to prevent it floating out and to deter fish from nosing through the top of the compost. Cut off old or damaged leaves.

4 BELOW Pass two strings through the basket and use them to lower it into the pool. Once it's on the bottom the strings can be withdrawn. The new leaves will soon grow to reach the surface of the water.

Marginal plants

LEFT Marginal plants can simply be taken out of their pots and pushed into the soft mud at the edge of the pool. Make sure that you plant them at the recommended depth of water.

BELOW If you buy a pre-formed pool it's likely to have shelves to take marginals, so you simply rest the pots on the shelves. Again, ensure that they're at the right depth.

BELOW **Oxygenating plants**

Oxygenating weed is very fast-growing, so don't buy too much. It comes in bundles, generally bound with wire; just throw it into the water and it'll sink to the bottom and root.

BELOW **Floating plants**

These are also simply thrown in, but bear in mind that some, like fairy moss and particularly duckweed, will grow very fast to cover the surface and are hard to get rid of.

Moving water

Moving water brings life, sparkle and a restful sound to the garden. On a more practical note, movement increases the oxygen content of water, keeping it fresh and clean. With the proviso that the type of water feature must be in sympathy with its surroundings (there should be no fountain in the wildlife pool, for example), movement is a great asset.

It's provided by an electric pump which circulates water around continuously. First be careful about installing the electricity supply. Pumps have built-in safety precautions, but unless you're an expert it's worth getting a qualified electrician to bring the power to the pool. Make sure especially that the cable is protected so that you don't risk putting your spade through it.

Pumps, of course, come in different sizes, so ensure that the one you choose is big enough for the job, particularly if you intend installing a waterfall. It takes a surprising amount of water to make a good show. Bigger pumps are non-submersible and will need to be housed in a pit at the side of the pool. If the pump is made to be lower than the water level, it will be primed by gravity, but if it's not, fit a footvalve and strainer unit to avoid continual priming. Take advice from the supplier and always err on the large side. It's easy to decrease the flow but not to increase it.

RIGHT By using rock and water you can transform a garden, but be very careful to ensure that the surrounding landscape is in sympathy with the feature.

Fountains

1 LEFT Fountains can easily be made with a submersible pump. Run the cable over the top of the liner and hide it with soil or plants. Then set the fountain unit on a few bricks to bring it to the right height and connect up.

2 RIGHT These submersible units will incorporate a valve which simply diverts water into the pool, so you can adjust the height of the fountain. There's also a filter which must be cleaned out periodically.

Building a waterfall

This is much like making a rock garden – the final design depends on the rock available, so you just have to make it up as you go along. First excavate a series of steps down the existing slope. Cover this with a liner and then set the rocks in mortar on top, forming a wide channel and perhaps a pool or two on the way down. If you do make pools, ensure that they'll remain full when the power is turned off.

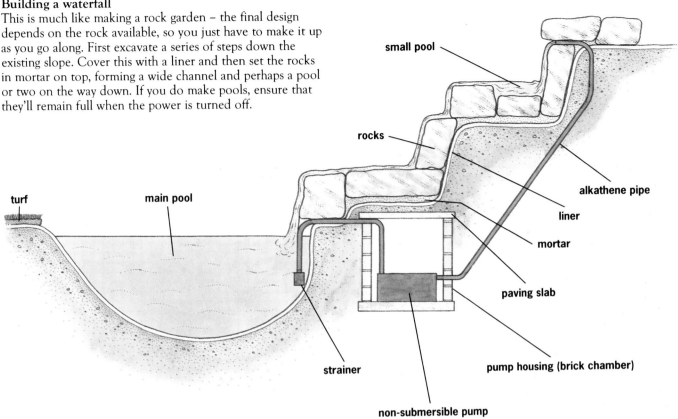

small pool

rocks

turf

main pool

alkathene pipe

liner

mortar

paving slab

strainer

pump housing (brick chamber)

non-submersible pump

Bubble pool

This will give you all the advantages of movement and sound without any of the danger of a conventional pool, so it's a good alternative if you have a young family.

Basin pool

In a very formal setting you can create a charming feature by fitting a sculpture to a wall and piping water through its mouth into a small basin pool beneath.

Stocking a pool with fish and other animal life

Introducing fish to a pool adds another interest but can have some disadvantages. In my experience too many fish can foul the water, causing clouding problems. They also, of course, eat other wildlife, so are not the best thing in the wildlife pool. Nonetheless the shine and sparkle of these creatures as they flash through the water and the fun of training them to come for food are almost irresistible attractions.

If you do decide to stock your pool with the more exotic types like goldfish or carp, avoid putting in any native species, especially sticklebacks, which will rapidly eat each and every goldfish egg as it's laid.

Other animal life will appear automatically in the pool. Water boatmen and whirligig beetles are sure to arrive and dragonflies might too. Water snails, which can be bought from an aquatic centre, make useful scavengers. You could also introduce frogs by collecting spawn from a friend who has a stocked pool. Alternatively contact your local nature club which should be able to put you on to a source. Never, of course, collect spawn from the wild. Take especial care of the wildlife when you pull out excess weed. Leave the weed in a pile in very shallow water for a day to allow any inhabitants to escape back to the pool.

Acclimatising fish to a pool Fish establish better if they're bought small; they'll travel better and, of course, they're cheaper too. They're generally transported in polythene bags, and you should acclimatise them to the lower temperature of the pool by putting the bags, unopened, into the water for a few hours. Then gently open the bags to release them.

Goldfish Good coloured specimens of goldfish are certainly the best bet. They're hardy and easy to rear and, once they've grown to about 13 cm (5in.), they'll breed quite freely.

Shubunkins Similar in shape to goldfish but with transparent scales. Some types have longer tails too. They're available in many colours, so it's best to visit a specialist and pick your own.

Golden orfe Longer and thinner than goldfish, these make a very attractive display. They're a little timid and should not be put into a pool less than about 3sq. m (3sq. yds) in surface area.

Koi carp Certainly the most exotic of all hardy fish as you'll see when you check the prices! They're available in a range of colours but again are not suitable for a small pool.

Maintaining oxygen levels Keep a supply of oxygen to fish at all times. In winter you may need a small pool heater to ensure that the surface doesn't freeze over completely. Alternatively maintain a hole by floating a rubber ball in the water.

Keeping the pool clear of leaves Leaves will inevitably fall into the pool where they'll eventually sink to the bottom and rot. Try to remove them before they sink or, better still, put a net over the pool in the autumn to catch them.

Herons These can be a big problem if you keep the pool stocked with fish. Again a net will foil them, though it does look rather unsightly. It's said that a single strand of fishing line on pegs around the pool frightens them off and after trying it I've not been troubled with them, but I must admit that this is hardly conclusive.

Secrets of success

In hot weather the oxygen level in a pool falls and fish will become listless. If the condition prevails for long they could be at risk, so introduce extra oxygen by turning on the pool pump to move the water. If you don't have one, stir up the surface with a jet from a hosepipe.

Feeding fish Feed fish twice a day in summer but don't overdo it. Give them only as much as they can eat in a few minutes and remove any they leave. During the winter feeding should be reduced and they'll probably stop feeding completely in very cold weather.

CHAPTER 10

ALPINE GARDENS

ALPINES GROW IN what seem to us gardeners the most impossibly inhospitable places. They spend much of the winter covered in a blanket of snow which thaws in spring to give them what is sometimes their only watering of the season. The rest of the year they suffer blazing sunshine and bitter winds. Add to that the fact that their roots are in clefts in rock or in pure gravel with no visible means of sustenance and you wonder how they survive at all. They then produce some of the most beautiful flowers you'll ever see.

These marvellous little plants can be grown in the rock garden, in a scree bed, between paving slabs, in the greenhouse, in containers – indeed, almost anywhere – and they'll put up with the same spartan conditions they have become used to in the wild.

They require virtually no attention except weeding and a periodic renewal of the mulch, and removal of dead leaves each autumn. Feed them only if they appear to be failing to grow and then with just a very light sprinkling of general fertiliser.

Alpines are one group of plants that have, on the whole, escaped the plant breeders' attentions, probably because it's very hard to imagine how they could be improved. As you may have realised, I'm an enthusiast. I make no apologies, because I can guarantee that as soon as any gardener grows one or two, he or she will become bewitched too.

An alpine feature can be as grand or as modest as you want to make it. It's the plants that provide the real fascination.

Making and planting a rock garden

The idea of growing alpines in a rock garden is to make them look as natural as possible by giving them something approximating to their natural environment. That's not as easy as it sounds. In a small, flat garden particularly, a contrived rockery looks like a heap of soil with stones stuck in it. It's essential that the contours should naturally lead to the slope of the rock garden and that the background should be as natural-looking as possible – which generally means a screen of plants. If you can manage this, you'll produce a wonderful feature that'll be a source of pleasure all year round. If you can't, it may be best to stick to a scree (see p. 224).

When ordering rock, it's strongly recommended that you go and actually choose each piece. Whichever way you buy it, try to make it look at home by opting for local stone if possible except, of course, natural limestone. Since transport is more expensive than the stone itself, it's a lot cheaper that way too. If you can't select your own, ask for pieces of various weights including a good proportion of large ones; and, if the stone is suitable, you'll find a few big, flat pieces very useful too.

When building, wear strong gloves and boots and, to avoid accidents, take lots of time. Bear in mind, too, that with heavy rocks, you'll need some help.

1 RIGHT A rock garden infested with weeds with running roots like couch grass or ground elder is a disaster and might as well be scrapped and redone. So before starting, get rid of all perennial weeds by spraying or covering with black polythene for at least a year. After ensuring that all the weeds are dead, cultivate the soil by single digging. Deep cultivation is not necessary.

2 The first layer of rocks is most important because it decides the line of all the others. All the rocks should be buried slightly to make them look natural. In most cases, burying a quarter of the rock, or even less, is sufficient.

3 The top of each rock should slant backwards a little into the slope. This looks more natural and directs water towards the plants. The horizontal line is important too, especially if the rock strata are well-defined.

4 The line of the first rock decides that of the others so, when you're satisfied that it's right, ram soil underneath the rock all round to ensure that it's very firmly anchored.

5 The rocks are set into a rough horseshoe pattern to provide planting pockets behind them. Make sure that the remaining rocks in the first row run back at the same angle and that their strata lines match those of the first rock. Be very careful here not to trap your fingers.

6 Once the first row is complete, fill in behind the rocks with compost to make planting pockets. The compost should be very well drained: use equal parts of good garden soil or bought-in loam, garden compost or bark and 3mm (⅛in.) grit. Don't use sand which can reduce drainage. Afterwards, firm well.

7 To move heavy rocks you'll find a sack-barrow with pneumatic tyres invaluable. You may need scaffold planks to make wheeling over soft soil easier. Large rocks can generally be manoeuvred into position with a crowbar, but don't try to lift rocks that are really beyond you – get help!

8 The second layer of rock goes in behind and, of course, slightly higher than the first in the same way. Again build them into rough horseshoes to accommodate plants, and fill with compost. Subsequent layers, if needed, are constructed similarly.

9 Most alpines are lime-lovers, so it's easy to provide them with suitable conditions. However, if you wish to grow acid-lovers too, like the beautiful miniature rhododendrons, you can fill some planting pockets with an ericaceous compost. Put these at the top of the rock garden to avoid limy water draining into them.

10 There's no need for fertiliser in the planting pockets since alpines are very undemanding feeders. Plant with a trowel and after planting mulch round the plants with coarse grit to set them off and to keep the leaves away from the wet soil. Alpines don't appreciate wet conditions.

Making your own rockery stones

Natural stone looks wonderful in the garden but, of course, by using it we are depleting our countryside. The answer is to make imitation stone – not difficult with a little patience, and the results are surprisingly convincing. Use a mixture of two parts coir (coconut fibre), two parts sharp sand and one part fresh Portland cement with a little colouring powder if you wish (I find yellow the most satisfactory), then mix with water to a stiffish consistency. Over time, algae and lichens will grow on the surface of the 'rocks' and add to their natural appearance. You could use your artificial stones to build a rockery or perhaps even a miniature version of the stunning natural stone pavements found in the countryside.

1 Dig a hole as a mould for each rock. Start with small holes: you can always make them bigger later for larger rocks.

2 Line the hole with strong polythene. Don't worry if it crinkles and folds – in fact this makes very attractive fissures in the imitation rocks.

3 Put some mixture in the mould and work it up the sides. This will ensure that the hollow rock is not too heavy to lift out – and saves money.

4 After a few days remove the rock from its mould. You may need help lifting larger rocks.

5 Peel away the polythene and leave the rock to dry out.

OPPOSITE Limestone pavements in County Clare, Ireland (bottom) and the Yorkshire Dales in England (top). Instead of being craggy and mountainous, these areas have been weathered flat and brilliant alpine plants – and occasionally trees – grow in cracks and crevices in the surface. With a stretch of the imagination and some dramatic miniaturization you can reproduce the same sort of effect in your garden, making an ideal alternative to the rock garden. I've seen a whole small front garden laid out with nothing but flat rocks and alpine plants, and very handsome it looked too. For the busy gardener it's also a great labour-saving alternative.

Making a scree bed

Though alpines grow in wild country and are, in the main, untouched by the hand of man, they can, surprisingly, be displayed very formally. Indeed, in my opinion it's much better to make an honestly artificial display than try to build a 'natural' environment in an alien situation. It's not easy to fit a full-scale rock garden into a small plot. I've built features in my garden at Barnsdale, one formally rectangular and another in a perfect circle, that are designed simply to show off a collection of alpines, relying on the plants rather than on the setting to impress. I think they work very well and they've certainly given me a great deal of pleasure.

ABOVE The scree bed will start the season with miniature bulbs and from then on should have something in flower right through to the coldest months of the year. Even in winter there should be something to see, perhaps dwarf evergreens early on or the first of the bulbs in late winter, but it's always at its best in late spring. As with all alpine plants, if you get the conditions right to start with there will be little maintenance to do later on.

1 Mark out the circular scree bed by scratching a line in the soil or, better still, by marking it with sand (see p. 139). You'll need the central peg when laying the edging bricks, so make sure that it stays in or that you clearly mark the spot if you remove it.

2 Put in a 7.5cm- (3in.)-deep concrete footing round the edge and lay paving bricks on this. Use the string to ensure that the bricks all face exactly into the centre of the circle.

3 Point between the bricks with mortar and then dig over the soil in the middle, mixing in compost or bark and coarse grit. However, if the soil's heavy, dig it out, break up the bottom and mix the soil with equal amounts of garden compost and coarse grit.

4 For better access to the plants for maintenance and for the close inspection they warrant, a path of stepping stones through the bed makes an attractive addition. They're set on compost (see p. 150).

5 Plant a few taller subjects like the truly dwarf conifers to add height and fill in with alpines. After planting, mulch with coarse grit.

RIGHT On heavy land a raised bed made from old railway sleepers is the ideal way to provide really sharp drainage. The sleepers are held by driving posts into the ground where they join and nailing the posts to them. Fill with a very well-drained compost.

The alpine house

As you would expect of plants that grow in the mountains, alpines are, on the whole, bone hardy. They'll stand any amount of frost, but what really makes them suffer is wet. In their natural habitat they're covered with a warm, dry blanket of snow all winter, so they resent the moist conditions of winters in countries whose climate doesn't provide this protection. For some species, therefore, especially those with woolly, grey leaves, the gardener must provide artificial protection. This generally means either a greenhouse or frame.

The protection of glass, even though full ventilation is given, will generally result in the plants flowering very slightly earlier than they would outside. In fact this is, for most gardeners, a distinct advantage since it extends the season of colour and activity and makes the alpine house a real joy in late winter when everything outside is still dormant.

Almost any greenhouse will do for alpines, but the bigger and airier, the better. Site it where it'll receive full sunshine in winter, even though this will mean shading it in summer. The main requirement is continuous ventilation on both sides of the roof.

RIGHT **Growing alpines on staging**
The other essential requirement is very strong staging. Ideally plants grown in pots should be plunged up to their rims in sand which is kept continuously moist. This means at least 15cm (6in.) of damp sand, which is very heavy indeed. Certainly normal greenhouse staging won't do. Alternatively plants can be planted direct in compost on the staging, making a very attractive miniature rock garden. Ideally use tufa rock which is very light, though the weight of the compost still necessitates reinforced staging.

Growing plants in tufa rock Tufa is a very porous rock and it's possible to grow plants directly in it. Make holes with an old screwdriver and plant with small seedlings or rooted cuttings. They'll find enough sustenance in the rock to survive and thrive.

LEFT **Alternatives to the greenhouse** As you might imagine, an alpine greenhouse is an expensive item. If the budget doesn't run to it, use a coldframe (though, of course, its disadvantage is that you can't actually get in it) or make a cover for beds outside. This one is made of wood and rigid PVC and slots into pipes at the corners of the raised bed so that it can be removed for the summer.

Alpine troughs

Alpines also look superb in troughs and, if your garden's small, this is an ideal way to grow them. There's no doubt that they look much the best in stone troughs, but there are many good concrete and reconstituted stone ones. Alternatively it's not difficult to make your own. First take a trip to the supermarket and beg a couple of strong cardboard boxes to make the mould. They needn't be very deep and the size, of course, depends on how big you want the troughs to be, but don't be over-ambitious. One box should fit inside the other to leave a gap all round of about 5cm (2in.). The material used for making the trough is called 'hypertufa' and is made with one part of sharp sand, one of fresh cement and two of sieved coconut fibre compost. Mix it quite wet.

1 Put a 2.5cm (1in.) layer of hypertufa into the bottom of the larger box and cover it with a piece of wire netting. The netting sold to make pea-guards is ideal, though small-mesh chicken wire will do. Cover that with another 2.5cm (1in.) layer of hypertufa.

2 Cut four pieces of broom handle 5cm (2in.) long and push them through the netting to make four 'legs' to support the smaller box. Then place this on top so that there's an equal gap all round between the boxes.

3 Cut some more reinforcing wire and join it to make a rectangle 2.5cm (1in.) larger than the smaller box so that it'll sit in the middle of the space between the two boxes.

4 Now fill in between the boxes with hypertufa, working it down with a stick and from time to time tapping the sides of the boxes to ensure that you get rid of any air spaces.

5 Soon the water in the hypertufa will soften the boxes, so they'll need supporting. Fill the inside box with sand or bricks and support the outside one with paving slabs or pieces of wood held in place with bricks.

6 Leave the boxes overnight. The following day you'll be able to remove the supports and tear away the wet cardboard. At this stage don't attempt to move the trough.

7 Before the hypertufa hardens, scrape away the corners and top edge to make them look weather-worn. Leave the trough in place for about a week, then knock out the pieces of broom handle to make drainage holes.

8 Set the trough in position on a couple of walling blocks to ensure good drainage. Fill it with gritty alpine compost (see p. 221) and plant.

CHAPTER 11
GROWING IN CONTAINERS

As GARDENS GET smaller, more and more plants are being grown in containers. It's a marvellous way to garden, because you have complete control over the plants and can site them just where you like. You can fill the patio with colourful tubs and troughs all year round, brighten up the front door with welcoming hanging baskets and even grow a few vegetables and herbs right outside the back door.

Smaller gardens have also exercised the brains of the plant breeders and the nurserymen with the result that there's a new range of plants suitable for container growing from fruit trees to flowering and foliage shrubs, vegetables and, of course, herbaceous plants and annuals.

The only disadvantage, if disadvantage it be, is that the containers depend almost entirely on you for their wellbeing. They need constant watering and feeding in particular, but they'll show their appreciation with healthy growth and a riot of colour. And few things do a gardener's heart more good than that.

Hard areas of paving or gravel will always look better if they're softened with plants in containers. Most plants will grow happily in tubs and troughs, if only for a few years. Even the exotic passionflower has been used here to form an unusual standard topiary.

Buying and making containers

Such is the range of containers available these days that gardeners are spoilt for choice. Prices vary considerably, from quite cheap plastic to real stone or lead. In between, you'll be able to choose from fibreglass that looks so much like lead it's hard to tell the difference, rustic or plain wood, concrete, terracotta and reconstituted stone. You'll have to decide which material most suits the plants you intend to use and its surroundings. Half-barrels, for example, look fine in a fairly rustic situation but can appear uncomfortable outside a new house, while alpines are at their best in

shallow stone or concrete troughs set on a low plinth.

During the summer, of course, you'll hardly see the container, but in small gardens bear in mind that it must look good in winter and early spring too when it'll be much more noticeable.

Containers are also quite easy to make. You could simply cut the top off a fruit-juice barrel or even use a plastic bucket. They need only drainage holes which you can drill or pierce with a hot poker. Alternatively, if you're handy with a saw, wooden containers are attractive and easy to make.

Making a wooden tub

1 A wooden tub can be made cheaply with outdoor-quality or marine plywood. The panels are formed by gluing and pinning the plywood to timber frames, using waterproof glue. Modern adhesives are very strong, so no joints are necessary.

2 A good coat of undercoat and paint or a wood preservative will ensure that it lasts for many years.

4 x 4cm (1½ x 1½in.) battens

battens 2.5 x 4cm (1 x 1½in.)

50cm (20in.)

50cm (20in.)

3mm (⅛in.) plywood

pins

2.5 x 4cm (1 x 1½in.) battens

drainage holes

4 x 2.5 x 15cm (1½ x 1 x 6in.)

23cm (9in.)

length of sill

15cm (6in.)

18cm (7in.)

all timber 2.5cm (1in.) thick

drainage holes

Making a wooden windowbox

1 Windowboxes are a possibility even in the smallest of gardens. No joints are necessary, so construction is easy. Glue and screw the timbers together and finish with paint or preservative.

2 The brackets must be strong and firmly bolted to the wall, since the soil in each box is quite heavy.

Lead containers are expensive but beautiful. However, you can buy fibreglass reproductions.

All kinds of old containers can be used to grow plants, but make sure that they have holes drilled in the bottom.

Wooden tubs can be bought cheaply and will last a long time since they're made to be waterproof.

Reconstituted stone urns can be weathered more quickly with a coating of dilute cow dung or sour milk.

Hanging baskets

Hanging baskets provide a cheerful, seasonal display to brighten up walls, fences or a pergola. They do need rather more attention than other types of container, but will reward you well.

While it's certainly possible to grow plants like ivies and winter-flowering pansies in baskets during the winter, I have never found them worth the trouble. I would suggest you try them only if you live in a warm area. From spring to autumn, however, baskets will gladden your eye and lift your spirits every day.

Very attractive, Japanese-style baskets are easy and quite cheap to make yourself.

Making a Japanese-style hanging basket

1 Cut sixteen pieces of 2.5 × 4cm (1 × 1½in.) timber 38cm (15in.) long. Drill holes 7.5cm (3in.) from each end.

2 Screw two pieces of similar wood on to the bottom two struts to make the basket base.

3 Pass strong plastic string through the holes to build up the basket.

Planting a hanging basket for summer

1 If choosing a ready-made basket pick the large-mesh type made of wire or plastic. The small, solid-plastic types make a poor show. Line the basket with moss or with a special fibre liner. Work with the basket resting in a large pot.

2 Put a square of polythene or a saucer in the bottom of the basket to retain water. Fill half-way with a soil-based compost which won't dry out as fast as a soilless one. You could add a controlled-release fertiliser (see p. 82).

3 Put a large, pot-grown plant like a fuchsia or a geranium in the centre to give height and fill round with a little more compost. Then place slightly shorter plants, such as petunias, salvias and marigolds, around the central one.

LEFT Summer hanging baskets make a superb, long-lasting display and are not difficult. The secrets are to use the right basket, fill it full to overflowing and water and feed regularly. It's well worth the trouble.

Secrets of success

Summer baskets should be crammed full of plants. Even when there's no room to fit in another one, I like to push in a couple of seeds of nasturtiums to provide a show of colour late in the season.

4 At the edge of the basket plant edging plants like lobelia, alyssum and ageratum together with trailing plants such as nepeta and trailing lobelia, helichrysums, geraniums and campanulas.

5 Hang up the basket and push trailing plants like lobelia through the moss and into the compost. Within just a few weeks the plants will have grown to create a complete ball of colour.

6 Water the basket regularly, probably every other day at first and then every day when the plants have filled the space. After about six weeks, start feeding with a liquid fertiliser if no controlled-release feed was added.

Summer tubs and troughs

Tubs and troughs are planted in much the same way as hanging baskets, with trailing plants at the edges and taller subjects towards the middle. By changing the planting schemes with the seasons, you could have colour and interest all year round. Start by planting half-hardy plants in the spring for a display throughout the summer. If the containers can be planted early and kept in the greenhouse until all danger of frost has passed, the plants could be in full flower from the day you put them out until the first frosts of the autumn.

Don't forget that, like hanging baskets, tubs and troughs rely on you for all their water (rain is *never* enough) and food. They may need watering two or three times a week and will have to be fed with a high-potash fertiliser at least once a week.

RIGHT Half-hardy annuals and perennials are the obvious choice for summer tubs because they'll go on flowering right through the summer. Picking off dead flowers helps the continuity. This container combines perennials and annuals, the half-standard fuchsia in the centre giving height with its bare stem hidden by geraniums and busy Lizzies.

ABOVE A lower, spreading tub containing white marguerites and purple lobelia which have soon grown to hide the container completely.

RIGHT There's no need to restrict the tubs to flowers. By planting vegetable fruits like tomatoes or courgettes you can have the best of both worlds with home-grown vegetables for the picking right on your doorstep. And they don't come any fresher than that!

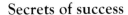

Secrets of success

If you surround the pot's 'legs' with the special grease sold to make grease bands on fruit trees, you'll prevent the wingless vine weevil crawling up to lay her eggs in the compost (see p. 347).

Planting

1 Before filling the containers, it's wise to stand them on 'legs'. A couple of pieces of wood underneath wooden containers is fine, but you can buy terracotta legs to match clay pots. Fill with a soil-based compost and ideally mix in a controlled-release fertiliser to avoid having to feed all season.

2 Start planting at the centre and work outwards, cramming the container as full as you possibly can. With most containers there's plenty of soil under the plants, so competition won't be too fierce.

3 Finally give the pots a good soaking to settle the compost round the roots. You won't need to water them quite so often as you would baskets, but never let them dry out. Feeding during the summer is essential using a high-potash liquid fertiliser until late in the season. When the plants begin to look a little tired, change the feed to one higher in nitrogen.

Spring tubs and troughs

After the summer-flowering plants have been pulled out of containers, the spring display can be planted immediately, including biennials like wallflowers and pansies. The soil will be somewhat impoverished, so it's best to tip it out and to mix in some more organic matter. A little bone meal is all the fertiliser the plants will need at this stage, though they'll benefit from liquid feeding in mid-spring when they're in flower. Bulbs need to be planted in early autumn, so you'll either have to curtail the flowering of the summer display or have another few tubs waiting in the wings.

As you would expect, spring-flowering containers are much more vulnerable to the harsher weather, so try to position them in as sheltered a place as possible and choose your plants carefully. This means avoiding plants that aren't fully hardy, of course, and also those that are too tall. Taller tulips, for example, will always flop in the strong winds that can be expected at that time of year. If you grow shrubs or conifers in tubs, they can be positioned to block the worst of the winter wind. It's also vital to avoid positioning tubs where they're likely to be covered by snow slipping from the roof.

With few trailing plants available at this time of year, and, it has to be said, somewhat sparser growth, spring tubs will look much better if you can group them together to make a really eye-catching display. A combination like this can give a much-needed lift to the spirits in early spring.

Crown imperials (*Fritillaria imperialis*) won't grow as tall in a pot as they do in a border, so they make a good subject for the patio. After flowering they can be transplanted to the garden where they'll flower again next year.

A few wallflowers grown from seed and transplanted in early autumn, plus several clumps of variegated aubrietia dug from the garden, cost next to nothing.

Planting a container of daffodils

1 To fill a tub completely with daffodil flowers, plant the bulbs in two layers with a little compost between. Though it may seem that you're planting one on top of another, they'll find a way through.

2 The result is a tub crammed as full as possible with flowers and making a fine show. After flowering, remove the bulbs with the foliage, heel them in in the garden and give them a high-potash feed to enable them to build up flowers for the following year.

If you use tulips, make sure that you choose shorter varieties. The long-stemmed ones blow about in the least wind and are likely to snap off. Naturally you should also ensure that they all flower at the same time. Mixed with a few winter pansies, they make an attractive pot.

Permanent containers

Permanent plants can be grown in tubs quite happily and it's surprising how even those that would become fairly large in open ground will last for many years where their root space is so confined. Naturally they'll need feeding and some will have to be pruned regularly to keep them down to size. Use the same soil-based compost recommended for hanging baskets (see p. 232).

RIGHT You may wish to grow permanent plants that are too tender for your location. The way to do it is to grow them in pots and bring them into a greenhouse in winter. This *Agave americana* gives a Mediterranean touch to an English summer garden but would not stand the winter outside.

Evergreen herbs like bay will not only provide an attractive, architectural shape but can also be sited right outside the back door within easy reach of the kitchen. In colder areas, evergreens will need the protection of a sheltered position.

Roses will do extremely well in containers and most can stay in the same one for many years. This one is 'Margaret Merrill', which is renowned for its perfume. Put it near a seat or by the door where it'll be most appreciated.

Some fruit trees will grow well in pots to provide attractive and productive plants. They're especially useful where space is limited, such as on a balcony or in a back yard. It's essential to choose trees that are grown on a dwarfing rootstock (see p. 290), or to select something like this genetically dwarf peach.

If you have to leave hardy plants outside in tubs during the winter, it may be worth protecting the roots from freezing. They're vulnerable to hard frosts and the whole plant could succumb unless they're protected. A few thicknesses of sacking tied around the pot will suffice.

You can have great fun with box planted in tubs by trimming the bushes into all kinds of shapes. They suit formal topiary very well and thrive in pots for years with few problems.

Some conifers are ideal in pots and make a good foil for other containers filled with flowering plants. However, after a few years they do begin to look a little sad and lack-lustre, so they're best then planted out in the garden.

Secrets of success

As permanent plants grow they need repotting into larger containers. Eventually the half-hardy ones become quite difficult to move in and out of the greenhouse for winter protection. In this case a sack-barrow with pneumatic tyres makes even the heaviest pot a one-man (or one-woman) job.

CHAPTER 12

VEGETABLES

THERE'S NOTHING QUITE so satisfying as growing your own fresh vegetables and they'll *always* taste better than those you buy. For a start, you have the opportunity to buy varieties that provide the best flavour. The commercial grower often rejects these in favour of varieties bred for increased yield or disease resistance, or so that they all mature at once, or just to look better.

Naturally, you'll never buy produce as fresh as that you grow yourself and you also know exactly what has or has not been sprayed on it. I like to grow mine organically (indeed I practise the same principles over the whole garden), and I have few problems with pests or diseases. As in the rest of the book, I have also included chemical methods in this chapter, so the choice is yours.

If your plot's small, grow first of all those crops you like and which do well on your land. You'll find that out only by trial and error, of course. Then go for the types and varieties that taste much better fresh – like spinach and sweetcorn – and, if you have space left, those vegetables that are expensive or difficult to get in the shops, like scorzonera and globe artichokes.

A well-tended vegetable garden is a joy to behold and a real pleasure to work in, quite apart from the high-quality produce you'll grow.

Crop rotation

Maintaining a continuity of fresh vegetables throughout the year takes quite a bit of good organisation or a formidable memory. You'll need, for example, to remember to sow lettuces every couple of weeks in summer; you'll need to think in April of one year about the green vegetables you'll be wanting in March the following year; and ideally you should have a plan of where in the plot you'll be growing each vegetable at any particular time. Quite a tall order.

The good news is that, if you do slip up by having a hundred lettuces one week and none the next, you're in good company. I don't believe anyone gets it right all the time and I'm quite sure I don't! Nonetheless, an attempt at planning certainly helps.

On a large plot, working out a crop rotation has its advantages. This is a very old system developed by farmers largely for pest and disease control before the days of pesticides, but it has less relevance in the garden. Alas, most pests can travel the short distances between crops however much you juggle them around, and diseases are carried all over on your boots and your spade.

But rotations certainly do help to make the most of your resources. By grouping all the heavy feeders together in one area you can maximise its value, making it necessary to manure only that one per year. The plot you manure is changed each year so that the whole garden is manured every three years. If you can get extra organic matter, you should not, of course, let the rotation plan stop you using it on all the plots. Note that, provided the manure is well rotted, you can grow root crops better with than without it.

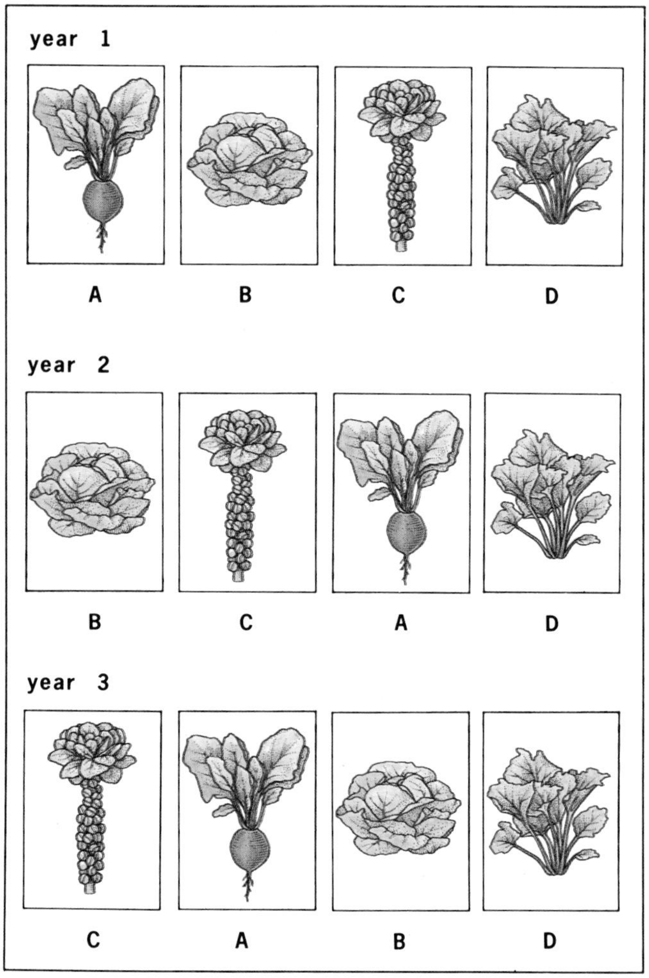

year 1

A   B   C   D

year 2

B   C   A   D

year 3

C   A   B   D

The rotation
Plots A, B, C and D are rotated as shown in the diagram.

Plot A
Dig in manure and use fertiliser too. Some longer-term crops will need extra fertiliser during the season. Use no lime.
Crops to grow: beetroot, carrot, celeriac, celery, courgette, fennel, garlic, leek, marrow, onion, Hamburg parsley, parsnip, potato, pumpkin, salsify, scorzonera, shallot, tomato. If space is limited, transfer some of the root crops to Plots B and C.

Plot B
Use fertiliser only every time a crop is sown or planted.
Crops to grow: globe artichoke, beans (all types), Swiss chard, chicory, land cress, endive, lettuce, peas, spinach, spinach beet, sweetcorn.

Plot C
Apply fertiliser before sowing or planting each crop. Lime in spring or autumn to bring the pH to 6.5–7.
Crops to grow: sprouting broccoli, cabbage, Chinese cabbage, calabrese, cauliflower, kale, kohl rabi, radish, Brussels sprouts, swede, turnip.

Plot D
This plot contains permanent crops and is not rotated. Use organic matter before planting anything new and mulch whenever possible. Use fertiliser at least twice a year.
Crops to grow: Jerusalem artichoke, asparagus, herbs, rhubarb, seakale.

ABOVE The well-maintained vegetable plot
Far from being ugly, a tidy, well-planned and well-maintained vegetable garden is something to be proud of and will delight the eye.

ABOVE Growing a catch-crop
Never let an area of soil remain bare for too long. If you harvest a crop and there are a few weeks before you need the land again for the next, use it to produce a fast-growing 'catch-crop' like baby beet or lettuce (grown for its young leaves).

LEFT Intercropping
Some longer-term crops need a lot of room when they're mature but much less in the early stages. To make the most of the space available, they can be 'intercropped' with faster-growing vegetables.

The deep-bed system

Small gardens in particular have little room to spare for vegetables, so it's vital to make full use of whatever space is available. To achieve the very maximum productivity from your land, you need a three-pronged approach: make the best use of space, extend the season as much as possible and ensure the highest yields of the vegetables you grow.

There are various ways to extend the season at either end and these are covered on p. 246, but the best way to achieve the other two objectives is to grow your crops on the deep-bed system. It has many advantages.

Crops are grown on 1.2m- (4ft)-wide beds, all the work being done from the side paths. The beds are first double dug and organic matter is worked in at all levels. This increases the fertility and the rooting depth of the soil and enables the crops to be grown much more closely together without any loss of yield. Drainage is also improved, so the soil warms up much more quickly in spring, allowing early sowing and planting. And, of course, the improved drainage makes the deep-bed system ideal for cold, heavy clay soils. When you compare it to the traditional method of growing in rows, you'll find that it doubles and even triples yields.

1 RIGHT To make a deep bed, mark it out with two garden lines 1.2m (4ft) apart and then double dig the area (see p. 90), working in manure, garden compost or spent mushroom compost through all levels of the soil. This will raise the bed about 15–23cm (6–9in.) above the side paths. Edging the beds with boards makes a neater job but is not obligatory. In subsequent years there's no need to double dig. Simply turn the soil over one spade deep, again incorporating organic matter. Eventually even heavy clay will become easy to work. Because the method is very intensive, you'll also need to use fertiliser before sowing or planting each crop.

2 ABOVE All crops are grown in blocks rather than in rows, thus saving the space between rows. Plant vegetables out in staggered rows to form the block, spacing them so that each plant just touches its neighbour when it's mature.

Secrets of success

The beds should never be trodden on during the season as all the work is done from the side paths. This does, however, make for a lot of walking, especially when sowing and planting, since you can't reach further than the middle of the bed. So make a simple wooden bridge high enough to span the bed and a low-growing crop. Fix a strong rope to each end to enable you to move it easily.

3 If plants are to be sown *in situ* and thinned out, the same principle applies. The easiest way to make shallow furrows for sowing is to push the edge of the planting board into the surface and move it backwards and forwards.

4 For crops that don't need transplanting, like radish, salad onions and pickling onions, sow in a wide band made with a hoe, scatter the seed thinly and cover by drawing soil over them with the back of the rake.

5 Peas can be sown in quite wide rows, with about 5cm (2in.) between each seed. If you use one of the self-supporting, co-called 'leafless' varieties, you'll be able to dispense with pea-sticks.

Extending the growing season

While growing on the deep-bed system will greatly increase productivity by improving yields, the other method of maximising harvests from the space available is to extend the season. A little protection from the weather will produce earlier crops in the spring and allow plants to finish cropping fully at the end of the season. Cloches are the easiest and cheapest method of protection and range from the more expensive glass structures to the very cheap 'floating' type (see p. 52).

To make the best of them, you'll need to plan your sowing and planting programme fairly carefully and here it's difficult to give precise advice. Sowing and planting dates will naturally depend on where you live and your local climate, so you'll have to take a few calculated guesses until experience tells you exactly when to do things. The main point to remember is to put the cloches out at least a couple of weeks before you want to sow in order to warm up the soil, and don't be in too much of a hurry. Most seed won't germinate before the soil temperature has reached about 7°C (45°F).

The cropping plan below offers some suggestions as to how you can best make use of your cloches.

Secrets of success

Clear polythene can also be used to good effect to keep soil dry and warm it up prior to sowing or planting. If left in position, it will warm the roots of some crops to bring them on too. There are two methods, one of which I have used successfully for potatoes (see p. 251) and the other for sweetcorn.

For raising sweetcorn without a greenhouse, make up ridges 60cm (2ft) apart and about 30cm (1ft) high and sow the seeds, two per station, in the bottom of the troughs about 30cm (1ft) apart. Stretch the polythene over the top of the ridges and, when the shoots of the sweetcorn touch the sheeting, cut a slit and help them through.

BELOW Plastic 'field frames' are ideal for covering deep beds.

CROPPING PLAN

Sow under cloches or plant out under them from the greenhouse in February (use early varieties):
Broad bean, beetroot, carrot, lettuce, spring onion, parsley, pea, potato, radish, spinach, turnip.

Remove cloches in April or May (in colder districts) and put them over:
Aubergine, French bean, runner bean, courgette, cucumber, marrow, pepper, sweetcorn, tomato.

Remove cloches in June or July. In August or September put them over the following crops in order to finish ripening:

Aubergine, courgette, cucumber, marrow, pepper, tomato.

Or cover the following crops which are sown unprotected in July or August:
French bean, carrot, corn salad, endive, lettuce, spring onion, potato, radish.

Or sow under cloches the following crops in September to November for overwintering and using in spring:
Broad bean, cauliflower, Swiss chard, chicory, lettuce, onion, spring onion, pea, spinach, spinach beet.

Forcing

The term 'forcing' is, I suppose, a little confusing. It's sometimes used to describe any method of bringing plants along a little earlier than usual. The traditional method of using a hot-bed (see p. 72) was referred to as 'forcing', for example. What I mean here is a method of encouraging growth from existing roots to produce blanched stems out of the normal season. It can be done indoors in a greenhouse or even in the kitchen since there's little or no mess. Alternatively it can be done outside where the plants are growing; as you would expect, harvests will be later than indoors though still a little earlier than normal. However, the flavour of blanched stems is much superior to those that remain unblanched, so it's still well worth doing.

Though perhaps not quite the same thing, the growing of mushrooms indoors is a similar technique to that of forcing other vegetables. Kits are available at garden centres and these are already 'seeded' with mushroom spawn. All that's necessary is to scatter a bag of special material over the top and add water.

Chicory

1 Chicory is sown in early summer in the garden and the roots are lifted from November onwards. They're hardy but, to avoid attack by soil pests, it's best to lift them all and to store some in damp sand or soil until required. Cut off the tops to leave no more than 1cm (½in.) of the leaves. Reduce the length of the roots by removing the thin end.

2 Set the roots upright in a deep box or tub and cover with at least 23cm (9in.) of moist garden compost or bark. Put the container in a warm spot and make sure that the material doesn't dry out.

3 Harvesting time will depend mainly on the temperature, but after four to six weeks you should be able to dig down into the container and pull our a root with a good growth of 'chicon' on the top. As you use the roots, replace them with more from your store to maintain a succession.

LEFT Rhubarb

If you want to force rhubarb, lift a root in November and, ideally, expose it to frost. Then put it into the bottom of a black polythene bag with its base bedded in compost or soil. Ensure that the compost is moist and then tie the top of the bag. Put it in a warm place and you should be able to harvest pale yellow sticks in about four to five weeks. Afterwards replant the root and don't use the same one for forcing in the following year.

An alternative with rhubarb is to put a small dustbin or, better still, a proper terracotta forcer over the top of a clump growing in the garden. Do this in late winter or early spring. To retain a little warmth, put some loose straw into the forcer and you should harvest blanched sticks in about six to eight weeks. After harvesting, leave the root uncovered to form more leaves and don't use the same root for forcing next year.

Harvesting and storing

Harvesting vegetables at the right time and eating them either cooked or raw while they're still fresh makes all the difference in the world to your enjoyment of them. Again the knowledge of just when to harvest comes with experience, but there are a few pointers.

Feel lettuce hearts with the back of your hand to ensure that they're firm and leave cabbages until you can feel that they're solid. You may have to lift a carrot or two to see its state of maturity, but never leave them to go hard and woody.

Leaf vegetables like spinach and Swiss chard are much tastier if pulled young, so harvest regularly to maintain a succession. The same rules apply to crops like French beans, courgettes, tomatoes and peppers, which will always produce more if you keep harvesting regularly.

Roots like beetroot and turnips are more succulent and have better flavour when pulled as 'babies', no bigger than a golf ball, though any intended for storage can be left to grow bigger.

Some vegetables can be stored for a while, and root vegetables are especially suitable, often lasting right through the winter if conditions are right. Some, like parsnips, are perfectly frost-hardy so could stay in the ground over winter. In my experience, though, it's best to lift all roots before really cold weather sets in to avoid attacks from pests, subsequently providing entry for disease. This will also, of course, free the land to enable you to get on with the winter digging and it means that vegetables will always be available even when the soil is frozen solid.

LEFT Many vegetables, especially roots, can be stored right through the winter and often until the new crop matures in the spring. But it's essential to make sure that they are free from frost and to inspect them regularly. Store only perfect vegetables and throw out or use immediately any that show signs of rotting.

ABOVE **Freezing and bottling** Many vegetables can also be stored for long periods in the freezer and this is the best way to avoid wasting an over-production of summer crops. Some can also be bottled in the more traditional way.

Potatoes These should be lifted carefully and any damaged tubers put on one side for immediate use. Store the good tubers in paper sacks in a frost-free shed. Ideally raise the sacks off the floor.

Other roots Carrots, turnips, beetroot, parsnips and other root vegetables are best stored in boxes. Separate the individual roots with a little garden compost, sand or bark and cover with about 5cm (2in.). Again, put the boxes in a frost-free shed.

Marrows and cabbages If marrows are first ripened in the sun, they can be stored in boxes until the end of the year, while cabbages will last a month or two if lifted with their roots and hung upside down in a cold spot.

LEFT **Onions** These can be strung together to form long ropes which should be hung in a frost-free shed. Alternatively beg a few mesh sacks from the greengrocer or put them into an old pair of nylon tights. The secret of keeping onions is to ensure that they've had a chance to ripen fully in the sun.

BELOW **Leaf vegetables** like lettuce quickly lose their crispness if they're not kept cold in a refrigerator. If possible, cut them and eat them straight away.

Secrets of success

In order to ensure that onions and shallots dry properly, lift them in August and put them on a wire-netting 'table' where they can receive full sunshine and also have air circulating around them. In wet weather they can be conveniently covered, but don't forget to remove the cover afterwards or fungus rot could set in on the skin. When they have dried out completely, clean off the dirt and loose skin; they're then ready for storage.

Growing instructions

The following brief sowing and planting information should be enough to ensure a regular supply of fresh vegetables throughout the year. Where no sowing depths are given, make the drill as shallow as possible. Ensure that the pH is above 6.5 (see p. 15) for all but potatoes and use fertiliser before sowing or planting.

ROOTS

Jerusalem artichoke
Plant in a single row 15cm (6in.) deep and 30cm (1ft) apart in early spring. Harvest throughout winter. This is a perennial, so always leave a few tubers in the ground to ensure a crop in the following year.

Beetroot
Multiple sow, two seeds per cell, in the greenhouse in early spring and plant out under cloches as soon as the young plants are big enough, setting the clumps 30cm (1ft) apart each way.

Sow under cloches two weeks later, putting two seed clusters 7.5cm (3in.) apart and 2.5cm (1in.) deep. Thin to leave one seedling per station.

Sow as above in open ground two weeks later until mid-summer.

Harvest throughout spring and summer when the roots are golf-ball size. Leave roots for storing to grow to tennis-ball size.

Carrot
Multiple sow round-rooted varieties, six seeds per cell, in a greenhouse in early spring. Plant under cloches when big enough, setting the clumps 15cm (6in.) apart each way.

Sow under cloches two weeks later in rows 30cm (1ft) apart. Thin to 7.5cm (3in.) apart.

Sow outside as above two weeks later until mid-summer.

Harvest when the roots are young. Harvest maincrop varieties in early winter and store.

Celeriac
Sow in the greenhouse in mid-spring. Plant outside in late spring 38 × 30cm (15 × 12in.) apart. Harvest in early winter and store.

Kohl rabi
Sow in a seed bed in mid-spring to mid-summer. Transplant 30 × 23cm (12 × 9in.) apart. Harvest during summer when the roots are a little less than tennis-ball size. Can be stored for a short time.

ABOVE AND FAR ABOVE **Hamburg parsley and parsnip**
Sow outside in early spring in rows 30cm (1ft) apart, setting three seeds in stations 15cm (6in.) apart. Harvest in early winter and store.

Potato

Set up tubers in the light in late winter to encourage them to sprout. Plant early varieties under polythene in early spring 60 × 30cm (2 × 1ft) apart and 23cm (9in.) deep. Protect from frost if necessary.

Plant early varieties in the open ground two weeks later at the same spacings. Earth up by pulling soil up to the plants once the shoots are about 23cm (9in.) high. If frost threatens, cover the young shoots completely.

Plant maincrop varieties two weeks later 75 × 38cm (30 × 15in.) apart. Earth up as described.

Harvest earlies in summer as they become ready and maincrop varieties in late summer. Store over winter.

ABOVE LEFT AND ABOVE RIGHT Salsify and scorzonera
Sow outside in mid-spring in rows 30cm (1ft) apart and 2.5cm (1in.) deep. Thin to 15cm (6in.) apart. Harvest in early winter and store.

Swede

Sow outside in late spring or early summer in rows 45cm (1½ft) apart. Thin to 30cm (1ft) apart. Harvest in early winter after frost and store.

Radish

Sow in a broad band under cloches in early spring and thin by harvesting selectively. Sow outside two weeks later and continue at weekly intervals until mid-autumn. Alternatively sow between crops and anywhere a space becomes available. Harvest and eat immediately.

Turnip

Multiple sow, three seeds per cell, in early spring in the greenhouse. Plant out under cloches 30cm (1ft) apart.

Sow under cloches at the same time as planting out, in rows 30cm (1ft) apart. Thin to 15cm (6in.) apart.

Sow in the open two weeks later, in the same way, until mid-summer.

Harvest when the roots are tennis-ball size. Maincrop varieties for storing could be a little larger.

Secrets of success

● Carrots make an attractive subject for the flower borders if room is short in the vegetable plot.

● For the very earliest radish, sow seed thinly in pots on the windowsill.

Growing instructions

SALAD VEGETABLES

ABOVE **Celtuce**
A type of lettuce that forms a thick stem and tastes of celery.

Sow in early spring, two seeds per cell, in modules in the greenhouse. Thin to leave one seedling. Plant out 30cm (1ft) apart either way under cloches as soon as the plants are 5cm (2in.) high.

Sow under cloches in early spring in rows 30cm (1ft) apart. Thin to 30cm (1ft).

Sow outside from mid-spring to mid-summer at similar spacings.

Harvest three to four months after sowing, but don't leave it too long or it becomes bitter.

RIGHT **Chicory**
There are two types – the greenleaf kind which forms a head like lettuce and the forcing varieties (see p. 247). Radicchio is simply red chicory.

Sow in early summer in shallow drills 30cm (1ft) apart. Thin to 23cm (9in.).

Harvest greenleaf types when they have filled out from autumn to early winter. They can be stored for several weeks by hanging in a frost-free shed. Harvest forcing types from early winter (see p. 247).

ABOVE **Endive**
Because of the somewhat coarser texture of summer varieties, in my view only winter types of endive are worth growing.

Sow in late summer in shallow drills 30cm (1ft) apart. Thin to 30cm (1ft). After three months cover each plant with a flower pot whose drainage hole(s) you have blocked with clay. This blanches and softens the endives. Alternatively tie the leaves together, lift the plants and replant in boxes in a frost-free place.

ABOVE **Land cress**
A good alternative to watercress where no running water or wet soil is available.

Sow from early spring to mid-summer in shallow rows 30cm (1ft) apart. Thin to 30cm (1ft). Harvest in about eight to ten weeks.

Lettuce
Start by sowing fast-maturing varieties in trays in the greenhouse in early spring. Plant out under cloches, allowing 15–23cm (6–9in.) either way for each plant.

At the same time as planting out, sow further rows under cloches. Thin and transplant to similar spacings.

Two weeks later sow outside and continue at two-week intervals until late summer. Thin and transplant at similar spacings.

Sow winter-hardy types in autumn and thin to similar spacings.

Mustard and cress
Sow throughout the spring, summer and autumn on damp blotting paper on a sunny windowsill. Sow from mid-spring at two-week intervals through to early autumn in small patches outside. Always sow the mustard four days later than the cress so that they mature together. No thinning is necessary.

Rocket
A spicy-tasting leaf to mix with other salads.

Sow at monthly intervals from mid-spring to mid-summer in a single row: not a great deal will be needed. Thin to 23cm (9in.) apart. Harvest the young tips as required.

Secrets of success

● Chicory can also be forced for a later crop outside simply by ridging up soil over the plants.

● If you run short of salad in winter, grow some sprouting seeds in a jar in the kitchen.

● The earliest crop of lettuce can be raised by using a small variety in pots on the windowsill.

● Lettuce grown to overwinter for early spring crops are best cloched to produce more tender leaves.

● BELOW Lettuce are prone to fungus attack at the base of the leaves, so transplant with the bottom leaves well above soil level.

● BELOW Grow a tasty crop of lettuce leaves by sowing thickly and cutting off just above the ground. They'll grow again to give a second crop.

Growing instructions

LEAF VEGETABLES

ABOVE Brussels Sprouts
Sow in shallow drills 15cm (6in.) apart in a seed bed in mid-spring. Transplant the seedlings when they are 5–7.5cm (2–3in.) high, setting them 75cm–1m (2½–3ft) apart each way. Harvest when the sprouts are firm, starting from the bottom and working up.

BELOW Cauliflower
Start with summer varieties sown in the greenhouse in early spring and planted out 23cm (9in.) square under cloches when the seedlings are 5cm (2in.) high. Never let cauliflower seedlings get too big before transplantation.

At the same time as transplanting, sow seed under cloches and transplant the results to similar spacings.

Sow outside in a seed bed at three-week intervals until late spring or early summer. Plant out at similar distances.

Autumn-maturing varieties should be sown in shallow drills in a seed bed in mid-spring and planted out 60cm (2ft) square.

Winter and spring varieties are sown similarly in mid- to late spring and planted out 75cm (2½ft) either way.

RIGHT Cabbage
It's possible to get a year-round supply of cabbages but you must be sure to choose the right varieties for harvesting at the appropriate time of year.

Start by sowing summer varieties in the greenhouse in early spring. Transplant 45cm (1½ft) square under cloches when the seedlings are 5cm (2in.) high.

At the same time as transplanting the greenhouse-grown batch, sow more seed under cloches and transplant at similar distances.

In mid-spring sow outside in a seed bed and transplant as above. Make further sowings in late spring and early summer.

Sow autumn and winter varieties and red cabbage in a seed bed in mid- to late spring and transplant 45cm (1½ft) apart either way when the seedlings are 5–7.5cm (2–3in.) high.

Sow spring-maturing varieties in shallow drills in a seed bed in mid- to late summer. Transplant in rows 45cm (1½ft) apart with 15cm (6in.) between plants when the seedlings are 5–7.5cm (2–3in.) high.

Harvest selectively, starting in mid-spring and taking some plants for spring greens to leave one plant every 45cm (1½ft); they'll mature to hearted cabbages.

Calabrese
Sow in shallow drills in rows 30cm (1ft) apart, putting three seeds per station 23cm (9in.) apart in mid-spring. Thin to leave one plant per station. Harvest the main head first to encourage side shoots to develop.

Kale
Sow in a seed bed in mid- to late spring. Plant out 45cm (1½ft) square when the seedlings are 5–7.5cm (2–3in.) high.

Pak choi
A succulent Chinese vegetable used in salads and stir-fry dishes.

Sow in early to mid-summer in shallow drills 23cm (9in.) apart, placing three seeds in stations 23cm (9in.) apart. Thin to single seedlings.

Chinese cabbage
Sow in well-manured soil from late spring to mid-summer at two-week intervals in drills 30cm (1ft) apart, putting three seeds per station 23cm (9in.) apart. Thin to leave one seedling per station.

Spinach
Start by sowing in modules, two seeds per cell, in early spring in the greenhouse. Thin to single seedlings and plant out 23cm (9in.) square under cloches when the seedlings are 5–7.5cm (2–3in.) high.

At the same time as planting out the seedlings, sow more seed in shallow drills 30cm (1ft) apart under cloches. Thin to 15cm (6in.) apart.

From mid-spring to mid-summer sow at three-week intervals outside.

Growing instructions

LEAF VEGETABLES

Sprouting broccoli
Sow in late spring in a seed bed. Transplant 75cm (2½ft) apart when the plants are 5–7.5cm (2–3in.) high. Harvest regularly from late winter to ensure a succession.

Swiss chard
Sometimes called seakale beet. There's also a red version called ruby or rhubarb chard.

Sow in mid-spring in shallow drills 38cm (15in.) apart, placing two or three seeds in stations 30cm (1ft) apart. Thin to single seedlings.

Sow again in mid-summer in the same way.

Harvest regularly, removing outside leaves to encourage a succession.

Spinach beet
Easier to grow in difficult soil than spinach. Being a biennial, it doesn't run to seed.

Sow in drills 2.5cm (1in.) deep and 30cm (1ft) apart in mid-spring and again in mid-summer. Thin to 30cm (1ft) apart.

Harvest the spring sowing in summer and cloche the summer sowing in November for harvesting during the winter months.

Secrets of success

● All members of the cabbage family like firm soil, so tread it down before planting.

● Plant with a dibber, firming the roots by pushing in the dibber slightly at one side.

● If frost threatens, break a few leaves over mature cauliflower curds for protection. Do the same to shield them against hot summer sun.

● Grow spinach well away from cucumbers if you can, because both are attacked by the same virus.

● **ABOVE** The tops of Brussels sprout plants can be eaten just like cabbage.

SHOOT VEGETABLES

Globe artichoke

The traditional method of growing globe artichokes is to buy 'suckers' from a specialist and plant them 1m (3ft) apart each way in mid-spring. I grow mine as annuals, sowing in gentle heat in early spring in modules, putting one seed per cell. I plant out in late spring, 45cm (1½ft) apart each way.

The next year I remove every other plant and grow a second crop in the normal way. The seed-raised plants crop well after the two-year-olds and this gives a long continuity of cropping.

Harvest when the flowers are still tightly closed.

Asparagus

Buy one-year-old crowns in mid-spring and plant them in well-drained soil 30cm (1ft) apart each way and 15cm (6in.) deep. Harvest a little in the second year, for about four weeks in the third and for six weeks subsequently. Always leave some shoots to help build the crown for the following year.

Celery

There are two types, blanched and self-blanching. Self-blanching varieties are not quite as crisp and succulent but much easier to grow.

Sow both types in gentle heat in early spring and transfer them to wider spacings in a seed tray when they're big enough to handle.

Plant out blanched types 30cm (1ft) apart in the bottom of a trench one spade deep and 45cm (1½ft) wide. Heap the excavated soil up either side. In mid-summer remove suckers from the base of the plants and wrap the stems with brown paper or corrugated cardboard. Refill with soil to the bottom of the leaves. Repeat this process twice more at three-week intervals as the plants grow.

Harvest self-blanching types before the first frost and blanched varieties throughout the winter as required.

RIGHT **Florence fennel**
The swollen stems of this fennel have a delicate flavour of aniseed.

Sow outside in shallow drills 45cm (1½ft) apart from mid-spring to mid-summer. Thin to 20cm (8in.) apart.

Sow in late summer and cover with cloches for winter use.

When the bases swell to the size of golf balls, earth them up. Harvest two to three weeks after earthing up.

Secrets of success

● I like to grow self-blanching celery in a block rather than in rows so that the plants tend to blanch each other, producing slightly more tender stems.

● Fennel can be grown in the greenhouse or coldframe but, since it dislikes disturbance, it's best done in modules: sow two seeds per cell and thin to one.

● When harvesting asparagus, cut underground right down to the hard root to get the tenderest part of the shoot.

● Globe artichokes make very fine architectural plants for the back of the border if there's no room in the vegetable plot.

● BELOW My soil is very heavy so I grow asparagus in raised beds. These bottomless wooden containers are filled with soil mixed with equal parts of garden compost and coarse grit.

Growing instructions

POD AND SEED VEGETABLES

ABOVE Broad beans
Sow the earliest crop in modules, one seed per cell, in the greenhouse in early spring, using a short variety. Plant out in a double row 10cm (4in.) apart just as the roots come through the bottom of the module.

At the same time as planting out, sow a short variety under cloches at similar spacings and also outside as soon as soil conditions allow. If you grow more than one double row, allow 1m (3ft) between them.

Another sowing of a hardy variety can be made in the autumn for an early harvest.

On exposed sites some support may be needed.

Climbing French beans
These are treated in exactly the same way as runner beans (see right).

BELOW Dwarf French beans
Start the first sowings in the greenhouse in modules, allowing two seeds per cell, in mid-spring. Thin to one seedling. Plant under cloches in late spring, in rows 30cm (1ft) apart with 20cm (8in.) between plants.

At the same time as planting, sow seed under cloches at the same distances, putting two seeds per station. Thin to one seedling.

Sow in the open ground at the same distances, starting in late spring, at three-weekly intervals until mid-summer.

Harvest regularly and while the beans are young and tender. At the end of the season some pods can be left on to turn brown and the seeds can be collected for bottling for use in soups.

RIGHT Runner beans
Ideally start plants off in modules in the greenhouse, putting one seed per cell, in mid-spring. Plant out in early summer, setting the plants against canes placed 30cm (1ft) apart in a double row with 60cm (2ft) between rows. Alternatively make a circular wigwam with the canes at the same distances and tied at the top.

To raise runner beans outside, sow 5cm (2in.) deep against the canes set at the same spacings, allowing two seeds per station, in late spring.

Harvest regularly to ensure a succession.

BELOW Sweetcorn

Sow in the greenhouse in mid-spring, putting two seeds in a 9cm (3½in.) pot. Thin to one seedling. Plant out in early summer in a block rather than in rows to ensure pollination, setting the plants 60cm (2ft) square.

Alternatively sow under clear plastic in the open ground in mid- to late spring (see p. 246), allowing two seeds per station 60cm (2ft) apart. Thin to one seedling.

Harvest when the tassels at the top of the cob turn brown.

ABOVE **Peas**

Start the first sowing in modules in the greenhouse in early spring using an early variety. Plant out under cloches just as the roots come through the bottom of the module. Set the plants out in double rows 15cm (6in.) apart with 7.5cm (3in.) between plants.

At the same time as planting out, sow an early variety under cloches in wide rows 60cm (2ft) apart with about 5cm (2in.) between seeds. No thinning is necessary.

Sow in the open ground from mid-spring using an early variety. Make drills about 5cm (2in.) deep with a spade and space the seeds about 5cm (2in.) apart.

Sow maincrop varieties at three-week intervals from late spring until mid-summer in the same way.

Peas must be supported with bushy twigs or plastic netting.

Secrets of success

● Broad beans can be grown in the flower borders, 10cm (4in.) apart in a circle with a cane in the middle for support.

● Early peas can be sown in lengths of guttering in the greenhouse. To transplant them simply slide them out into a prepared drill.

● The earliest crop of dwarf French beans can be grown in large pots in the greenhouse or on the windowsill.

● When any bean crop has been harvested, cut off the tops for the compost heap but leave the roots in to supply nitrogen to the soil.

Growing instructions

VEGETABLE FRUITS

Cucumber
Sow bush and trailing types in mid-spring in the greenhouse, putting two seeds per 7.5cm (3in.) pot. Thin to single seedlings.

Plant out bush varieties in late spring under cloches, setting them 45cm (1½ft) apart. Plant trailing varieties outside in early summer, setting them 1m (3ft) apart, and trim them as necessary to prevent them spreading beyond bounds.

Alternatively sow two seeds of either type per station at similar spacings outside in late spring. Thin to one seedling.

Harvest regularly to ensure a succession.

Pumpkin and squash
These are grown in just the same way as courgettes and marrows, though they are not suitable for cloche culture. If ripened in the sun and stored in a frost-free place, they'll last well into the winter.

Courgette and marrow
These are both grown in the same way, the only difference being the time of harvesting.

Sow in gentle heat in mid-spring, putting two seeds per 7.5cm (3in.) pot. Thin to one seedling.

Plant bush varieties in late spring under cloches, setting the plants 60cm (2ft) apart each way. Plant outside in early summer at the same spacings. Trailing varieties are not suitable for cloching and should be planted outside in early summer 1m (3ft) apart each way; trim occasionally to prevent them spreading too much.

Alternatively sow two seeds per station at similar spacings outside in late spring. Thin to one seedling.

Harvest courgettes regularly when they're about 15cm (6in.) long to ensure a succession. Allow marrows to grow bigger.

RIGHT Tomato
Sow in trays in the greenhouse in mid-spring, transferring the young plants to 9cm (3½in.) pots as soon as the seed leaves are fully formed.

Plant out bush varieties in late spring under cloches, setting them 60cm (2ft) apart each way, or in early summer in the open ground. Upright varieties should be planted against 1.2m (4ft) canes set 60cm (2ft) apart.

Bush varieties need little maintenance, but upright types must be tied in regularly and should also be 'side-shooted': remove all lateral shoots as they appear in the leaf joints.

Secrets of success

● A great deal of space can be saved by growing trailing varieties of marrow and squash up a decorative pergola or arch. Naturally they need regular tying in and the fruit must be supported as it ripens.

● Cucumbers can be grown up a wigwam of canes to save space. Make sure that you keep up with the job of tying them in or they'll become tangled and difficult to deal with.

● At the end of the season encourage upright varieties of tomato to finish ripening by taking the plants off their canes, laying them on a bed of straw and covering them with cloches. Bush varieties simply need covering.

● When sowing courgettes, marrows, pumpkins and squashes, it's a good idea to put the flat seeds into the compost on their sides to avoid water lying on them and rotting them.

BULB VEGETABLES

Shallot
Start the sets in the open ground in mid-spring. Starting too early could lead to bolting. Put them 15cm (6in.) apart in rows 30cm (1ft) apart. Harvest in late summer, dry and store (see p. 249).

Leek
Leeks should not be sown too early or they'll run to seed. Start them in the greenhouse in modules in late spring, putting six seeds per cell. Plant out the clumps 30cm (1ft) apart each way. There's no need to blanch the stems since the close spacing will suffice.

Alternatively sow them in a seed bed in late spring. In early summer prepare to plant them out by dibbling holes about 10cm (4in.) deep and 15cm (6in.) apart in rows 30cm (1ft) apart. Place the seedlings in the holes and water them in. Don't refill the holes, which will later get filled up during weeding and so on. If you plant the leeks in rows, blanch the base of the stems by drawing up soil around them.

Harvest during winter.

Onion
Start by sowing onions in the greenhouse in early spring. Sow in modules, putting six seeds per cell. Plant out the clumps when the roots have filled the cells, setting them 30cm (1ft) apart each way.

Alternatively sow outside in mid-spring in rows 30cm (1ft) apart and thin to 7.5cm (3in.) apart.

Another way, particularly good for heavy soil, is to start with small bulbs or 'sets' in mid-spring. Plant them in rows 30cm (1ft) apart with 7.5cm (3in.) between sets.

Harvest in late summer, dry and store (see p. 249).

Pickling onions, such as 'Giant Zittau', should be sown fairly thickly in wide bands but not thinned. Harvest in late summer while the bulbs are still small.

Salad onion
Start by sowing in modules in the greenhouse in early spring. Put about six seeds per cell. Plant out under cloches as soon as the roots have filled the cells, setting the clumps 7.5cm (3in.) apart each way.

At the same time as planting out, sow in wide bands under the cloches, scattering the seed sparingly to avoid thinning.

At monthly intervals from mid-spring until late summer, sow in wide bands or, if space is limited, in rows in the open ground. No thinning is necessary.

Secrets of success

● Plant all sets of bulb vegetables in shallow drills. Simply pressing them into the soil could lead to the bulbs pushing themselves out when they start to form roots. Remove dead foliage to prevent birds pulling them out.

● LEFT If you need the space where your leeks are growing, perhaps to get the winter digging done, lift them and heel them in to a corner of the plot. They'll stay sound for several months.

CHAPTER 13

HERBS

HERBS HAVE BEEN grown for centuries for use in a variety of ways. Before the advent of modern drugs, they were the basis of curative medicine and indeed many herbal extracts are still used.

Herbs were widely used in days gone by to mask bad smells and there's still a place for them in this capacity in modern houses. I much prefer the sweet perfume of lavender or a mixed *pot-pourri* to the synthetic chemical odours sold in aerosol cans these days as 'air fresheners'.

However, the most important function of herbs was in the kitchen, and it's there that their main contribution continues. These days everyone travels much more, with the result that all kinds of herbs are in demand for dishes first experienced abroad as well as for the traditional ones.

Most of us wouldn't dream of eating lamb without mint sauce or turkey without sage and onion stuffing, but surprisingly the vast majority of cooks are unaware of the difference made to the flavour of these and other dishes when the herbs used are harvest-fresh. Even after drying, home-grown herbs are quite superior, so there's every reason to spare a little space for them either in the borders or in a special herb garden.

In fact, so accommodating and attractive are they that you can grow herbs just about anywhere from a pot on the kitchen windowsill or a container on the patio to an ornamental knot garden covering your whole plot.

Even if you don't use them, herbs will delight your eye and your nose every time you step into the garden.

Traditional herb garden
A relatively elaborate herb garden like this would need to be fairly big – at least 5 × 3m (16 × 10ft). Each of the separate beds would contain one herb with the paths giving easy access to all of them. The border on the outside of the garden could be filled with scented or taller herbs and cottage flowers like mullein, foxglove and valerian mixed with old roses.

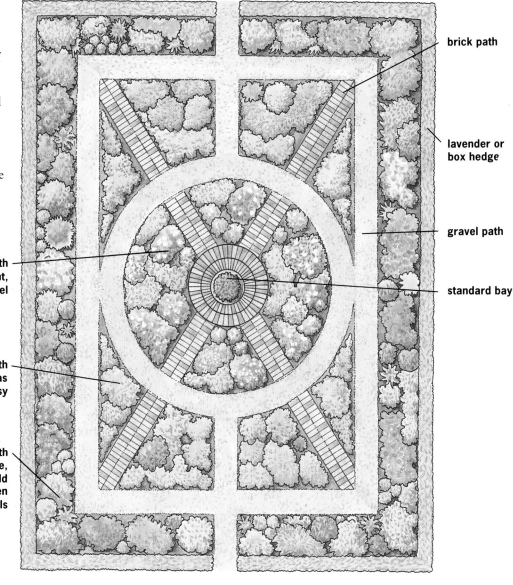

brick path

lavender or box hedge

gravel path

standard bay

inner beds planted with culinary herbs such as mint, parsley and sorrel

centre beds planted with medicinal herbs such as feverfew, chamomile and tansy

outer border planted with scented herbs such as thyme, lavender and rosemary, old roses and cottage garden perennials

all beds planted with culinary herbs such as marjoram, borage, mint, thyme, rosemary, sage, garlic, sorrel, tarragon and parsley

paving-stone path

brick path

box hedge

Simple herb garden
A more basic design could be reduced in size to about 2.5m (9ft) square. This would be enough for several culinary herbs like mint, parsley, thyme, sage, rosemary, chives and basil, but care should be taken to exclude any tall or rampant growers.

Making a herb garden

There's a tradition, dating back, I suppose, to the first Elizabethans, that herbs should be grown in a special formal garden all to themselves. There's absolutely no reason why we should continue the style, since herbs can be grown quite happily in the mixed border or in the vegetable plot where they'll look good and grow well. No reason, that is, except that the traditional way happens to suit herbs very well indeed and we gardeners tend to warm to the idea of continuing well-tried horticultural traditions.

Herb gardens can be as large or as small as you wish and can include other cottage-garden plants to add colour and interest. Be sure to check the eventual size of the plants, though. The lovage plant, for example, that looks so diminutive in its pot in the garden centre will grow to a massive 3m (10ft) and quickly swamp the rest. If space is limited and such herbs are considered a 'must', it's best to grow them in the borders where they can spread out.

If you decide to build a special herb garden, site it in a sunny spot, ideally in a position where it'll be handy for the cook to harvest just prior to use. The fresher herbs are, the better. Be careful not to make the surrounding hedges so high that they shade the whole garden, for most herbs prefer sunshine. If your soil is heavy, try to raise the borders a little and incorporate coarse grit to improve drainage.

ABOVE In really small spaces, herbs can be grown in a container, though you'd obviously have to be even more careful to select plants that wouldn't grow too big or take over. A container like this will supply most of the day-to-day requirements in the kitchen. Again, site it in a sunny spot as near the kitchen as possible.

A small herb garden to supply the kitchen can easily be incorporated into the design of the whole plot. It's often easiest to site it near the house where the lines of the garden are generally more formal. This is, of course, also the most convenient place from the cook's point of view!

Making a parterre

The French *parterre*, which was translated on the English side of the Channel into the Elizabethan knot garden, consists of a formal pattern of dwarf hedges. Sometimes they were used to edge beds of informal plantings of herbs, herbaceous plants or roses; often they simply made intricate and elaborate patterns with gravel between. In the past some huge schemes were constructed in the grounds of stately homes throughout Europe and superb examples can still be found at Villandry in France, Hatfield House in England and many other great houses. But the beauty of the parterre is that it can be shrunk to almost any size to fit any garden.

Perhaps because of this, the idea has found favour again recently. The formal designs are ideally suited to small plots where they can be used as a part of the overall scheme or to form the complete garden. And they make the perfect setting for a collection of low-growing herbs.

Because box (*Buxus sempervirens*) is expensive, even a small knot garden could be quite costly. However, if you have the patience, it's not difficult to propagate your own plants. The very simple garden illustrated in picture 5 took five years to make, all the box having been grown from cuttings taken from one mother plant (see p. 112).

RIGHT The Château at Villandry boasts probably the most extensive *parterre* in the world.

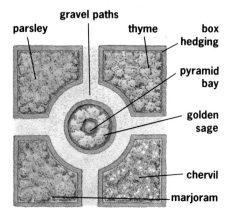

parsley | gravel paths | thyme | box hedging | pyramid bay | golden sage | chervil | marjoram

For a small *parterre* it's best to keep the design simple. I used this traditional design at Barnsdale.

1 Mark out the shape of the garden using a wine bottle filled with sand to indicate the planting lines clearly.

2 Plant the box, setting the plants about 15cm (6in.) apart. This is a job best done in mid-spring.

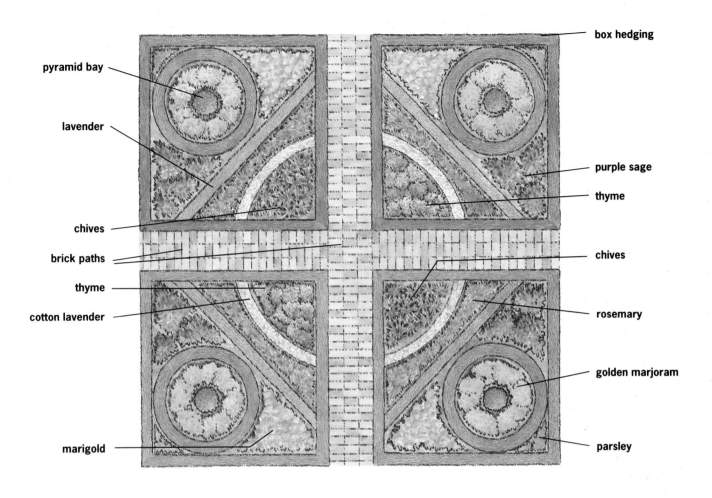

pyramid bay

lavender

chives

brick paths

thyme

cotton lavender

marigold

box hedging

purple sage

thyme

chives

rosemary

golden marjoram

parsley

ABOVE Originally, *parterres* and knot gardens were based on designs taken from oriental carpets and were very complicated. This more elaborate design is a compromise between the two extremes and would suit a larger garden.

3 Level the paths, trample them firm and cover them with a shallow layer of gravel.

4 The beds formed by the box edging can now be planted with herbs. Be sure to choose low-growing varieties.

5 After a year or two the hedges should be trimmed annually to make a formal contrast with the herbs.

Sowing and planting herbs

It needn't cost a lot to start a herb garden. Many plants can be raised from seed and indeed the annuals and biennials have to be done this way. Most perennial herbs can be easily increased from cuttings too – if you have a friend who has an existing herb garden; alternatively it may be possible to divide one plant bought from a garden centre at the right time to produce several.

LEFT **Sowing outdoors** The easiest and most straightforward way to grow herbs from seed is to sow direct where the plants are to grow. This is particularly suitable for some annuals which will run to seed quickly if transplanted. Sow as recommended for hardy annuals (see p. 96) in straight rows in patches or drifts. The best time to sow most herbs is mid- to late spring when the soil is warm.

There's nothing like fresh herbs, and if you grow a small mixed bed of them outside the kitchen door, you'll never get them fresher and they'll bring butterflies, hoverflies and other insects right to your door. Choose carefully, avoiding the really large or spreading types, and keep them in check with regular harvesting.

Sowing under cover Alternatively you can sow seeds in the greenhouse or on the windowsill. This can be done earlier than outside, giving you a head start and at the same time protecting the young seedlings from slugs. Transfer the seedlings to individual pots as soon as they're large enough to handle and harden off before planting out in late spring.

Propagation by softwood cuttings
Many of the perennial herbs can be increased from softwood cuttings taken in early summer, exactly as described for shrubs (see p. 110).

Propagation by root cuttings Some herbs like mint have running roots which will very easily produce plants. In autumn lift a plant and remove a few roots. Cut them into pieces and lay them horizontally on some compost in a seed tray. Cover with 13mm (½in.) of compost and place in gentle heat or even in a coldframe where they'll soon produce shoots. Fresh mint can be produced over winter in this way on a warm windowsill.

HERBS TO RAISE FROM SEED
Annuals: *Anise, basil, borage, chervil, coriander, cumin, dill, mustard, nasturtium, purslane, rocket, summer savory, sweet marjoram*
Biennials: *Angelica, caraway, parsley*
Perennials: *Chives, fennel, feverfew, French marjoram, garlic chives, hyssop, oregano, sage, salad burnet, sorrel, sweet cicely, thyme, Welsh onion, winter savory*

HERBS TO GROW FROM CUTTINGS
Curry plant, French tarragon, hyssop, lavender, lemon verbena, marjoram, rosemary, sage, thyme, winter savory

HERBS TO DIVIDE
Chives, lemon balm, lovage, marjoram, sorrel, tarragon, thyme

HERBS TO GROW FROM ROOT CUTTINGS
Comfrey, horseradish, mint

Increasing by division Some of the bulbous herbs like chives can simply be split up in the early spring. Divide the root by pulling the individual bulbs away and replant them immediately about 15cm (6in.) apart. Clump-forming herbs are split as described for herbaceous perennials (see p. 122).

Secrets of success

A whole collection of annual herbs could be sown in a plastic module since most require exactly the same temperature and moisture regime. Germinate them in a temperature of about 15°C (59°F). Sow a small pinch of seed in each cell and no thinning will be necessary. The plug of roots will eliminate root disturbance, so the plants won't run to seed.

Rules for planting When planting herbs remember that most require a well-drained soil which will at the same time hold water. So prepare the soil with manure, compost or one of the alternatives and further lighten heavy soil with coarse grit. Then plant with a trowel in the normal way.

Collecting and storing herbs

Some cooks might disagree with me but I reckon that herbs should always be used fresh whenever possible. Somehow the flavour they impart is so much better than that of the dried equivalent sold in grocers' shops.

Try therefore to keep them growing as long as possible by starting early in the greenhouse and under cloches, and by forcing some on the windowsill. Herbs like mint, basil and parsley are very well suited to this kind of cultivation.

Still, at the end of the season you won't want simply to sacrifice those herbs that are about to die down, so it's worthwhile cutting and drying them then. Timing is perhaps the most important secret of success.

RIGHT **Picking fresh herbs for instant use**
Gather fresh herbs in the morning just as the sun has dried the dew from the leaves but before it gets hot enough to disperse the essential oils. Pick leaves and shoots carefully to avoid bruising and never strip plants completely.

Freezing fresh herbs
An alternative way of preserving herbs is to bundle them into small bunches, lay them flat on a tray and freeze them. Then store them in the freezer in rigid containers. Alternatively put the leaves into ice-cube trays, cover with water and freeze.

Pot-pourri
Pot-pourri is the original air freshener and a million times more appealing than chemical aerosols. Use a mixture of paper-dry flowers and herbs and add a fixative like orris root which you can buy in most handicraft shops. Blend gently by hand and store for six weeks in sealed jars in a warm, dry, dark place to 'cure'. Display in open or covered glass bowls.

Your own dried herbs

1 Cut herbs for drying just before the flowers open. Again the best time to do this is the early morning. Cut into a shallow basket, avoiding crushing or bruising so as to retain all the flavour and aroma.

2 Small herbs are best spread on a muslin frame to dry but larger subjects may be tied into small bunches and hung in a shady, cool place so that air can circulate freely around them.

3 When the leaves are dry and brittle they can be removed and stored in airtight jars. Make sure that the jars are perfectly clean and dry beforehand. Store in a cool, dry, dark cupboard.

Drying herbs look very attractive in a country kitchen and they'll fill the room with a delightful, fresh fragrance.

Cultivation and use of herbs

If you're starting a herb garden, the main herbs you'll want to grow will be the culinary ones. Those used for aromatic purposes are perhaps best grown in the borders. The following list contains most of those you'll need.

HERB	DESCRIPTION	CULTIVATION	USE
ANGELICA (*Angelica archangelica*)	A tall perennial, growing to about 2.4m (8ft). Generally self-seeds, so only the original sowing is necessary. It may take a few years before it flowers, after which it dies.	Prefers a shady spot. Sow in August where it's to flower.	Used to counteract the tartness of rhubarb and gooseberries; may also be candied.
BALM (*Melissa officinalis*)	A 1m- (3ft)-tall hardy perennial with vigorous underground runners which could colonise. The leaves have a strong lemon aroma.	Prefers a semi-shaded position and moist soil. Sow in spring, take cuttings in late spring, or divide clumps.	Chop the leaves and add them fresh to salads or to fruit or vegetables before cooking. Can also be added to tea.
BASIL (*Ocimum basilicum*)	There are several varieties of basil including bush, sweet and lemon basil. Grown as a tender annual, it rarely reaches a height of more than 45cm (1½ft).	Grow in full sun, protected from wind. Best sown in the greenhouse in mid-spring and planted out in early summer.	The spicy leaves are used in salads, soups, egg and fish dishes and, most notably, in tomato dishes.
BAY (*Laurus nobilis*)	A high ornamental evergreen shrub which can grow to 12m (40ft) but is often clipped to formal shapes and kept small.	Grow in full sun in well-drained soil. Propagate by half-ripe cuttings taken in late summer. It's not reliably hardy so should be grown in a pot in colder areas and taken inside for winter.	Used in recipes for vegetables and fish when these are cooked in liquid. Always remove bay leaves before eating the dish or liquidising.
BORAGE (*Borago officinalis*)	A very decorative annual, 45–60cm (1½–2ft) tall, with clusters of bright blue, starry flowers with a black cone in the centre.	Grow in a sunny, well-drained position. Sow in spring, after which it will seed itself readily.	The young leaves can be used in salads or infused in tea. The leaves and flowers are floated on summer drinks.

HERB	DESCRIPTION	CULTIVATION	USE
CARAWAY (*Carum carvi*)	A biennial or perennial up to 60cm (2ft) tall with white or pink flowers.	Grow in a sunny, well-drained position. Sow in late spring. Seed heads set in late summer when they should be cut and hung to dry before storing.	Used in cakes, rye bread, soups and cheese and fish dishes.
CHERVIL (*Anthriscus cerifolium*)	A quick-growing annual that looks somewhat insignificant, like a weedy form of parsley, but is invaluable in the kitchen.	Grow in part-shade in moist soil to prevent it running to seed. Sow in early to mid-spring. After flowering, leave a few plants to reseed, which they should do continuously.	The spicy, aniseed flavour adds a freshness to many dishes and is especially good with new potatoes, egg and vegetable dishes and on salads: sprinkle over before serving. Also makes an excellent soup.
CHIVES (*Allium schoenoprasum*)	A low-growing perennial with onion-like foliage. It grows no more than 23cm (9in.) tall so is often used to edge beds. The rounded, pink flowers are very attractive.	Will grow almost anywhere and should be propagated by division in spring or autumn. Can also be raised from seed sown in early spring.	Chop up the leaves and use them fresh as a delicate onion garnish to salads, soups, and cheese and egg dishes.
DILL (*Anethum graveolens*)	A hardy annual up to 60cm (2ft) tall with a distinctive 'bitter-sweet' flavour.	Grow in a well-drained sunny spot, sowing the seeds in spring where they're to flower. Pinch out most of the flowers, leaving just a few to provide seed for successional sowings during the year.	Use to make dill vinegar and in sour-cream dishes or to flavour fish, cheese, chicken and egg dishes.
FENNEL (*Foeniculum vulgare*)	A vigorous, hardy perennial growing to 1.5m (5ft). Most varieties have attractive, green, feathery foliage and there is also a bronze form.	Grow in a sunny, well-drained soil, but not near dill or coriander as they'll cross-pollinate. Sow in late spring or divide in autumn. Remove the flower heads if you want only the leaves; otherwise collect the ripe seed.	All parts of the plant have a pleasant aniseed flavour. Use the strongly flavoured seeds crushed and sprinkled on fresh fruit or cooked apples. The leaves are chopped over salads and cooked vegetables and in soups and fish dishes.
GARLIC (*Allium sativum*)	You'll want to grow a lot of this, so you may prefer to have a row or two in the vegetable plot. It reaches about 30cm (1ft) in height.	Divide the bulbs and plant the cloves 7.5cm (3in.) apart in autumn. Lift and dry in late summer. Save a few bulbs for replanting.	Use in salads, meat, vegetable and fish dishes.

HERB	DESCRIPTION	CULTIVATION	USE
HORSERADISH (*Armoracia rusticana*)	A vigorous perennial which can become invasive. It grows large, dock-like leaves to about 60cm (2ft) high.	Prefers a rich, moist, well-manured soil. Plant pieces of root about 15cm (6in.) long, 30cm (1ft) apart in a trench in late winter. Water well during the season. Ideally leave them growing on for two seasons and then lift all the roots for storage in moist sand.	Use to make horseradish sauce to serve with meat and oily fish dishes.
JUNIPER (*Juniperus communis*)	A native conifer growing to about 2.4m (8ft) if not trimmed.	Grow at the back of the border in a sunny spot. Start with plants bought from a nursery, putting male and female plants together to ensure berries. If you need more plants, take softwood cuttings in June (see p. 110).	Pick the berries when they're ripe and black and dry them on trays at room temperature. Store them in airtight jars in a cool, dark place. Alternatively, they'll freeze quite well. They're used to flavour strong game and pork dishes.
LOVAGE (*Levisticum officinale*)	Not a plant to grow in the small herb garden since it'll reach about 3m (10ft).	Prefers a moist soil with plenty of organic matter. Raise plants from seed sown in summer and transplanted about 1m (3ft) apart in autumn or spring.	The leaves have the flavour of peppery celery, so use them sparingly in salads, soups, stews and casseroles or wiped over meat before roasting.
MARJORAM **POT MARJORAM** (*Origanum onites*)	A perennial shrub growing to about 60cm (2ft) with pale pink or white flowers. It's attractive and easy to grow but the least flavoursome of the three.	Raise from seed sown in spring and give a warm, sheltered spot.	Use in all dishes that otherwise have a bland flavour; also chop fine and sprinkle over salads and vegetables just before serving. Dries and freezes well.
SWEET MARJORAM (*Origanum majorana*)	Grown as a half-hardy annual. It reaches to about 30cm (1ft) and has small white or pink flowers.	Sow in early spring in gentle heat and plant out in early summer 15cm (6in.) apart.	As for pot marjoram.

HERB	DESCRIPTION	CULTIVATION	USE
WILD MARJORAM (*Origanum vulgare*)	A European native growing to about 75cm (2½ft), it has a stronger flavour than the other marjorams.	Likes a well-drained, sunny spot and is easily raised from seed sown outside in spring.	As for pot marjoram.
MINT **APPLE MINT** (*Mentha rotundifolia*)	Probably the most commonly grown herb for the kitchen. It has slightly hairy, green leaves and a very distinctive aroma and flavour. If not harvested it grows to about 1m (3ft).	All mints prefer a moist soil and will do well in shade but are very invasive. For this reason they should be grown in a bed of their own or in a bottomless container to prevent them taking over. Propagate by digging up a plant and planting out pieces of root in spring or autumn. Mint can also be forced for a winter supply by putting pieces of root in a box of compost on a warm windowsill (see p. 269).	Use to flavour meat, especially lamb, and for all vegetables. The fresh leaves are best, so force a continuous supply or freeze them in ice cubes (see p. 270).
SPEARMINT (*Mentha spicata*)	Grows to about 60cm (2ft) and has a very distinct, clean flavour of spearmint, so is valuable for use with meats that tend to be fatty.		As for apple mint.
PARSLEY (*Petroselinum crispum*)	A well-known and widely used herb with two main varieties, plain-leaved and curly. It grows to about 23cm (9in.) and makes an attractive edging to herb beds.	Likes a fertile, well-manured soil and will do well in shade. A biennial, it's generally sown each year to prevent it running to seed. Sow in modules in gentle heat in early spring and outside in mid-spring, planting out or thinning to about 15cm (6in.) apart. Note that it takes a long time to germinate.	Used to make sauces for fish dishes, for garnishing almost all dishes and in salads and sandwiches.
ROSEMARY (*Rosemarinus officinalis*)	A hardy evergreen shrub growing to about 1m (3ft) if not trimmed. Has attractive, aromatic foliage and clear mauve or blue flowers.	Grow in full sun in well-drained soil. After flowering, cut back with shears to prevent it becoming straggly but never cut into old wood since it won't grow out. Plants are best replaced every six to seven years. Propagate by half-ripe cuttings in late summer.	The shoots can be harvested and dried in an airy shed; store the dried leaves in airtight jars. Use to flavour meat, especially lamb, pork, veal, rabbit and poultry.

HERB	DESCRIPTION	CULTIVATION	USE
SAGE (*Salvia officinalis*)	A hardy shrub growing to about 60cm (2ft). There are several forms of sage with variegated leaves which are more attractive than but perhaps not as long-lived as the common form. They are as useful for cooking.	Plant in well-drained soil in full sun. Prune back after flowering but not into old wood.	Pick the leaves before flowering or the flavour will be impaired. They can be dried successfully; store them in airtight jars. Alternatively freeze them (see p. 270). Use to make stuffings and as a flavouring for cheese dishes, in sausages, pies and soups.
SAVORY **SUMMER SAVORY** (*Satureja hortensis*)	A rather loose, floppy annual growing to about 15–23cm (6–9in.). It has whitish or purple flowers and is a very effective bee attractor.	Sow in a sunny spot where it's to grow in mid-spring and thin to 15cm (6in.) apart.	Can be dried and stored in jars. Use in bean and tomato dishes and with veal, mushrooms and salads.
WINTER SAVORY (*Satureja montana*)	A perennial growing to about 30cm (1ft).	Prune back hard in spring to induce soft growth. Propagate by half-ripe cuttings in late summer.	Doesn't need preserving since leaves are available all winter. Uses are as for summer savory.
SORREL **COMMON SORREL** (*Rumex acetosa*)	Produces broad, dock-like leaves with an acidic taste – it is the least acid of all the sorrels. Grows to about 45cm–1m (1½–3ft).	Prefers a rich, moist, acid soil and will do well in partial shade. Raise from seed sown outside in early spring. Pick the leaves regularly and remove flower heads as they appear. Lift and divide the roots every three to four years.	The leaves can be dried: lay them flat on trays at room temperature and store in airtight jars. Use the fresh leaves to make soup, as a salad ingredient and to flavour meat and fish dishes.
GARDEN SORREL (*Rumex rugosus*)	As for common sorrel.	As for common sorrel.	As for common sorrel.

HERB	DESCRIPTION	CULTIVATION	USE
FRENCH SORREL (*Rumex scutatus*)	As for common sorrel.	As for common sorrel.	As for common sorrel.
TARRAGON (*Artemisia dracunculus*)	There are two types of tarragon, French and Russian, but only the French is worth growing. It's a fairly hardy perennial reaching a height of about 75cm (2½ft).	Likes a sunny position and a well-drained but rich soil. Plant about 45cm (1½ft) apart. Propagate by division, which should be done every three or four years. The roots become rather tangled and should be separated carefully. Washing them in a bucket of water will help.	Cut the shoots early in the summer and dry them, though some of the flavour will be lost this way so the leaves are best used fresh. They can also be frozen. Considered by cooks as an essential herb, tarragon is used to flavour sauces, fish, game, salads and, of course, tarragon vinegar.
THYME **COMMON THYME** (*Thymus vulgaris*)	Low-growing, bushy perennial reaching 23–30cm (9–12in.) in height. Produces small, pale lilac flowers over a long period. There are various forms, including much lower-growing, spreading types.	Prefers a sunny, well-drained soil, ideally stony and limy. Can be grown from seed but is easily propagated by half-ripe cuttings in late summer. Alternatively just pile a little soil on to the crown of the plant and shoots will root into it. They can later be detached and replanted.	Dry the sprigs and store them in airtight jars. The dried leaves are more aromatic than when fresh. Use in meat and fish dishes, casseroles and stuffings and to flavour soups and salads.
LEMON THYME (*Thymus citriodorus*)	Has a distinct lemon aroma and paler pink flowers than common thyme.	As for common thyme	As for common thyme.
CARAWAY THYME (*Thymus herba-barona*)	A prostrate shrub growing to about 10cm (4in.). It has rose-pink flowers and dark green leaves with a distinct aroma and flavour of caraway.	As for common thyme.	Used mainly to flavour beef.

CHAPTER 14

FRUIT

There was a time when, to grow fruit in the garden, you'd need a hectare of orchard – no longer, alas, possible for most of us. Fortunately research into fruit growing has advanced so fast and so far in the last fifty years that some kind of 'orchard' can now be a part of every garden.

Trees on dwarfing rootstocks are now the norm, giving the gardener a choice of plants that can be pruned and picked from the ground. Then there are genetic dwarfs which are naturally small and there are even trees that grow no side branches at all, so that several can be crammed into the tiniest back yard. If you do have the space, those original full-size trees are, of course, still available. The great thing is that the choice is now yours.

There are cultural methods of saving space too. You could use your walls and fences to support trained trees, you could make an attractive ornamental and productive hedge to edge your property, or you could create a 'fruit cocktail' with one small tree growing up to three varieties.

Even better, there's no need to be put off growing fruit by the complicated pruning instructions we've all tried to come to grips with in the past. Those have been simplified to make them easy to grasp and more productive. No longer a luxury for the landed gent, fruit growing is something every gardener can and should do.

If you have space, a traditional orchard is much to be desired – but it's by no means necessary.

Fruit tree shapes

You can do almost anything with the shape of fruit trees and the type you choose will depend on how much room you have and how decorative you want your trees to be. The smaller the garden, the greater the need to create trees that take up little space but look attractive.

Most of the information on fruit growing available to gardeners has come from research aimed at commercial growers. That has the great advantage that all the legends and old wives' tales have been eradicated. But it has also made fruit growing appear much more complicated than it actually is. With this in mind, you won't find here any mention of 'delayed open centre' pruning or of the 'renewal system'. Instead I've limited myself to simple yet highly effective methods that are readily accessible to the gardener.

The shapes of trees suggested on this page will cover all the gardener's needs and, best of all, you don't need an honours degree in botany to grasp the pruning instructions.

ABOVE Cordons These consist of single stems bearing short, stubby 'spurs' of branches along their length. It's here that the fruit is produced. The trees are grown at an angle to restrict the sap flow, discouraging exuberant growth and encouraging fruiting. They need the support of a fence or wall or, better still, a free-standing post-and-wire structure. They make a decorative and productive hedge and are often used to divide the vegetables from the ornamental part of the garden. This is an ideal way to grow apples and pears particularly. Plant them 75cm (2½ft) apart.

Fans Trained either on wires fixed to a wall or fence or, less often, on a post-and-wire structure, these look very decorative and produce good crops while taking up no more than a few centimetres of garden space. The warmth of a south-facing wall will help protect tender flowers from frost damage and encourage fruit ripening too. So this is an excellent method for pears, peaches, nectarines and apricots in particular. Plant 3–3.6m (10–12ft) apart.

Espaliers A variation on the fan shape, espaliers have an attractive appearance and will also derive some protection from a wall or fence. They are often used for apples and the training is far less complicated than that for a fan. The 'tiers' of branches are spaced out about 30cm (1ft) apart and the height is restricted only by the height of the supporting wall. Plant 3–3.6m (10–12ft) apart.

Step-overs Nothing more than single-tier espaliers and pruned in exactly the same way. They are generally trained on a single wire about 23cm (9in.) above the ground and can be used to make a decorative and productive edge to a path or border. Plant 3m (10ft) apart.

Bushes These are a more conventional shape and could grow into large trees. So, if your garden is small and you want this type of tree, make sure that it's on a dwarfing rootstock (see p. 290) and keep on top of the pruning. The main idea with bush shapes is to maintain an open centre to the tree to let in light and air. Planting distances will depend on the rootstock used, the type of fruit and the variety, but should be between 1.5 and 4.9m (5 and 16ft).

Dwarf pyramids Free-standing trees grown to form the rough shape of a Christmas tree. This is a shape generally reserved for apples and pears. Buy them on a rootstock that will restrict growth (see p. 290) and plant about 1.5–1.8m (5–6ft) apart.

Festooning A method of tying down branches rather than pruning them. This restricts the sap flow, increasing fruiting and encouraging shoots to grow out along the curves. These are pruned back to form 'spurs' as in cordons. Plant about 1.5m (5ft) apart.

Column trees Restricted to apples, these are a type genetically programmed to produce only short side shoots on which the fruit is borne. No pruning is necessary. Plant 75cm (2½ft) apart.

Pruning fruit trees

The main principle to remember about pruning a fruit tree is that you prune in the summer for fruit and in the winter for growth. So, in the early stages when you're building up the framework of the tree, some pruning is done in winter. Later, when the tree has grown to the shape and size you want, you do all the pruning in summer.

When pruning always use sharp secateurs and cut at an angle just above a bud, sloping the cut so that the water runs off away from the bud. Avoid leaving a long stub which will die back to the bud and could allow the entrance of disease.

RIGHT For small gardens, trained fruit trees are by far the best. Don't be put off by the pruning which is all done in the pleasant summer weather and is very easy to master. The best time for summer pruning is when the shoots are just beginning to stiffen at the base – generally in late summer.

Pruning cordons

1 Cordons are an ideal way to grow apples and pears in a small garden. They're the model for pruning other shapes of tree, so once you've mastered them the rest follow naturally. Start with a one-year-old (maiden) tree and, after planting, cut any side shoots back to leave them about 7.5cm (3in.) long and prune the main stem (leader) back by about a third. That's all the winter pruning the tree will ever need.

2 Late the following summer, and in all subsequent summers, look for shoots that have grown directly from the main stem and cut them back to 7.5cm (3in.). Then look for shoots that have grown from side shoots pruned the previous year and cut those back to 2.5cm (1in.). Eventually you'll produce stubby 'spurs' which bear the fruit. When the tree has grown as long as you want it, treat the top growth like a side shoot.

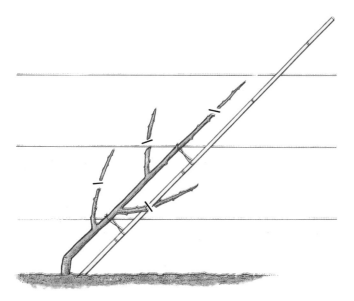

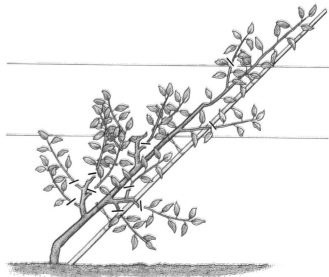

Pruning espaliers

1 Espaliers are generally used only for apples and pears. They can be bought ready-trained but it's not difficult to shape your own from scratch. Start with a maiden tree and plant it against wires stretched horizontally at 60cm (2ft) intervals. After planting cut the main stem back to a bud just above the lowest wire.

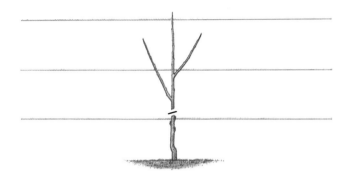

2 In the first year three shoots will grow out. Two of these should be trained horizontally and the third vertically. Any other shoots should be rubbed off while they're still green. In the winter cut back the main stem to a little above the second wire to form the second tier.

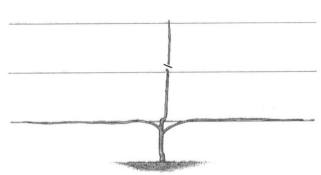

3 In the following summer treat the second tier as you did the first, tying in two shoots horizontally and one vertically. The branches of the first tier are pruned in late summer, just as if they were each cordons: you cut back the side shoots to 7.5cm (3in.) and any shoots arising from those to 2.5cm (1in.). In the following winter simply repeat the process to make a third tier.

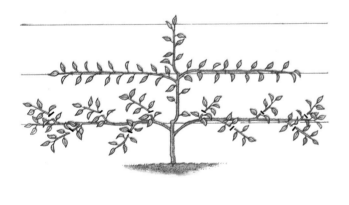

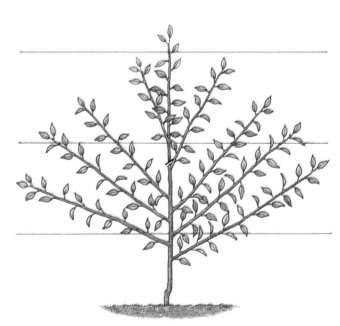

Pruning step-overs
Prune these annually as single-tier espaliers trained on a single wire stretched 23cm (9in.) above the ground.

Pruning fan-trained apples and pears
Fans can be used for apples and pears and are much better bought ready-trained, when the nurseryman will have selected those trees that were best shaped for the job. Alternatively buy a maiden and cut it back to about 45cm (1½ft) above the ground. Allow shoots to grow out and train them into a fan shape. In late summer simply treat each branch as if it were a cordon.

Peaches, nectarines, apricots, plums and sweet and acid cherries are also grown as fans but the pruning is somewhat different (see pp. 284–5).

Pruning fruit trees

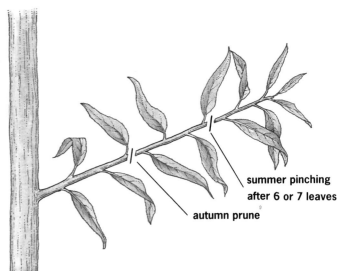

It's best to do all pruning of plums and cherries when the plants are growing vigorously and will heal quickly to lessen the risk of attack by the silver-leaf fungus.

summer pinching
after 6 or 7 leaves

autumn prune

Pruning fan-trained plums, sweet cherries and apricots
These fruit on both old and new wood, so pruning is slightly different from that of other fruit fans. Buy a ready-made fan and train it in the way recommended for peaches. In spring, when the tree starts to grow, pinch out shoots growing towards or away from the wall and select shoots for fruiting (these can be spaced slightly closer than on peaches). Pinch out their tips when they've made six or seven leaves. Then, after picking the fruit, shorten those shoots again by half. Repeat the process each year.

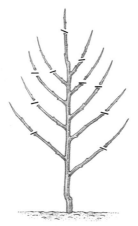

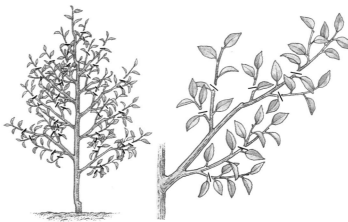

Pruning dwarf pyramids

1 Dwarf pyramids are a convenient way to grow small, free-standing apples and pears. Start with a maiden tree planted in the winter and cut it back to 60cm (2ft) above ground level immediately after planting.

2 In the second winter prune the lower branches to 25cm (10in.) long to form the lower tier. If there are branches above these, cut them back to 15cm (6in.) to form the second tier. Reduce the leading shoot to 30cm (1ft) above the topmost branch.

3 In late summer look first at the main branches and cut back new growth to leave it 15cm (6in.) long. Then look at side shoots and cut those to leave the new growth 10cm (4in.) long. Any shoots coming from them are cut back to 5cm (2in.). When the tree has reached the size you want, prune it back twice as hard each summer. You'll finish up with a tree that's much the same shape as a Christmas tree and easy to reach for picking fruit and pruning.

Pruning fan-trained peaches, nectarines and acid cherries

1 These are pruned in the same way as dwarf pyramids and they're easier than you think. Most books will give complicated instructions for the initial pruning to shape, but that's not necessary. It's much better to allow the nurseryman to train the original fan. Plant it against wires on a south-facing wall or fence if you can, tying in the shoots to form a fan shape. As side shoots grow, you select one every 10cm (4in.) or so and tie it in; rub the others out while they're still young and soft.

2 When pruning annually, remember that fruit is borne on wood the tree made the year before. Once you grasp that, the pruning is quite logical. Early in the year remove shoots that are growing towards or directly away from the wall. Then look for shoots that were made last year and, as soon as they have produced four to six leaves, pinch out the tip. They will also make one or two shoots at the base and these should be allowed to remain to make the fruiting shoots for next year.

3 After you have picked the fruit, cut out those shoots that bore fruit just above the shoots that you have selected as replacements. Tie these in and next spring start the whole process again.

BELOW **Pruning festoons**
Plums, apples and pears can be kept small by festooning. Start with a maiden tree and, in summer while the growth is still soft, bend the main shoot downwards very carefully and tie it to the base of the tree. Any other side branches can be treated in the same way. This induces growth and fruit along the curves in particular and the resulting shoots should be pruned as for cordons (see p. 282).

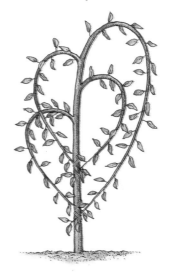

Planting and training fruit trees

As with all planting, it's worthwhile taking trouble over fruit trees since good initial preparation will result in higher and, particularly, earlier yields. If it's done properly, you can certainly expect a fair crop of apples, for example, in two years and a full crop in four or five. Prepare the ground as recommended for ornamental trees (see p. 182), cultivating the whole area to be planted rather than digging isolated holes in otherwise uncultivated soil.

Planting methods will vary a little depending, in the case of apples, on the type of rootstock used (see p. 290) and, in all types of fruit, on the chosen method of training. For autumn planting, field-grown trees should be available more cheaply than those in containers.

RIGHT **Planting at the correct depth**
Fruit trees are generally grafted on to a special rootstock which will control the vigour of the tree (see p. 290). It's obvious, then, that the advantage of the stock will be lost if the variety is allowed to root into the ground. The bend in the stem that marks the union between the stock and the variety is easy to see, and it's important to ensure that this is far enough out of the ground to prevent rooting of the variety. Plant it high enough to allow for a thick mulch around the base too.

BELOW **Staking and tying**
This is done in exactly the same way as for ornamental trees (see p. 182), except that with varieties on really dwarfing rootstocks the stake will be required for the life of the tree. It's therefore much more important to ensure that it'll last, so spend a little more on stakes that have been pressure-treated with preservative. Again, use a proper plastic tree tie tacked to the stake and check it annually.

BELOW **Planting against a wall**
If you're planting against a wall, remember that this is always the driest part of the garden, so add extra organic matter to retain moisture in the soil. After planting mulch around the tree with a good, thick layer of compost or manure to reduce water loss further. Make sure too that you keep an eye on the soil and water if necessary, because trees are less likely than smaller plants to show signs of stress early.

ABOVE **Lollipop trees**
Apple and pear trees can be trained to almost any shape. This 'lollipop tree' was trained round a former made with 13mm (½in.) alkathene water pipe. Each of the four branches is treated just like a cordon, and the side shoots summer pruned to form fruiting spurs. When the branches meet at the top they can be 'splice' grafted together (see p. 126) or simply pruned back each year.

Planting trained trees

1 BELOW When planting trained trees, set stout, galvanised wires about 60cm (2ft) apart. On the wall they can be fixed with vine eyes (see p. 199), but a row of free-standing trees will need posts at about 3m (10ft) intervals. Again buy specially treated posts and place a strut at each end and also, in the case of a long run, at about 9m (30ft) intervals.

2 If the branches are fixed directly to the wires, there's bound to be a certain amount of chafing of the bark. So tie canes to the wires with either nylon twine or wire and then tie the branches to the canes using soft string. Never fix any tree with nylon string, which will eventually cut into the bark.

Training cordons and espaliers

To encourage fast initial growth, train cordons fairly upright for the first year. Then pull them down and retie the canes to the wires at an angle of about 45 degrees to restrict growth and encourage the production of fruit buds. The same applies to the branches of espaliers.

Training cordons over an arch

This is a more decorative way to grow cordon fruit. Plant the trees at each arch support and simply tie them in. Their upright position encourages initial growth which is slowed down after they're bent over the top. When the two trees touch they can be cut off or grafted together.

General care of fruit and harvesting the crop

Those big, gnarled, old fruit trees that used to be common in traditional orchards had very little attention and yet they would produce fruit year after year. So why should the modern gardener need to bother with regular maintenance?

The fact is that old-style orchards may well have produced good yields, but most of them were far below their real potential in terms of yields per square metre. And, with restricted space at our disposal, that's of vital importance to gardeners. Modern research has been aimed at getting maximum crops from smaller trees. The methods were, of course, designed for the fruit farmer, mainly to reduce labour and increase profits. But the self-same methods have obvious advantages for the gardener who may have room for only a few trees and so also needs to derive the biggest yield possible. Attend to a few annual chores and that's exactly what you'll do, from both fruit trees and soft fruit bushes.

RIGHT We tend to look on fruit trees as purely productive plants, but any tree that's covered with flowers in spring, followed by large, colourful fruits, is extremely decorative too. Plant apples at the back of the border to form a superb backing to flowers.

LEFT **Feeding** All fruit trees and bushes need feeding at least once a year. I use pelleted chicken manure or blood, fish and bone meal supplemented with a mulch of well-rotted manure. If you garden chemically, rose fertiliser is the one to use, having a high potash content. Fertiliser should be applied in late winter or early spring.

RIGHT **Keeping weeds at bay** Keep the base of newly planted trees free from competition from weeds and grass. Either hoe lightly but regularly round the trees or put a piece of polythene on the soil round the base on planting – it can be hidden by covering with a little soil or compost.

BELOW Encouraging growth on bare branches Sometimes fruit trees can produce branches with long, bare areas. Examination shows that wood buds exist but simply refuse to grow out. The gardener can control this by diverting growth-retarding substances sent down from the topmost bud. The purpose of these substances is to reduce competition, so ensuring that the top bud grows fastest to enable the tree to reach the light rapidly. The growth retardants are in vessels running just below the bark, so a small nick cut out just above a bud will divert the retardants and encourage the bud to grow.

ABOVE **Watering** Most fruit trees will benefit from additional water, especially at a time when the fruit is swelling. However, avoid the temptation to put on a little in times of drought since this will encourage surface roots to form which will be even more vulnerable in hot sun. A hose and sprinkler are essential, and the water should be left on for at least an hour in hot weather.

BELOW Thinning With apples, small fruits are often to be preferred, especially when there are young children in the family. However, if it's bigger fruit you're after, some thinning may be necessary: it's normally enough just to remove the 'king fruit', which is the one in the centre of each cluster. With fruits like gooseberries you can harvest the early berries a little under-ripe for cooking, leaving some to grow bigger for eating raw.

RIGHT **Harvesting** Always harvest fruit very carefully. Pick it when it parts easily from the branch and put it into a basket lined with cloth. See under individual fruit for specific storage instructions and times.

Apples

Before buying apple trees there are two factors to be taken into account – rootstock and variety. The rootstock will control the size of the tree, so it's important to know just what you're buying. If your local nursery or garden centre can't tell you, go elsewhere.

The variety takes even more thought. First, of course, you want one you'll enjoy eating and, if you grow more than one tree, you'll want a succession of harvesting. You must also bear in mind that, to give a full crop, all apples need pollinating with a different variety. Though there are some exceptional ones (known as triploids) which won't pollinate anything, it's generally simply a matter of combining varieties that flower at the same time. Gardeners in colder areas would be well advised

to choose varieties which flower late in order to avoid frost damage.

In fact there's no doubt that the very best way to choose varieties is to ask around your own area, seeking advice particularly from older gardeners who've been growing there for some years because they'll know the varieties that'll do best.

Most apple varieties store well after harvesting, usually for several months. Put small quantities of perfect fruit into sealed polythene bags (do not mix varieties within a bag), make one or two (no more) pinpricks in the bags and store in a very cold but just frost-free place. Inspect the fruit regularly and remove any that show signs of rotting.

Rootstocks There are really just three rootstocks you'll need to remember. The smallest trees are produced on M27 stocks, while M9 makes slightly larger trees. Both these are ideal for trees grown in containers but both really need quite fertile soil and will have to be staked all their life. On poorer soil and for bigger trees it's best to go for MM106 which is certainly the best general-purpose rootstock.

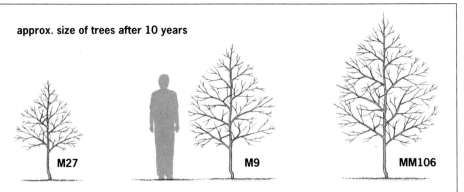

approx. size of trees after 10 years

M27   M9   MM106

SUGGESTED VARIETIES

Unless marked T, which indicates a triploid, the following varieties will pollinate others in the same group.

Early-flowering varieties
'Egremont Russet': One of the best-flavoured russets with crisp and nutty flesh. Use October–December.
'Idared': Pale green with a bright red flush. Good flavour for cooking and dessert. Use November–March.
'Lord Lambourne': Bright-coloured apples with a juicy, sweet flesh. Use September–November.

'Egremont Russet'.

'Idared'.

'Lord Lambourne'.

Mid-season-flowering varieties

'Blenheim Orange' (T): Large fruits that are crisp and well-flavoured. Keeps well. Use November–February.

'Bountiful': A good, new cooker with an excellent flavour. Smaller and more compact than 'Bramley'. Use October–February.

'Bramley's Seedling' (T): The most popular cooker with a superb flavour. Good keeper but very vigorous. Use November–March.

'Cox's Orange Pippin': A very popular dessert apple with a fine flavour but it's a poor cropper and very prone to disease. Not recommended for gardens. Use November–January.

'Discovery': Orange-red fruits produced very early with a superb flavour and texture. Doesn't keep. Use August–September.

'Fiesta': A new variety with a 'Cox' flavour. Red and yellow fruits with a crisp, juicy texture. Keeps well. Use October–March.

'Greensleeves': Greenish-yellow fruits with a crisp, juicy flesh and excellent flavour. High yielder. Use September–November.

'James Grieve': Excellent green and red fruits with a superb flavour if eaten straight from the tree. Bruises easily and doesn't keep. Use for cooking and eating in September–October.

'Jupiter' (T): A new variety with a 'Cox' flavour. Excellent texture and keeps very well. Use October–January.

'Katy': A superb, crisp, juicy and well-flavoured early variety. Heavy-cropping and reliable. Use September–October.

'Spartan': Deep red fruits with a firm, juicy flesh and excellent flavour. Keeps well and is disease-resistant. Use October–December.

'Sunset': Firm and juicy with a 'Cox' flavour. Disease-resistant and keeps very well. Use November–March.

'Blenheim Orange'.

'Bramley's Seedling'.

'Discovery'.

'Cox's Orange Pippin'.

'Greensleeves'.

'James Grieve'.

'Spartan'.

'Sunset'.

Late-flowering varieties

'Ashmead's Kernel': An old favourite with a superb flavour. Keeps well and has the bonus of the best blossom of all. Use December–March.

'Gala': A fairly new variety with a typical 'Cox' flavour. Hardy. Use November–March.

'Howgate Wonder': A very large cooker with not quite the flavour of 'Bramley'. Use November–March.

'Orleans Reinette': A very old apple but still widely grown for its prolific habit and fine flavour. Use December–February.

'Suntan' (T): A fairly new variety with a wonderful 'Cox' flavour and good keeping qualities. Highly recommended. Use November–March.

'Ashmead's Kernel'.

'Suntan'.

Pears and quinces

Pears are not as easy to grow as apples and, since they flower earlier, it's best to choose a sheltered spot for them. If you have a south- or a west-facing wall, they'll do best as fan-trained or espalier trees, deriving some protection from the storage-heater effect of the wall.

There are not so many varieties of pears available as there are of apples but the same rules for pollination apply. The variety 'Conference' will, in fact, produce quite reasonable crops on its own pollen but the pears are long, thin and misshapen, so it's always best to have another variety to pollinate it. There's less variation in flowering time, therefore most varieties will pollinate each other.

Rootstocks are limited too. The smallest trees are budded on to Quince C stocks but they're really only for very fertile soils. Trees budded on to Quince A rootstocks will produce more vigorous growth. However, pears are not as strong-growing as apples, so my own advice would be to stick with Quince A unless your soil is very fertile and to control growth by pruning.

Because pears are slightly earlier than apples, trained trees should be pruned a week or two earlier in the summer than apples but are otherwise treated in exactly the same way.

Pears won't keep as long as apples once harvested, so store them in open trays or on a shelf in a cool place for a few weeks and bring them into a warmer atmosphere for final ripening two days before eating.

Quinces, which are self-pollinating, are grown in the same way as pears, though less pruning will be necessary. The harvested fruits will keep a little longer than pears.

Pear trees flower early, so give them as protected a spot in the garden as possible.

Quince trees are attractive in flower and the fruit makes fine jams and jellies.

SUGGESTED VARIETIES

Pears

'Beth': A fairly new introduction with relatively small but very sweet and juicy, yellow fruit. Use September.

'Beurre Hardy': A strong-growing, old variety bearing good crops of reddish fruit. It can be used for dessert or cooking. Use October–November.

'Concorde': An excellent new variety producing double the yield of most others. The fruits are medium to large, light green turning yellow, and the flavour and texture are excellent. Highly recommended. Use October–December.

'Conference': One of the most popular pears because it's a very reliable cropper. The fruits are longish and green with an excellent flavour. Use October–December.

'Doyenné du Comice': One of the best-flavoured pears, with very juicy flesh. The skin is golden-yellow with a slight russet tinge, sometimes flushed red. Use November–December.

'Louis Bonne of Jersey': A very fine-flavoured fruit with white, juicy flesh and regular high yields. It's partially self-fertile but will not pollinate with 'Williams'. Use October–November.

'Onward': Greenish-yellow fruits with juicy flesh and an exceptionally good flavour. Good cropper but doesn't keep long. Will not pollinate with 'Doyenné du Comice'. Use September–October.

'Williams Bon Chrétien': The best-known and most popular variety with pale yellow skin and juicy flesh with the finest flavour. Use September–October.

'Winter Nelis': A useful winter pear for cooking or dessert. Good flavour even when green and keeps a relatively long time. Use November–January.

Quince

BELOW 'Vranja': The best variety for culinary use, this produces large, yellow, pear-shaped fruits with a fine, juicy flesh and excellent flavour. Use late summer–autumn.

Pear 'Beth'.

Pear 'Conference'.

Pear 'Concorde'.

Pear 'Onward'.

Pear 'Beurre Hardy'.

Pear 'Doyenné du Comice'.

Plums, damsons, gages and apricots

Plums and damsons are closely related and both are fairly easy to grow, doing well as dwarf pyramids or fans. They're very vigorous trees, so make sure that you buy a variety which has been budded on to a dwarfing rootstock. The stock St Julien A is semi-dwarfing but will still make big trees; in a small garden, therefore, stick to the much smaller Pixy.

Gages are really much the same as plums, though said to be sweeter and more aromatic. They're slightly more difficult and will do best trained as fans on a south- or west-facing wall.

Apricots, though grown in much the same way, are more temperamental, so need the warmth of a south-facing wall for best results.

Since all varieties of plums, damsons, gages and apricots are subject to attack from silver-leaf disease, it's bad practice to prune in winter when wounds will take a long time to heal and so could allow disease to enter. Prune either immediately after harvesting or in early spring just as the trees start into growth.

In a good year it may be necessary to thin plum fruits to about 7.5cm (3in.) apart and to support heavily laden branches.

Plums are best eaten straight from the tree and they can be stored by bottling.

RIGHT 'Merton Gem' is a good dessert or cooking plum producing large, very juicy fruit. It's partially self-fertile and crops in early September.

SUGGESTED VARIETIES

The list below indicates which varieties are self-fertile and suggests pollinators for those that aren't.

Plums and gages
'Cambridge Gage': Small fruits with yellowish-green flesh and a superb flavour. Pollinate with 'Victoria', 'Czar' or 'Marjorie's Seedling'. Harvest August–September.
'Czar': One of the best cooking plums with an acidic flavour. Medium-sized, dark purple fruits. Self-fertile. Harvest August.
'Denniston's Superb': Large, round fruits with a darker stripe. Good flavour and excellent for colder gardens. Self-fertile. Harvest August.

'Cambridge Gage'.

'Czar'.

'Denniston's Superb'.

'Edwards': An American variety producing large, blue fruits with a succulent orange flesh with excellent flavour. Good for dessert or cooking. Pollinate with 'Victoria', 'Czar' or 'Cambridge Gage'. Harvest September.

'Early Laxton': The earliest to ripen. Fair flavour and good for dessert or cooking.

Pollinate with 'Victoria' or 'Czar'. Harvest July.

'Marjorie's Seedling': Large, oval, purple fruits with a juicy yellow flesh and superb flavour. Excellent for dessert or cooking. A good variety for colder gardens. Self-fertile. Harvest September–October.

'Opal': Red/purple fruits

with a juicy flesh and good flavour. Self-fertile. Harvest July–August.

'Victoria': Still the most popular variety and the best if you want only one tree. Heavy crops of pale red fruits that are sweet and juicy. Self-fertile. Harvest August–September.

'Merryweather': Large, well-

flavoured fruits. A good all-round variety. Self-fertile. Harvest September.

'Shropshire Damson': Very juicy, well-flavoured fruits and probably the best for cooking. Compact growth, so good for smaller gardens. Self-fertile. Harvest September–October.

'Edwards'.

'Early Laxton'.

'Marjorie's Seedling'.

'Opal'.

'Victoria'.

'Merryweather'.

Apricots

LEFT 'Moorpark': The most popular variety with large, pale yellow fruits with a red flush. Juicy, orange flesh and a fine flavour. Self-fertile. Harvest in late August. There is an earlier-fruiting variety called 'Early Moorpark' which is similar but crops in July.

'Alfred': An American variety which shows no sign of the die-back often associated with others. Fruits are large, round and orange with a pink flush and

a good flavour. It tends to be biennially bearing, so protect the flowers from frost because, if a crop is missed, the biennial habit is likely to be established. Self-fertile. Harvest July.

Cherries

Cherries are wonderfully decorative trees, covered in blossom in spring and pretty attractive when they're full of fruit too – if you can stop the birds demolishing the lot in about five minutes flat. Unfortunately cherries are big trees and not really suitable as free-standing specimens in small gardens. It's virtually impossible to protect the fruit from birds in the normal way. However, all is not lost.

The good news is that, like other types of fruit, they too have a relatively new dwarfing rootstock. The bad news is that it's not *very* dwarfing. Still, make sure that anything you buy is grown on a Colt rootstock, which will reduce normal tree size by a third.

The other way to reduce size is by pruning and I would always recommend a fan-trained tree for small gardens. You can grow sweet cherries against a south- or west-facing wall, but bear in mind that even with a dwarfing stock and some hefty pruning you'll still finish up with quite a big tree. None the less, this shape of plant is very easy to cover with netting against birds.

Acid or cooking cherries are useful in that they can be fan-trained against a north-facing wall.

Prune sweet cherries like plums (see p. 284) and acid cherries like peaches (see p. 285). Because they too are subject to silver-leaf disease, prune in early autumn or just as growth begins in spring.

SUGGESTED VARIETIES

Sweet cherries
There are dozens of varieties of sweet cherries but most need another variety to pollinate them. In the majority of gardens two trees would be difficult to accommodate, so my recommendation would be to shun the older varieties in favour of new, self-fertile ones. The choice is pretty limited but all the new varieties are as well-flavoured as the older ones.
'Lapins': Large, dark red fruits with a good resistance to splitting and an excellent flavour. Heavy cropping. Harvest late August.
'Stella': The first of the new self-fertile varieties, carrying red fruits with an excellent flavour. Harvest late July. There is also a more compact form called 'Compact Stella' which seems to produce more fruiting spurs and therefore heavier crops and is a little smaller too. Harvest late July.
'Sunburst': Heavy crops of large, black fruits with a very juicy flesh and excellent

flavour. Good resistance to splitting. Harvest early July.
'Merton Glory': This is not self-fertile but I include it because it can be pollinated by 'Morello' which many gardeners might grow to cover a north wall. It's a very early, yellow cherry with large fruits. Harvest late June–July.
'Merton Bigarreau': Another that needs 'Morello' to pollinate it. This produces large, black, juicy fruits with a quite exceptional flavour. Harvest July.

'Stella'.

'Merton Glory'.

'Lapins'.

'Sunburst'.

'Merton Bigarreau'.

Acid cherries

Both these varieties of cooking cherries are self-fertile.

'Morello': The best-known and oldest variety, producing heavy crops of cherries, black when ripe, with an excellent flavour. Harvest August.

'Nabella': A recent German introduction which is heavy-yielding and compact. The fruits, black when ripe, have a fine flavour. Harvest August.

'Morello'.

'Nabella'.

RIGHT Provided you can keep the birds at bay, cherries will produce heavy crops. But even without fruit at all the trees are still valued for their fine spring blossom.

Peaches and nectarines

Peaches and nectarines, which are close relatives, are grown in the same way. The difference is that nectarines have a hairless skin and a subtly different flavour and are slightly smaller than peaches.

Both are fairly tolerant of most soils except where drainage is bad. A south-facing wall is usually the best growing position for a fan-trained tree, though the newer dwarf varieties can be grown as small bushes in pots. These need virtually no pruning except thinning of branches if they become overcrowded. The great advantage with these genetic dwarfs is that they can be prevented from contracting peach leaf curl disease. This disease is carried by spores in rain, so if plants can be protected from rain between January and late May, they'll escape completely. It's not too difficult to contrive a cover over fan-trained trees on a wall or fence, but it's even easier to grow dwarf peaches in pots

and keep them under cover during the critical period.

Peaches and nectarines can also be grown in a well-ventilated greenhouse or conservatory. Their treatment is the same as for those grown outside except that more pinching of young shoots and pruning may be needed to check their more vigorous growth. For pruning instructions for fans see p. 285.

Since peaches flower very early when there are few pollinating insects about, it may be necessary to hand pollinate the flowers with a paintbrush. This is nearly always necessary in the greenhouse.

For fan-trained trees it's best to use the slightly more vigorous rootstocks. Ask for St Julien A for most purposes but Brompton if the soil is very poor. Buy trees budded on to Pixy rootstocks if you want them to remain small. Like all dwarfing rootstocks this also encourages fruiting early in the life of the tree.

Peaches are not nearly as difficult to grow as their exotic nature may make you believe. And you would be quite mistaken to be put off by the complicated traditional pruning instructions. This tree, for example, has not been pruned at all for the past nine years and yet it produces a bumper crop every season without fail. That's not to say, of course, that you won't get more satisfaction, a better-looking tree and an even bigger crop if you do it the right way. But it's encouraging to know that leaving it to nature is far from a total disaster.

SUGGESTED VARIETIES

Since peaches and nectarines are self-fertile, only one tree is necessary.

Peaches
'Amsden June': The earliest variety, bearing very pale green fruits with a red flush and an excellent flavour. Not a particularly heavy cropper. Harvest mid-July.

'Early Rivers': A heavier-cropping variety with yellow and red fruits, juicy and well-flavoured. Harvest July.

BELOW LEFT 'Duke of York': A deservedly popular variety with juicy and delicious crimson fruits. Harvest late July.

BELOW CENTRE 'Peregrine': A variety with large, juicy fruits with an exceptional flavour. Probably the best of all.

Harvest early August.

BELOW RIGHT 'Rochester': One of the easiest and most reliable varieties, especially in colder areas. The large fruits are well-flavoured. Harvest mid-August.

Nectarines
LEFT 'Lord Napier': The best-known and most popular variety. It regularly produces large, very well-flavoured and aromatic fruits. Harvest early August.

ABOVE 'Pineapple': A good variety in warmer areas or under glass. The large yellow/red fruits have a distinct flavour of pineapple. Harvest early September.

Figs

Though considered very much warm-country plants, figs will do remarkably well outside in quite temperate areas and in a cold greenhouse or conservatory in cooler regions. In these places they produce tiny fruits in late summer which overwinter to swell and ripen the following summer. They're best grown fan-trained on a south- or west-facing wall.

Figs are quite soil-tolerant, though they require good drainage. Indeed, too rich a soil is to be avoided or growth will be lush at the expense of fruit, so feed judiciously.

In winter you can protect embryo fruits by tying the branches together and covering them with straw.

Figs are grown on their own roots and are self-fertile.

RIGHT Figs are decorative and productive plants to grow against a warm wall.

Prune by removing weak, damaged or overcrowded shoots in early spring. When growth starts tie in the shoots to form a fan shape, and before mid-summer pinch out the tips of young growths when they have reached five leaves.

SUGGESTED VARIETIES

All these varieties should be harvested during the summer as their fruits become soft, indicating ripeness.

RIGHT ABOVE 'Brown Turkey': Probably the best-known and most successful for growing outside. The fruits are reliably and freely produced and are juicy and well-flavoured.

RIGHT BELOW 'White Marseilles': A fine variety for outside or under glass. The large, almost transparent fruits have a rich flavour.

'Bourjassotte Grise': A richly flavoured variety with red flesh and thick juice. Ideal for pot culture under glass.

Grapes

Grapes can be successfully grown for wine making even in quite cold areas, but for eating they need warmer conditions either in a favoured location or in a cold greenhouse (see p. 323). They thrive on well-drained, rather poor soil in a sunny spot and are self-fertile.

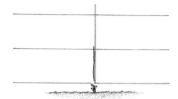 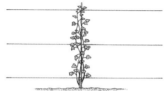

Planting and training

1 Plant vines 1.5m (5ft) apart against a post-and-wire structure. This should consist of three wires, the top one 1.2m (4ft) high. After planting cut back the main stem to leave three buds.

2 During the following summer train the subsequent three shoots up a central cane.

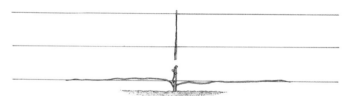

3 The following autumn train two of those shoots horizontally either side of the wire and cut the other back to three buds. The three shoots that will subsequently grow from the central one are again trained up the central cane.

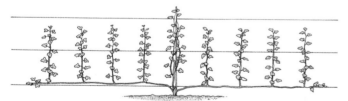

4 Shoots growing from the two horizontal ones should be trained vertically and pruned off when they reach the top wire. They'll bear the fruit, after which they should be cut off and replaced with the new shoots that have been trained up the cane.

'Seyval Blanc' produces good wine grapes outside.

SUGGESTED VARIETIES

Harvest these grapes when they are ripe, usually in mid- to late autumn, depending on the region.

'Madeleine Sylvaner': A white grape ripening quite early, so useful for colder areas. Good flavour, making excellent wine. A heavy cropper.
RIGHT ABOVE 'Muller Thurgau': Golden grapes with a superb, sweet flavour, making a fruity wine.
'Seyval Blanc': A later ripener for warmer districts where it can be grown for dessert use or wine making.
RIGHT BELOW 'Brandt': Will produce heavy crops of black grapes in warmer areas. Makes a good rosé wine and can also be eaten.

Strawberries

Strawberries are one of the most rewarding of the soft fruit crops. They rarely fail to provide a bumper harvest and they'll produce fruit just ten months after planting. Most varieties are self-fertile but it obviously pays to grow more than one to give a continuity of harvesting over a long period. It should be possible to harvest fruit from early summer through to the first frosts.

Strawberries grow best in well-drained soil in a sunny spot. On heavy land it pays to raise the beds to improve drainage. Fertiliser is needed only on very poor soil. Too much feeding could result in good crops of leaves but little fruit. After the crop has been picked, sprinkle a little potash fertiliser along the row – about a handful per metre/yard run.

SUGGESTED VARIETIES

The following varieties are recommended in order of ripening:

'Pantagruella': The earliest to ripen and excellent for forcing. Crops are not quite as heavy as those of other varieties and the berries are slightly smaller.
'Honeoye': An American variety bearing large fruits with a good colour and texture and excellent flavour.

'Idil': An early summer variety, producing heavy crops with a fine flavour. Perhaps its most striking characteristic is that it seems to be very disease-resistant.
'Elsanta': The most widely grown commercial strawberry, producing mid-season crops of large berries with excellent texture and flavour. Can be prone to mildew, so make sure that it doesn't go short of water.

'Pandora': A fairly new variety, bridging the gap between the summer- and autumn-fruiting types. Unlike most varieties it is not self-pollinating, but all the other varieties recommended here will do the job.
'Aromel': The best of the autumn fruiters with a quite superb flavour and heavy crops. Remove flowers in the spring to ensure later fruiting.

'Honeoye'.

Planting Plant in late summer or early autumn, setting the plants 45 × 60cm (1½ × 2ft) apart. Make sure that the crown of each plant, where the leaves join the roots, is exactly at soil level to prevent rotting or lifting.

Using polythene sheeting Plants can be grown through black polythene sheeting to retain moisture, prevent weed growth and keep the fruits off the soil. Ideally install a seep-hose underneath the plastic for watering (see p. 93). With this method you may experience some slug problems.

Early crops under cloches The earliest harvest comes from early varieties covered with cloches. However, strawberries need a cold spell in order to initiate fruit formation, so cloches should not be put on until late winter or early spring after the plants have been subjected to frost.

'Idil'.

'Elsanta'.

'Pandora'.

'Aromel'.

Secrets of success

Strawberry plants are attractive in leaf, flower and fruit, so they can be grown very happily in the borders alongside flowers. In fact the variety 'Serenata' has eye-catching pink flowers and extremely good fruit too.

Strawing When small fruits have set, raise them slightly off the ground by tucking straw underneath the leaves. Alternatively use special strawberry mats. This will help keep the fruits clean and will deter slugs too. Don't straw too early, though, or you'll insulate the flowers from the warming effect of the soil and they may suffer frost damage.

Removing old leaves after fruiting Protect the plants from birds by netting and pick the fruits regularly as they ripen. After harvesting is finished completely, trim over the plants with a pair of shears to remove the old leaves right down to the new young crown. Then put the leaves and straw on the compost heap.

Growing in a barrel Strawberries can also be grown quite successfully in barrels. Before planting put a piece of drainpipe down the middle of the barrel and then fill around it with a soil-based compost. The drainpipe enables water to reach the bottom plants.

Gooseberries, red currants and white currants

Gooseberries are the earliest of the soft fruits and are welcome just for that. They're all self-fertile, so there's no need to grow two varieties. Ideally give them a well-drained soil in sun. In fact they will tolerate semi-shade but the berries will ripen later. It's worth buying a variety that's resistant to mildew, especially in a dry area.

They can be grown as bushes or cordons. Bushes are planted 1.5m (5ft) apart and cordons so that there's a distance of 30cm (1ft) between the upright 'arms'. Single cordons therefore go in at 30cm (1ft) intervals, doubles at 60cm (2ft) and triples at 1m (3ft). They take up only a tiny space when grown against a wall or fence. Alternatively, train them on to a free-standing post-and-wire structure to make a productive fruiting 'hedge'. Gooseberries grown alternately with red currants look very attractive.

Red and white currants are grown in exactly the same way as gooseberries and they too are self-fertile.

RIGHT Cordons These can be trained against a wall or fence or on a free-standing post-and-wire structure. Prune them in summer immediately after harvesting, reducing the side shoots to about 2.5cm (1in.) from the old wood.

Free-standing bushes These are grown on a 'leg' or short stem. In winter reduce the leading shoots by about half and remove any crossing, dead, diseased or overcrowded branches. In summer the side shoots should be reduced to about 7.5cm (3in.).

Mulching After pruning, mulch around the plants, especially gooseberries, with a thick, weed-inhibiting mulch. Gooseberries are difficult and painful to weed by hand!

Feeding Like all fruit bushes, gooseberries will respond well to a dressing of fertiliser in early spring. Use a high-potash rose feed or, if you're organic, pelleted chicken manure.

SUGGESTED VARIETIES

BELOW LEFT TO FAR RIGHT **Gooseberries**

'Early Sulphur': A very early variety bearing yellow fruits with an excellent flavour for cooking and dessert. Has no disease resistance.

'Whinham's Industry': A red-fruited variety with an excellent, sweet flavour. It fruits in mid-season and does well in shade. It has no inbred disease resistance.

'Invicta': A fairly new variety which has replaced the old favourite, 'Careless'. It produces large, green fruits with an excellent flavour and has a high resistance to mildew.

'Jubilee': Another variety bred to replace 'Careless', this has been cleaned of all virus diseases and also shows some resistance to mildew. The flavour is excellent for cooking and, if the fruit is left to ripen further, for dessert too.

Red currants

BELOW 'Laxton's No. 1': A very early variety and an old favourite. It reliably produces good crops.

'Red Lake': Very much like 'Laxton' but cropping a little later.

FAR BELOW 'Stanza': A new mid-season variety which flowers late so should miss late frosts. The flavour is exceptional.

White currants

'White Versailles': The best white currant variety, deserving to be grown more. Flavour and quality are excellent for all purposes.

Secrets of success

Both gooseberries and red currants can be grown on a standard stem. They make attractive bushes, ideally suited to a small garden, allowing you to grow other plants underneath.

Black currants

Black currants take up a lot of room but are popular and well worth growing. Their flavour is unsurpassed for eating raw, for cooking or for making drinks and they're very high in vitamin C. Unfortunately there's no really successful space-saving way to grow them, so gardeners with a small plot are best advised to restrict themselves to the one compact variety available. The plants are vigorous and hungry; plant then 1.2m (4ft) apart.

1 Unlike red and white currants, black currants are grown on a stool rather than a leg so they should be planted slightly lower in the soil than they grew in the nursery.

2 After planting cut all shoots right down to ground level to encourage strong, vigorous growth from the base. This means that no fruit will be borne the following year but a good, strong bush will be built up. The following winter no pruning is necessary.

3 In subsequent winters those shoots that have borne fruit should be cut out completely to encourage further growth from the base. It may not be possible to cut right to the ground, so prune to just above a new shoot as near the base as possible. In early spring feed with a high-potash general fertiliser.

SUGGESTED VARIETIES

RIGHT 'Ben Lomond': A heavy-cropping, mid- to late variety, producing superb-quality, large fruits with good flavour. Excellent for all purposes and shows good resistance to mildew.

RIGHT CENTRE 'Ben More': A very late-flowering variety, so good for colder gardens. Produces very heavy crops of large, well-flavoured berries. Mildew-resistant.

FAR RIGHT 'Ben Sarek': A new, compact variety which can be planted 1m (3ft) apart and so is ideal for smaller gardens. Crops are very heavy and the flavour is good.

Raspberries

Raspberries are almost an essential in most gardens since they're easy to grow and crop very heavily. The berries can be eaten fresh, cooked or frozen and, of course, made into jams and preserves. By choosing varieties carefully it's possible to harvest from mid-summer through to the first frosts, but note that the autumn-fruiting varieties are grown quite differently from the others. All raspberries need well-drained soil.

Growing summer-fruit varieties

1 Summer-fruiting raspberries are grown on a post-and-wire structure about 1.8m (6ft) high with the wires 45cm (1½ft) apart. After planting the canes 45cm (1½ft) apart with 1.8m (6ft) between rows, prune them back hard and, as they grow, tie them in at about 10cm (4in.) intervals.

2 The following year they'll fruit, after which the fruited canes should be pruned right out and the new canes tied in their place. In spring feed them with a high-potash general fertiliser.

3 Raspberries are vigorous growers and will produce canes quite some distance away from the supports. Those growing where they're not wanted are best pulled out.

SUGGESTED VARIETIES

Summer-fruiting
BELOW 'Glen Clova': A vigorous, early to mid-season variety, producing very large crops of excellent flavour.
'Glen Prosen': A mid-season variety producing heavy crops of well-flavoured fruits. Resistant to virus diseases.
'Leo': A late-fruiting variety, heavy-cropping and well-flavoured. Resistant to aphids and virus.

Growing autumn-fruiting varieties
Autumn-fruiting raspberries need no support. Prune them in late winter, cutting them right down to ground level and feed them with a high-potash fertiliser. The best variety is 'Autumn Bliss'.

Secrets of success

In small gardens there may not be room for a full row of raspberries. In this case erect a single post with two cross-bars nailed to the top and bottom. Fix wires to these and plant the canes in a circle around the post. Tie them to the wires in the normal way.

Briar fruits

Briar fruits are a bit of a mixed blessing really. While loganberries, for example, are delicious and, if you choose the thornless variety, not difficult to train, the rest can be a problem. It's essential to train them in as they grow. Blackberries and hybrid berries make vigorous, thorny bushes which can easily get out of control and they take up a lot of space which you might consider could be better used. However, for large

gardens that may not be a problem, and their vigour means that they'll do well on poor soil which might not suit other fruits. They can also be grown in semi-shade and, because of their thorns, they make an excellent boundary when grown against, say, a wire fence.

Perhaps the greatest value of briar fruits is that they come late in the season, following on from the raspberries. Allow at least 3m (10ft) between plants.

1 The supports can be much the same as those recommended for raspberries (see p. 307) with the difference that the wires are set 30cm (1ft) apart. After planting cut the canes back to within 23cm (9in.) of the ground.

2 Training is simple provided you realise that the fruit is borne, like raspberries, on canes made the year before, so after picking remove the old canes. This means separating the old from the new, and the best way is to train one year's canes to the left and the new canes made the following year to the right. It's essential to tie in the new canes as they grow. If you leave the job, the new canes will pile up on the ground into a tangled mess and they'll become quite unmanageable.

3 The only other cultivation necessary is to mulch round the plants with a good layer of manure or compost to add some nutrients and inhibit weeds.

SUGGESTED VARIETIES

RIGHT **Loganberry**
'LY 654 Thornless': Though blessed with a most unromantic name, this is the only variety worth growing and generally the only one you'll be offered. The fruits are large – about 5cm (2in.) long – and juicy.

RIGHT **Tummelberry**
A newish hybrid which comes from crossing two tayberries. The fruits are rounder and redder and the flavour's good. It's very hardy, so is good for colder districts. There is only one variety available.

ABOVE If you have the space, blackberries make a productive addition to a hedge.

Blackberries

ABOVE LEFT 'Ashton Cross': There are lots of cultivated varieties that are a pale shade of the wild ones in flavour. This gets very near to the real thing and at least you can be sure that it hasn't been covered with chemicals as those in the hedgerows may have been. Fruits are normal size and it's heavy-cropping.

ABOVE CENTRE 'Himalayan Giant': A very vigorous, thorny blackberry which can be recommended for a barrier, but beware if your garden's small. The berries are large and the flavour is good – if you can get near enough to pick them!

ABOVE RIGHT 'Merton Thornless': Truly thornless and compact. Flavour and cropping are both good.

RIGHT **Tayberry**
A cross between a raspberry and a blackberry, producing large, elongated berries of excellent flavour and quality. It's mainly used for cooking but can be eaten fresh if allowed to ripen well. Needs protecting from birds, which seem to like it more than any other briar fruit. It's fairly vigorous and thorny. There is only one variety available.

CHAPTER 15

GREENHOUSE

AND COLDFRAME

A greenhouse is probably the most expensive single item you'll buy for your garden, so you'll need to think twice about what you choose. But don't think twice about buying *something*.

The fact is that it'll extend your gardening activities right through the winter and early spring, it'll bring you hours of joy and it'll pay for itself in a few years.

A greenhouse can, of course, be as much of a tie as a dog or cat, though it needn't be if you plan things right. If you're at work all day, invest in a bit of automation which, on our scale, is cheap and effective. And when you go on holiday – cultivate your neighbour!

One final word of warning: buy the biggest model you can afford because, however big it is, I can assure you that within a couple of months it'll not be big enough.

If you do buy a greenhouse you'll really need a coldframe too. When you raise plants in heat inside, it's important to acclimatise them gently to the lower temperatures outside.

If you don't have a greenhouse, a coldframe becomes almost obligatory for propagation and to produce plants both ornamental and vegetable that would otherwise be grown in a greenhouse. It'll increase the scope of your gardening considerably and it'll pay for itself quite easily in the first season of use.

We can't all run to a real Victorian greenhouse but try to choose one that matches your own garden style.

Aluminium greenhouses Cheaper and with a contemporary appearance, these need no maintenance except cleaning. They are also available with a plastic-coated frame, generally white though green and brown are obtainable too. They suit modern houses and gardens very well and they admit maximum light.

Hexagonal greenhouses Available in both wood and aluminium, these will fit well into most gardens. They make maximum use of space and are quite deceptive in the large number of plants they'll accommodate. Because they can be sited almost anywhere, they're especially useful for very small gardens.

Plastic greenhouses Cheap and not by any stretch of the imagination beautiful. However, for areas where aesthetics don't matter they make excellent, cheap growing houses. Generally the plastic cover needs replacing about every three years, but it's still a long time before the cost reaches that of a glass structure.

Choosing a greenhouse

You can't really apply the same criteria to buying a greenhouse for the garden as those the professional grower would. A lot will depend on aesthetics, of course. You may feel that a wooden greenhouse will fit in better with your old house or that aluminium sits well in a more modern garden. That choice naturally has to be yours.

I'm quite convinced that the arguments the grower would apply – that aluminium lets in more light, though wood retains more heat and so on – are irrelevant to amateurs. For example, most of us don't start using our greenhouses for propagating young plants until early spring when there's plenty of light about anyway. It won't be long before we're actually shading to reduce the light. The two important factors to consider really are looks and price.

LEFT **Traditional wooden greenhouses** These look very attractive, especially in older gardens. But unless they're made of expensive cedar they'll need regular maintenance. Whether of cedar or cheaper softwood, they're still likely to be more expensive than aluminium.

Round, igloo-type greenhouses These have been around for a long time and find favour with many gardeners who prefer a slightly eccentric look. They certainly grow plants very well because they trap all available light, whichever direction it comes from. Like hexagonal greenhouses they're easy to site because they don't face in any particular direction. Glazing broken panes may be tricky if you're not used to glass cutting.

Conservatories These are becoming popular and can also be used to grow plants though not without some problems. They do tend to heat up very considerably, causing violent fluctuations in temperature. If they're furnished it may not be possible to raise the humidity high enough to provide ideal growing conditions. Certainly shading should be provided. Since light comes in from only two or three sides, they're not so efficient for plant raising; nonetheless they should be adequate for most purposes.

Secrets of success

All greenhouses will need adequate ventilation, so make sure that there's at least one roof vent either side for each 2.4m (8ft) run, plus side vents to match.

Equipment and special techniques for the greenhouse

Greenhouses require constant attention and cannot be left for long periods unless most of the routine work is automated. That's possible but expensive. Watering, humidity, ventilation and heating can all be controlled electronically and worked automatically, and this will find a place in some gardens. For me it defeats the object and reduces the great enjoyment of raising plants by sheer craft. But if you're at work and can adjust the heating and ventilation only in the morning and evening, it's often wisest to invest in a little technology.

Watering with a can
Young seedlings are best watered with water that has been warmed to greenhouse temperature in a tank. This is especially important in spring. You'll therefore have to apply it with a can. It's worth buying a good, long-spouted one to reach to the back of the staging and a fine rose. Initially the water will come out of the rose in a flood, so start with the can held away from the seedlings until the water's running finely and evenly.

If you do use a tank, keep it covered to prevent the build-up of green algae in the water. If it's stored under the staging, put it on three broomstick rollers so that it can easily be pulled in and out for access. Make refilling the tank your last job at night.

Watering and damping down
Later in the season a hose can be used for watering and this will, of course, save a lot of time. Make sure that you use a fitting that will provide a fine spray. If it doesn't include a pressure-control device, you can adjust the flow of water simply by kinking the hose.

As well as daily watering, the atmosphere must be kept humid, especially in hot weather. This is achieved by damping down the paths and stagings every morning and, if possible, at mid-day too. If you use capillary matting you must try to ensure that it always stays wet except in winter.

Staging
All manufacturers supply staging and it's best if you can buy from them. However, this is one area where the do-it-yourselfer can save a little money. Many stagings have a slatted top but I've found this unsatisfactory. I recommend covering the top with a sheet of waterproofed plywood. Cover this in turn with strong polythene and then with a sheet of absorbent capillary matting. This system makes watering much easier and more controllable.

Ventilation

Correct ventilation is important. As a rule you should always try to get some air movement through the house during the day by opening the ventilators even just a crack. This discourages fungus disease. If you heat with paraffin or gas there should be a tiny amount of ventilation at all times. In summer you may need to ventilate day and night. If you're away during the day you'll have to rely on automatic openers, in which case a thermostatically controlled fan is best.

Providing bottom heat

For propagation, some form of bottom heat is needed. A small electric propagator will suffice for a few plants, but I use a heated blanket which covers a large area. It's laid on a piece of polystyrene and then covered with polythene followed by capillary matting. To arrive at three different temperatures I set the thermostat to about 18°C (65°F), then put anything that needs a slightly lower temperature on an upturned seed tray and those that want more heat under a polythene cloche.

Space heating

I prefer electricity because of its convenience and, provided your heater has a thermostat, it's cheap. If you don't have an electricity supply, use bottled or mains gas or paraffin. In winter fit panels of polystyrene to the glass below the staging and bubble polythene to the glazing bars above it. Remove them in early spring. You'll need to know the lowest temperature at night and the highest by day, so a maximum/minimum thermometer is essential too.

Shading

During the summer it's most likely that some form of shading will be necessary. Shades that can be drawn up and down are ideal and there are types that fit inside or outside the greenhouse, but they are fairly expensive. Green polythene sheeting can be fixed inside the house for the summer but this can cause some condensation problems. I prefer to paint the outside with a special shading paint.

Using manufactured composts

It's generally recommended that manufactured composts should not be mixed with anything else, but there are certain cases where some 'doctoring' is an advantage. I generally use coir compost and to this I add a controlled-release fertiliser to avoid supplementary feeding during the season. If you do add fertiliser, work with as large a quantity of the mix as you can to ensure even distribution.

Using soil composts

Soil composts like the John Innes range can also be adjusted for specific plants. For alpines I use JI No. 1, but I add an equal amount of extra grit to make a really well-drained compost. Some gardeners utilise garden soil or make use of stacked turves for the loam content, and they sterilise it in a microwave oven. I've never done this but have heard that it's successful for small amounts.

Making the best use of a coldframe

If you have a greenhouse an almost obligatory accessory is a coldframe. If you don't have a greenhouse, a frame's absolutely essential. It's quite surprising how much you can raise without any heat at all, and if you add a special heater you have a complete mini-greenhouse that can be used in much the same way as the full-scale version. Naturally, because the space is so much more limited, a coldframe is very cheap to heat, but there's the obvious snag that you can't actually get inside it yourself. While the plants can be kept snug, therefore, it's not quite as comfortable for the gardener.

There are several models available at garden centres and it's not too difficult to make your own (see p. 56).

RIGHT A brick-built frame is attractive and retains heat well in winter.

LEFT **Hardening off** One of the great secrets of raising plants successfully is to keep them growing smoothly without a check. So, when transferring greenhouse-raised plants to the open ground, acclimatise them slowly to the lower temperatures. This is known as 'hardening off' (see p. 103).

BELOW **Rooting cuttings** Frames are extremely useful for propagation. If the base is lined with wet sand, the humidity is very conducive to rapid rooting. Cuttings can be put into pots or rooted direct into a bed of compost. Covering with a sheet of very thin polythene and then closing the frame lid is a well-tried method.

Winter sowing In winter the coldframe is the ideal place to germinate seeds of alpines and other plants that require a cold spell before they'll germinate. They'll still be subjected to freezing weather but the frame covering will protect them from excess rain. Always ventilate the frame a little, day and night.

Spring and summer sowing In spring and summer many seeds can be germinated and grown on in pots, trays or modules in the frame. Subjects like hardy annuals, many herbaceous perennials and most hardy vegetables require no extra heat for germination but will relish protection from excess heat and wind.

Raising early vegetables Early vegetables can also be raised in frames in exactly the same way as that recommended for cloches (see p. 246).

The heated coldframe If the frame is heated with either a low-wattage electric or a paraffin heater or soil-warming cables, it can be used in exactly the same way as a greenhouse to produce plenty of seedlings and to grow on vegetables and flowers to maturity over a very much extended season.

Greenhouse vegetables

The greenhouse can be used to grow vegetables much earlier than could be achieved outside and to produce some types that would be impossible out of doors. First you need to decide whether or not to heat the house. While heating will naturally allow you to produce earlier crops, the cost often outweighs the advantage. For the majority of amateur gardeners it's probably most sensible to use a small heated area for propagation – perhaps a propagator or a part of the staging cut off from the rest by polythene curtains – and to save the cost of heating the whole greenhouse. Alternatively young plants could be raised indoors and transferred to the unheated greenhouse later to advance harvesting and improve quality. Naturally timing is important.

Tomatoes

The tomato is certainly the most popular greenhouse vegetable and with good reason. You'll easily supply all your summer needs from a small greenhouse and the earliest fruits will be harvested when those in the shops are expensive.

1 LEFT Sow in early spring in seed trays in a temperature of about 18°C (65°F) and transfer to 9cm (3½in.) pots as soon as the seed leaves have completely unfurled. Handle with care since damage to even one seed leaf will result in a smaller, later plant.

2 Make sure that the young plants have plenty of space on the staging. This will necessitate spacing them more widely as they grow, in order to produce strong, bushy plants.

3 By mid-spring the weather should be warm enough to plant them out into an unheated greenhouse. The minimum temperature needs to be about 10–13°C (50–55°F). Plant either directly into well-prepared soil, or into growing bags, or into 23cm (9in.) pots of soilless compost. To support the plants tie a strong nylon string to the greenhouse structure immediately above each one and bury the other end under the root ball.

4 As the plants grow they should be twisted round the strings regularly. It's also necessary to remove the shoots that will appear in the leaf joints. Do this while the shoots are still small.

5 After the first three weeks, start to feed the plants regularly with a liquid tomato fertiliser. Recommendations vary, but I feed mine at every watering except once a week when I use clear water to flush away any build-up of mineral salts. If the top growth of the stem begins to look thin, change to a fertiliser high in nitrogen. The bottom leaves should be removed only when they have started to turn brown and are obviously not performing a useful function. Take them off just as far as the truss that's ripening. Harvest regularly to encourage further production of fruit.

Aubergines

Aubergines can be grown in the same greenhouse as tomatoes and peppers, and in much the same way. They make bigger, more vigorous plants than peppers.

1 Sow in the same way as tomatoes and at the same time. Prick out into 9cm (3½in.) pots and then straight into their final 23cm (9in.) size.

2 Stake and tie the plants as they grow and feed as recommended for tomatoes. With aubergines and peppers, however, there's no 'side-shooting' to do as there is in the case of tomatoes.

Greenhouse vegetables

Cucumbers

Most of the problems of cucumbers have been overcome by the plant breeders. With all-female varieties, there's no longer any need to prevent insects pollinating flowers by removing male flowers or netting doors and vents. These new F1 hybrids also have the advantage of increased vigour so that there's now no problem with growing them in the same greenhouse as tomatoes. It goes without saying, therefore, that you should start by buying an all-female F1 hybrid variety.

1 RIGHT Germinate seeds in mid-spring in 9cm (3½in.) pots of soilless compost in a temperature of about 21°C (70°F). Because the seeds are flat, they're generally pushed into the compost on their sides to avoid water lying on them and rotting them. Sow two seeds per pot and remove the weaker seedling.

2 Plant into growing bags or 23cm (9in.) pots of soilless compost. Do this a little later than for tomatoes since cucumbers require a slightly higher temperature. They can be supported in the same way as tomatoes (see p. 318).

3 LEFT Unlike the older types, new varieties of cucumber bear fruit on the main stem, so don't remove any young fruits. As side shoots develop, trim them back to leave two leaves. Feed with a tomato fertiliser twice a week. Harvest regularly to encourage further production.

Sweet peppers

Similar to tomatoes in their requirements, sweet peppers are fairly easy to grow though not quite so prolific. They'll live happily in the same house as tomatoes.

Sow them just like tomatoes and pot into 7.5cm (3in.) pots. Peppers have a small root system, so don't surround them with a mass of cold, wet compost. It's better to pot them on into a 10cm (4in.) pot and finally into a 20cm (8in.) one for cropping.

Stake and tie the plants with a short cane and soft string. Feed as recommended for tomatoes (see p. 319). It's often suggested that the number of fruits should be restricted, but I've never found this necessary. The plants will produce reasonable crops of good-sized fruits. Commercial growers now grow peppers up strings just like tomatoes.

French beans

Dwarf French beans can be sown in the greenhouse at the beginning and end of the season to prolong harvesting. They're very welcome at these times and, of course, more expensive to buy. Sow in early autumn and again in early spring. They need a temperature of about 10–13 °C (50–55 °F). Use 23cm (9in.) pots of soilless compost, placing five or six seeds round the edges. A stake in the middle will allow you to tie each plant in as necessary. Spray the plants daily with water to help pollinate the flowers and feed weekly, starting three weeks after germination.

Potatoes

The very earliest crop of potatoes can be produced in the greenhouse, though it's not a good idea to grow them in the same borders as tomatoes since they're subject to similar diseases. Instead put three tubers into a 30cm (12in.) pot. I prefer to use a soil-based compost like John Innes No. 3 to which extra garden compost has been added. Half-fill the pot before setting the tubers and then fill almost to the top. Feed with a liquid fertiliser six weeks after the foliage appears.

Herbs

A tub of herbs brought into the greenhouse for winter will provide a fresh supply during the coldest months.

Lettuce

There are really two seasons for growing greenhouse lettuce. They can be planted directly into the border soil in the autumn and overwintered for spring harvesting; alternatively a few plants can be potted in early spring for the earliest harvest of the year.

Greenhouse fruit

There are several fruiting plants which can be profitably grown in a cool greenhouse, many of them requiring nothing more than frost protection. Indeed, citrus fruits, for example, will relish being put outside during the summer, releasing valuable space.

RIGHT Citrus fruit
Though oranges, lemons and grapefruit can be grown from pips, there's no guarantee when they'll flower or what the fruit will be like. It's much better to buy a named variety from a specialist nursery. They're easy to grow but must be kept cool in summer when it's wisest to put them outside. In winter they need to be kept just frost-free. Then simply water as necessary, feed once a week in summer and prune out overcrowded or crossing branches in winter.

RIGHT Strawberries
Strawberries can be forced under glass for the earliest crops of the year. Pot up some runners in summer (see p. 8) into 18cm (7in.) pots and leave them outside. In autumn turn the pots on to their sides to keep the plants dry and bring them inside in late winter after they've been subjected to frost. It's a good idea to hand pollinate by dabbing each of the flowers with a soft brush to increase pollination.

BELOW Peaches
Peaches are grown in the greenhouse like fan-trained peaches outside, with one important variation. Under glass they'll flower earlier, so there will be few, if any, insects to pollinate them. You will therefore have to do this yourself by transferring pollen from flower to flower with a soft brush.

BELOW Melons
Grow melons in 23cm (9in.) pots of coir compost and feed them at every other watering with a tomato fertiliser, but bear in mind that they'll require less water than cucumbers. Otherwise grow them in the same way. Support the fruits as they grow and harvest when the flower end feels soft.

ABOVE Figs
Figs can be grown in the border soil but the roots will need to be restricted with a lining of bricks in the planting pit. They do very well grown in pots filled with a soil-based compost. Prune by cutting out old wood in winter or early spring. When the fruit is swelling, feed weekly with a tomato fertiliser. Grow figs either trained as fans against a lean-to wall or as standards.

Grapes

1 Grapes are the most popular greenhouse fruit and, since they're not at the mercy of the weather, they'll usually produce a good crop every year. Plant a young plant at the end of the greenhouse in the border soil and, in the first year, train the resulting main stem up a cane until it reaches the ridge and then tie it in along it. Pinch back and tie in side shoots after they've made five leaves and sub-laterals after one leaf.

2 At the end of the season cut back the side shoots to leave one good bud and reduce the main stem by a third of the wood it made that year. This pruning should be done every year immediately after the leaves have fallen.

3 In the following year look for embryo bunches of grapes and pinch back those shoots two leaves beyond the bunches. You want one bunch every 930 sq. cm (1 sq. ft), so rub out the rest. Tie in selected shoots.

4 As bunches of eating grapes grow, they should be thinned to produce good-sized fruit. This is simply a case of removing some berries to allow others more space. Start when they're the size of pearl barley and look at them a second time when they're as big as peas. You'll almost certainly find then that you haven't removed enough, so go over them again.

5 Grapes can also be grown as standards in pots. Allow the main stem to run up to the required height and then prune it back to encourage branching. Pinch out the side shoots in the usual way as the fruits set. All grapes need maximum ventilation and should be sprayed over with water twice a day, if possible, until the fruit begins to ripen. Feed weekly with tomato fertiliser after flowering.

Pot plants from the greenhouse

There's an enormous range of flowering and foliage pot plants that can be grown in a cool greenhouse for use in decorating the house or the greenhouse itself. However, for most of us it's feasible to grow only those that need lower temperatures. The days of the old-fashioned stovehouse disappeared, alas, with the Victorians and cheap coal.

However, this still leaves a very wide range, so I have stuck to those plants that need a minimum winter temperature of 7°C (45°F). Most of the plants described here will need extra heat for germination, of course, so an electric propagator or a heated bench will be required. In summer the maximum daytime temperature should be kept as near 18–21°C (65–70°F) as possible, which may mean shading the greenhouse and will certainly require full ventilation during the day and sometimes at night too.

All the following plants can be grown in soilless compost and fed with a liquid fertiliser high in potash. A year-round succession of colour is quite possible.

BELOW **Florist's carnations** These can't be raised successfully from seed, so you'll have to buy plants and propagate them from cuttings. Pot up young plants in spring and pot them on as required to 15–18cm (6–7in.) final pots. Keep them in the coldframe from early summer onwards and pinch out the main stem to produce bushy plants. This pinching should continue until mid-summer. Stake and tie them as necessary and bring them into the greenhouse in late summer, still keeping them as cool as possible. When the shoots start to produce buds, remove all but the one at the tip of the shoot to make larger flowers. Feed weekly. Propagate from cuttings taken in late winter or early spring.

ABOVE **Chrysanthemums** Early-flowering varieties can be grown outside like most herbaceous plants (see p. 186), but late flowerers will need a greenhouse. Start with plants bought from a specialist and pot up into 23cm (9in.) final pots. The plants go outside in May where they're staked and tied regularly. The nurseryman's catalogue will tell you when to pinch out the tops and the resulting shoots should be tied in as they grow. Disbud (as for carnations) to produce larger flowers and feed weekly. Bring into the greenhouse in late summer for flowering. After flowering cut down the plants and leave them just moist until early spring when they can again be put on the staging and sprayed over to produce cuttings.

Asparagus ferns (*Asparagus sprengeri*; *A. plumosus* 'Nanus') Attractive foliage plants. Sow them in early spring in a temperature of 18°C (65°F) in 7.5cm (3in.) pots and pot them on as their roots fill the pots. *A. sprengeri* will need a 13cm (5in.) final pot, but *A. plumosus* 'Nanus' can be kept in a 9–10cm (3½–4in.) one.

Slipper flowers (*Calceolaria* hybrids) Easy to grow, these have quite stunning flowers. They're best sown in mid-summer in a coldframe. Grow them on there until early autumn, potting them on as their roots fill the pots. They'll need final pots of 9–18cm (3½–7in.), depending on their size. They hate being too hot and should never be allowed to dry out completely, so you may need to shade them in summer. Feed weekly.

Cigar plants (*Cuphea ignea*) Pretty little plants that are easy to grow from seed. Sow in early spring at 18°C (65°F) and pot into final 9–10cm (3½–4in.) pots when the seedlings are big enough using a standard soilless compost. Feed weekly with a fertiliser high in potash. Dispose of the plants after flowering.

Cinerarias These indispensable plants can be had in flower over winter and spring. Sow in early summer at 18°C (65°F) and transfer the seedlings to small pots when they're big enough. Pot on as required to final 18–20cm (7–8in.) pots. The plants should spend summer in the coldframe and be brought inside in late summer. Give them plenty of room to develop and feed weekly. Shading may be necessary in summer.

Flame nettles (*Coleus blumei*) Attractive foliage plants in a variety of colours. Sow in early spring at 18°C (65°F) and pot into small pots when the seedlings are big enough. Pot on into 13–18cm (5–7in.) final pots as necessary and feed weekly. Good plants can be propagated from cuttings.

Half-hardy annuals Many half-hardy annuals can be grown as pot plants in the greenhouse. They can all be raised from seed sown from early spring right through to late summer. Sow them in a temperature of 18°C (65°F) and finally pot them into 9–10cm (3½–4in.) pots. Feed weekly.

Indian shot (*Canna indica*) A tall and striking plant for the back of a display. Sow in early spring, soaking the seeds overnight first and germinating at 21°C (70°F). Pot on as required, finishing in a 15–20cm (6–8in.) pot. Water freely and feed twice weekly.

Pot plants from the greenhouse

Fuchsias Generally raised from cuttings, so you'll have to start by buying plants in early spring. Pot them into 9cm (3½in.) pots and continue potting on into successively larger pots. They can be flowered in pots of 10–18cm (4–7in.) in diameter. Pinch out the tips of the branches to make bushy plants, but stop pinching six weeks before flowers are required. Keep them reasonably cool during summer and spray them often with clear water. Feed twice weekly. In autumn gradually dry them off and overwinter them under the staging, where you should keep them quite dry. Bring them back on to the staging in early spring and prune the bushes back quite hard. Increase the watering and spray them overhead to induce growth. This is also a good time to take cuttings to increase stock, though I make sure I overwinter enough strong, young plants taken from cuttings in August. They need only to be kept frost-free during the winter.

Cyclamen Popular plants for a cool greenhouse and excellent for winter and spring display. Sow at 15–18°C (60–65°F) in late summer for flowering at Christmas of the following year and in late winter for flowering in spring of the next year. Prick out into seed trays and keep the seedlings constantly moist. Grow them on at 10°C (50°F). When they have made good roots, pot them on successively to their final 13–15cm (5–6in.) pots. Put them in the coldframe for the summer and feed weekly. In autumn bring them in for flowering. After flowering, dry them off and store them in their pots until mid-summer. Then repot the tubers and start again.

RIGHT **Roses** The miniature and patio roses particularly make good pot plants and cut flowers. In autumn pot new plants into 18–23cm (7–9in.) pots, depending on their size. Prune them as recommended for outdoor roses (see p. 197). Feed twice weekly once they start to grow. Flower them inside and after flowering put them out. In autumn prune them again and repeat the process. Eventually you'll need to repot them.

Regal pelargoniums Bought plants should be potted into small pots and moved on until their final 13–18cm (5–7in.) pots. Grow them as cool as possible and, after they have flowered in mid-summer, put them into a coldframe. Cuttings can then be taken and the plants should be cut back quite hard, repotted and sprayed to induce new growth. Bring them in to overwinter and start them into growth with increased light, watering and spraying in late winter. Feed weekly.

Winter cherry (*Solanum capsicastrum*) Easy to grow as an annual. It can be pruned and grown for a second year, but will probably be of poorer quality. Sow in early spring at 18°C (65°F). Pot the seedlings into small pots and successively to their final 10cm (4in.) pots. In early summer they're best grown outside and fed weekly. Bring them into the greenhouse to berry in early autumn.

Gerberas Easy to raise from seed sown in early spring at 18°C (65°F). Pot the seedlings into small pots and successively up to the final 18cm (7in.) size. They can be grown on in the coldframe during summer or kept as cool as possible in the greenhouse. In winter reduce watering and just keep the plants 'ticking over' until restarting them into growth in early spring.

Gloxinias Handsome, tuberous-rooted plants which can be started in late winter by simply buying tubers and half-burying them in a pot of soilless compost. They can also be raised from seed sown in late winter or in late summer at 18°C (65°F). Pot the seedlings on successively to final 10–15cm (4–6in.) pots. Give them plenty of light and feed weekly. In winter reduce watering and allow the tubers to rest until repotting in late winter.

Exacums Flowering from June to October, these are also easy to grow. Sow in early spring at 18°C (65°F) and pot into final 9–10cm (3½–4in.) pots when the seedlings are big enough. Feed weekly and spray over with clear water frequently, because they prefer a humid atmosphere.

Primulas The best for pot plants are *Primula obconica*, *P. malacoides*, *P. kewensis* and *P. sinensis*. Sow *P. sinensis* and *P. malacoides* in late spring and again in early summer at 15°C (60°F). Sow *P. kewensis* and *P. obconica* in early spring. Pot the seedlings into small pots and successively into their final 13cm (5in.) pots. Keep them cool and shaded at all times. In summer they're best in the coldframe. Feed weekly.

Cape primroses (*Streptocarpus*) Sow in late winter at 18°C (65°F). Pot the seedlings into small pots and successively move them on to their final 13–15cm (5–6in.) pots. Avoid firming them too hard. Grow the plants on at about 13°C (55°F), providing shading if necessary. Feed weekly when the plants are growing vigorously. Good specimens can be increased by leaf cuttings (see p. 117).

327

CHAPTER 16

PESTS AND

DISEASES

This is a difficult chapter for me. I firmly believe, and indeed have proved to my own satisfaction, that chemical pest control is counter-productive. There's no doubt that, in the commercial field, pests are now a greater problem than ever they were before we started using chemical controls in a big way, and I see no reason to repeat this in the garden.

The fact is that most sprays, even the so-called 'organic' ones, are pretty indiscriminate, killing the enemies of the pests as well as the pests themselves. And because almost without exception the pests will breed faster and re-establish themselves more quickly than their predators, spraying can only make things worse in the end.

Mind you, I have to admit that it does take two or three years to build up a balanced local ecology with good colonies of predators in the garden or regularly visiting. So you'll almost certainly have problems initially. In my view it's much better to grin and bear it and wait for a peaceful harmony to become established. If you feel you have to use chemicals, however, do so with the greatest caution.

I have *never* sprayed my garden in the nine years I've been there and I have few problems. I do use some physical controls, but I'm careful only to protect plants and not to kill other wildlife.

Methods of chemical control

All chemicals for use in the garden have to be treated with the greatest caution. Most are poisonous to a greater or lesser degree and will do much harm if used in any way contrary to the makers' instructions. If that sounds alarmist, I make no apologies.

Used properly, they'll certainly do all that's claimed of them, so the very first step must be to read the instructions on the bottle or pack or on any accompanying leaflet carefully and to stick to them.

The best time to spray is in the early morning or the late evening when there are fewer insects about and the sun is not strong enough to scorch the plant leaves.

Always wait for a calm day and never spray in strong sunlight. Spray as soon as you see the first signs of attack.

If you're spraying vegetables or fruit, check the required delay between spraying and harvesting.

Never spray open flowers or you kill pollinating insects. Bees are particularly vulnerable to chemicals.

In most countries it's illegal for amateur gardeners to use products recommended only for professionals or to use anything not approved by the legislating body – and that includes washing-up liquid and boiled rhubarb leaves!

BELOW **Safe storage** Chemicals are at their most dangerous in the concentrated state, so it's vital to ensure that bottles or packs can't fall into the wrong hands. Always store them out of reach of children and pets and preferably under lock and key. Keep them in their original packs or bottles so that you know exactly what they are. In the United Kingdom and other EC countries chemicals are marked with symbols denoting their dangers. Get to know them and be aware of the risks. If you lose the labels from the bottles, it's safest to dispose of them: contact your local council, which will generally operate a safe disposal scheme.

✖ **harmful**	✖ **irritant**
oxidising	**highly flammable**
toxic	**explosive** **corrosive**

ABOVE **Measuring as instructed**
Measure out chemicals carefully and never put in a little extra 'just for luck'. All have been carefully formulated and tested to give the best results with the greatest degree of safety, so stick by the instructions to the letter. Mix only the amount required for the job in hand since you shouldn't store diluted chemicals. Sometimes separate chemicals can be mixed, but again this should only be on the advice of the manufacturers. You should certainly never mix two chemicals from different makers. If you do mix, say, a fungicide and an insecticide together, remember that you'll need one measure of each in the *same volume* of water. If you're in doubt, it's generally possible to buy a 'cocktail' made up by the manufacturers in concentrated form.

BELOW **Disposal of 'left-overs'** After spraying, dispose of any unused solution on to uncultivated soil or on a path and wash it off with a hose. It's essential to wash out the sprayer thoroughly. Don't trust yourself to remember what you had in it last time, for that could lead to disaster. It's much better to start with clean equipment and finish with it clean too.

BELOW **Using a hand sprayer** When you're applying a contact insecticide, the pests have to be drenched with the chemical, so here a thorough soaking on top of and beneath the leaves is the order of the day. In the greenhouse a small hand sprayer is ideal for this and very cheap. In fact many sprays are now packed in trigger sprayers, so you may not need to buy a separate one and there's no danger of leaving residues of another spray in it.

BELOW **Dusting** Some insecticides are available in dust form and this can be a handy way of applying them in small quantities. Give the container a good shake first and hold it some way away from the plant so as to create a fine dusting rather than a thick coat.

Using a pressure sprayer Certainly the best bet for most chemicals. Remember that some chemicals need to be taken into the plants' tissue to be effective, so you should try to ensure that the tiny drops of liquid remain on the leaves. Once they start to join together, the surface tension is lost and most of the spray will run off. With these 'systemic' insecticides, therefore, a light spray over is most effective.

When handling *any* chemical spray you should wear gloves, and for most it's worthwhile going the whole hog just to be on the safe side. That means rubber boots, gloves, goggles and a face mask and preferably an old waterproof coat too. Even then, wash your hands thoroughly when you've finished.

Methods of chemical control

PESTS OF ORNAMENTALS

Some pests of ornamental plants are easy to identify. A heavy infestation of greenfly, for example, is not difficult to spot. Some attacks, though, have to be recognised by the symptoms alone and that can be more tricky. There's a great danger of over-reacting to small holes or marks on leaves which are often caused by physical damage, frost, wind or rain, or sometimes by an isolated pest which will not present great problems. It would be a mistake in these instances to splash too much chemical spray about, so wait until you see regular signs of damage. Even then always remember that most insecticides will kill indiscriminately.

Some pests of ornamentals will also attack fruit and vegetables. If you don't find a reference here, check pp. 334–7. Sometimes organic controls are much more effective than chemicals, so you should also see pp. 344–7.

RIGHT AND FAR RIGHT **Eelworms and narcissus fly** Bulbs in particular are attacked by eelworms, which can't be seen but which cause softening and rotting. When the bulb is cut open, dark rings are revealed inside.

Narcissus fly attacks daffodils, also causing rotting but no brown rings. When the affected bulbs are cut open, the maggots may be visible.

There's no cure for either pest, so throw away infected bulbs and don't plant on the same plot for five or six years.

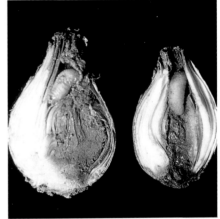

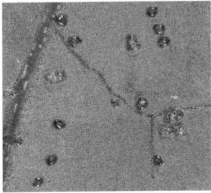
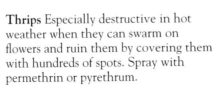
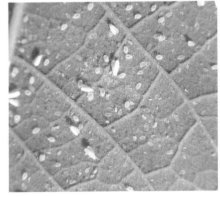

Leaf miners These burrow inside leaves and are a particular pest of chrysanthemums. They're difficult to get at, so a systemic insecticide is useful. One containing permethrin and heptenophos is effective.

Thrips Especially destructive in hot weather when they can swarm on flowers and ruin them by covering them with hundreds of spots. Spray with permethrin or pyrethrum.

Whitefly Most troublesome in the greenhouse. Though they do attack outdoor plants, particularly members of the cabbage family, they do little damage, generally arriving only late in the season. Inside spray with permethrin or insecticidal soaps (see p. 347), but because they have a very short life cycle, be sure to do so at least three times at intervals of not less then seven days.

Leafhoppers These cause small, yellow spots on leaves and are commonly seen on geraniums and primulas. They may carry virus diseases, so control, by means of malathion, pirimiphos-methyl or fenitrothion is advisable.

Aphids Greenfly and blackfly are among the most persistent pests in the garden and between them will attack almost anything. Some have a wide range of hosts while others attack only one plant. They're easy to recognise and to kill with a contact or systemic insecticide. There are dozens available but one containing pirimicarb is best since it will kill only aphids and, alas, the hoverfly larvae that feed on them.

Caterpillars There are many kinds which attack many different plants, eating holes in the centre and edges of leaves and sometimes skeletonising leaves or completely defoliating trees or shrubs. Spray with permethrin, derris or pyrethrum bifenthrin.

Slugs and snails These are widespread and exist in huge numbers – so much so that complete control is impossible. Use pellets containing metaldehyde or methiocarb, but be sparing. Research has shown that they are most effective when placed at 18cm (7in.) spacings and that put closer they repel rather than kill.

Woodlice These feed mainly on decomposed material but will also attack live plants, especially those that have already been damaged. They cause large, irregular holes in leaves. Control is difficult, but slug pellets help.

Capsid bugs These attack many flowering plants, particularly dahlias and chrysanthemums. They make spots on the leaves which eventually enlarge to holes and they eat the petals inside forming buds, causing gross distortion of the flowers. Spray with fenitrothion or pirimiphos-methyl as soon as damage is seen on the leaves.

Vine weevils Extremely damaging pests. The adults attack the leaves of shrubs, rhododendrons being especially at risk. The larvae are most dangerous, though, since they'll feed on the roots of almost any plant both in the greenhouse and outside. They can be controlled biologically in two ways, but there is no control available chemically (see p. 347).

Methods of chemical control

PESTS OF VEGETABLES

Because you're eventually going to eat them, extra care must be taken when spraying food plants. Make sure that the chemical you intend using is specifically recommended for food crops and take careful note of the harvesting interval – the time that must elapse between spraying and eating. Wash all vegetables carefully prior to eating them, whether or not they're going to be cooked: don't be tempted to eat them raw in the garden before they've been washed. And, of course, never make the chemical spray solution stronger than is recommended. Finally spray only as a very last resort.

I have included chemical controls alone here, so please check the organic methods on pp. 344–7 too. Some are more effective than chemicals. For control of whitefly, slugs and snails see pp. 332–3.

Flea beetle This pest attacks mainly young seedlings, though I've seen it devastate large Chinese cabbage plants too. It's found mostly on turnips, swedes, radish, Chinese cabbage and all members of the cabbage family. It makes numerous tiny holes in the leaves and should be dealt with as soon as the first symptoms are seen. Dusting with derris is very effective.

Blackfly This aphid attacks all kinds of beans – broad beans in particular – clustering round the young growing tips and sucking the sap. It's very easy to identify. Generally it's enough just to nip off the tip of the plant, or you can spray with pirimicarb. Other aphids are treated in the same way.

Pea and bean weevils U-shaped notches in the edges of the leaves are signs of these pests. They generally cause little damage, but if seedlings are attacked, spray with malathion, permethrin or pirimiphos-methyl.

Cabbage white butterflies The caterpillars of these and many other species of butterfly can be a nuisance, making holes in leaves and, if left, completely skeletonising them. The caterpillars can be seen in clusters under the leaves. Spray with derris.

Carrot fly Attacks carrots, parsnips, Hamburg parsley, celeriac, celery and parsley, tunnelling into the roots to make characteristic brown marks. This often leads to fungus diseases getting a hold too. Dust pirimiphos-methyl down the drills at sowing time and repeat in August if necessary.

Red spider mite Attacks cucumbers and tomatoes in the greenhouse, but also French beans, courgettes, marrows and cucumbers outside in hot, dry weather. The individual mites can only just be seen, but they cause speckling and discoloration of the leaves which eventually dry up and die. Spray weekly with bifenthrin or pirimiphos-methyl or insecticidal soap if the infestation is severe.

Cutworms, leatherjackets, chafer grubs and wireworms All these attack below the ground or, in the case of cutworms, just at ground level and are particularly troublesome in recently cultivated soil. They can be controlled by hoeing bromophos into the soil.

The cockchafer beetle does no harm itself but should be picked off before it produces its very damaging grubs.

ABOVE AND FAR ABOVE
Cutworm and leatherjacket.

Wireworm.

Mice Can be a problem early in the season when they dig up and eat pea and bean seeds. They're difficult to control with chemicals but can be deterred with mothballs or by setting traps.

Onion fly The most serious pest of onions and leeks, causing the outer leaves to yellow and wilt in early summer. Little white maggots can be found at the base of the plant, and these can kill small plants. Dust rows with pirimiphos-methyl to control when the seedlings are small and again two weeks later.

Pea moth A common pest of peas, producing the well-known maggots inside the pods. It's only necessary to worry about it affecting plants flowering between June and August, when you can spray with permethrin a week after flowering.

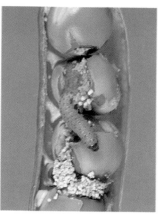

Cabbage root fly The maggots of this pest feed on the young roots of all members of the cabbage family. The first symptoms are lack of growth and a bluish colour, but plants quickly wilt. Then it's generally too late to rectify the problem. Dust seed rows with pirimiphos-methyl at planting time.

Methods of chemical control

PESTS OF FRUIT

Commercial fruit growers keep up a constant
programme of spraying whether there are attacks or not.
It's not necessary for gardeners to go quite this far, but
once you commit yourself to chemical controls you'll
have to do a certain amount of preventative spraying
even though the plants may look perfectly clean.

RIGHT **Aphids** All kinds attack most fruit trees. They may
look identical to the ordinary greenfly and blackfly that you
find on roses and other plants or they may be covered in a
grey, mealy coating. Woolly aphid (illustrated) actually cloaks
itself with a protective coat of a white, waxy material, which
makes it very difficult to control. Many aphids also excrete
sticky honeydew on which black, sooty moulds grow. Destroy
overwintering eggs with a winter wash of tar-oil when the
plants are completely dormant and spray with a systemic
insecticide just before or just after flowering. To control
woolly aphid, the spray will need to be forceful to break
through its protective coating. Apple and pear suckers look
rather like aphids and they feed on flowers. Control them in
the same way.

Raspberry beetle This feeds on the
ripening fruit and can often be seen at
harvest time. It also attacks briar fruits.
Spray raspberries with derris when you
see the first pink fruits. Spray
blackberries just as the first flowers
open and loganberries after flowering
and when the fruits start to colour.

Strawberry seed beetle A shiny, black
beetle that feeds on the fruits. Spray
unripe fruits with bifenthrin at dusk to
control.

Winter moth The caterpillars eat new
leaves and flowers of apple trees and are
a serious pest. Spray with permethrin as
leaves emerge from buds.

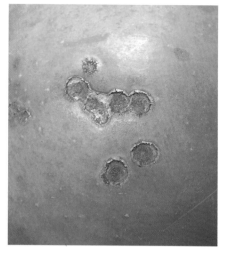

Apple sawfly The larvae burrow into fruit after feeding on the surface. You can recognise an attack by characteristic, ribbon-like scars on the skin. Spray with permethrin about a week after the blossom has fallen, soaking the young fruits. Also pick up and destroy apples that fall in June.

Capsid bug Not a serious problem for amateur gardeners but it does damage to apples and currants in particular. It tends to cause a puckering and distortion of leaves, giving them a tattered appearance, and is responsible for small bumps on the skin of apples. If you feel it's absolutely necessary they can be controlled by spraying with permethrin when the petals have fallen.

Pear midge Attacks fruitlets, turning them black. They eventually fall and, if you cut one open, you'll see tiny grubs inside. Pick up fallen fruits and burn them and, if attacks are regular, spray with fenitrothion or pirimiphos-methyl at the white bud stage.

Red spider mite This attacks some fruit trees, causing the same sort of symptoms seen on vegetables – spotting and eventually drying of the leaves. Spray with bifenthrin, pirimiphos-methyl or fenitrothion.

Codling moth The most serious pest of apples. The maggot-like caterpillars tunnel into developing fruits and feed inside. They leave a powdery, brown 'frass' on the outside and will often be found within. Spray with permethrin four weeks after the petals fall and again three weeks later.

Big bud gall mite Attacks blackcurrants, causing buds to swell. It also transmits a virus called 'reversion virus' which dramatically reduces crops. Look for enlarged buds in winter and pick them off. Spraying with the fungicide carbendazim as the first flowers open gives some incidental control. If attacks are severe, the bushes will have to be destroyed.

Gooseberry sawfly The larvae can devastate bushes within days, completely stripping off the leaves. Attacks are likely in late spring and can continue until autumn. As soon as they're seen, pick off as many as possible and if the attack continues spray with derris.

Methods of chemical control

DISEASES OF ORNAMENTALS

The first step with all diseases of ornamental plants is to remove infected areas/plant parts immediately. Get rid of them completely by putting them in a plastic bag and confining them to the dustbin. Never put them on the compost heap or leave them lying beside the infected plant. An eagle eye and quick action can often make chemicals unnecessary. Remember that you can't usually cure fungus diseases: you can only stop them spreading.

Powdery mildew A result of dry conditions, this causes characteristic, white, mealy growths on leaves and stems. Spray with carbendazim or bupirimate with triforine and repeat at two-week intervals if it persists.

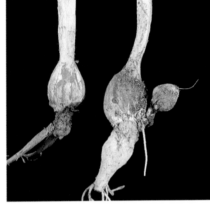

Tuber rot Attacks mainly dahlias in store. Inspect them regularly, and if you see any parts turning brown and soft, cut them out to healthy tissue and treat the cut area with sulphur powder.

Leaf spots These come in all shapes and sizes from brown blotches to round, reddish spots and concentric circles of spores. Most are difficult to control, but regular sprays with mancozeb will help.

Virus diseases These show in various forms and sometimes do no damage at all. Often they cause leaves to turn yellow and this could be the reason for the attractive leaf colour of some variegated plants. Leaves may also be spotted, streaked, crumpled and distorted, and plants can be stunted. There's no cure except digging out, but spraying against insects may prevent these diseases being spread.

Rust This photograph of the top of the leaf shows this serious disease, which attacks roses in particular and many herbaceous plants. It causes red, yellow or brown spots on the underside of leaves. It's extremely difficult to control but fortnightly sprays with myclobutanil will help. As with most diseases there are some varieties less prone to attack than others, so search them out if you can.

Petal blight Not a life-threatening disease, but it can spoil prized blooms, attacking mainly chrysanthemums, dahlias, anemones and cornflowers. It causes water-soaked spots to appear on petals and eventually the flowers are destroyed. Pick off affected blooms and spray with mancozeb at weekly intervals.

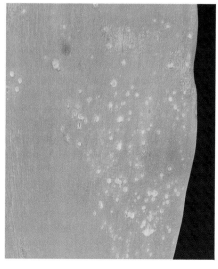

Damping off A fungus disease that attacks small seedlings, mainly those grown under cover. The base of the seedling shrinks and turns brown and eventually it topples over. Remove affected seedlings as soon as you see the first signs and water with copper fungicide. It also helps greatly to improve the flow of air around the plants by sowing more thinly and ventilating whenever possible.

Tulip fire This attacks leaves and bulbs. It causes scorched patches on the leaves and the stems may be covered in a grey mould. The bulbs show eruptions of fungus on the outside. Dig up infected plants and get rid of them, and spray the rest with carbendazim. To guard against attack, dip bulbs in carbendazim before planting and after lifting. Planting late, even up to November, helps avoid attack.

Foot rot Something like damping off, this attacks older plants, causing the base of the stem to blacken and shrink. Often the fungus is carried in the compost, so use only new compost, remove infected plants immediately. No chemical control available.

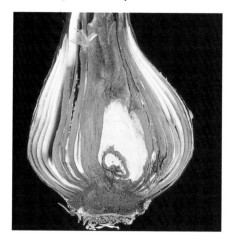

Bulb and corm rots These show themselves in different ways, sometimes starting at the base and turning the bulb soft and slimy or erupting on the sides of the bulb as brown mould. Corms can sometimes become quite hard and produce brown spots on the outside. There's no cure, but if one of the diseases does strike, dip new bulbs in benomyl before planting and again after lifting.

Downy mildew Attacks a few ornamentals in wet weather. It causes the upper side of the leaves to produce yellowish patches, while underneath is found a greyish, white mould. Spraying with mancozeb or myclobutanil helps.

Botrytis or grey mould fungus Very common and can attack leaves, stems and flowers. It's particularly bad in wet conditions, showing as a fluffy, grey mould. Remove the offending part and spray with carbendazim as soon as you see the first signs of attack.

Methods of chemical control

DISEASES OF VEGETABLES

Don't think that, because fungicides are designed to kill plants rather than animals, they'll be harmless to us or to wildlife. Great care needs to be taken, especially when you're spraying food crops; so, as always, follow to the letter the manufacturer's instructions on the pack.

RIGHT **Blight** A serious disease of potatoes and tomatoes. Yellowish patches develop on the leaves in mid-summer and these turn brown and eventually black, spreading into ugly blotches. White fungal threads can be seen under the leaves. The spores can be washed or blown on to the soil to infect the tubers too, causing brown marks under the skin which creep inwards. On tomatoes, stems and fruit are affected in the same way. Spray in mid-summer with copper fungicide or mancozeb and again two weeks later. Remove plants at the first sign of infection and destroy them.

Chocolate spot Attacks broad beans and is well named. Eventually the spots may spread to form brown patches. Make sure that the soil is limed and well supplied with potash fertiliser. Destroy all the crop debris from infected plants and rotate the crop if possible. Should the disease have been experienced before, spray with carbendazim when the first leaves have opened.

Neck rot Attacks onions in store, showing as a grey mould on the neck. Eventually the bulb rots. There's no cure, but the disease can be lessened by ripening the bulbs well before storing and avoiding feeding too much nitrogen when growing them, especially towards the end of the season. Don't bend over the tops to hasten ripening but let them fall naturally.

Rust Attacks mainly leeks, showing as bright orange pustules. It's very difficult to control. Avoid excessive use of high nitrogen fertilisers and dress the soil with sulphate of potash.

Blossom end rot This causes depressed, black patches on the underside of tomato fruits. It's a physiological disorder connected to the transport of calcium in the plant. It can be avoided to some degree by keeping the supply of water as even as possible. Never let the plants dry out.

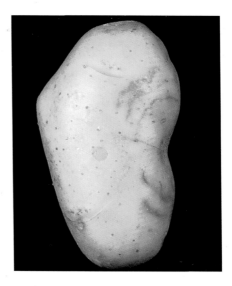

Canker A serious disease of parsnips which causes reddish-brown marks on the shoulders of the roots. Don't confuse them with carrot fly attack (see p. 334). There's no real cure, but some varieties are resistant.

Scab This attacks potatoes, causing corky, brown marks on the skin. It has little effect on the crop and can be peeled off, but it ruins exhibition tubers. There's no cure, but it helps if you make sure that the soil remains acid. There are varieties that show some resistance.

Spraing Another potato disease, this time caused by a virus. It shows as reddish-brown, arc-shaped marks on the inside of the tubers. There's no cure except to destroy the tubers and grow the next crop on a new site. Some varieties are more likely to be attacked than others.

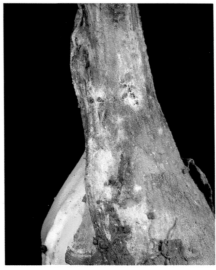

Clubroot Feared by every gardener since it attacks all members of the cabbage family and there's no known cure. It causes a swelling and distortion of the roots which eventually become slimy and rotten. Ensure that the soil is well limed and grow on raised beds to improve drainage. Dip the roots in a paste made with thiophanate methyl before planting. The organic controls work best (see p. 346).

White rot Affects leeks and onions, attacking the roots and the base of the bulb. Diseased plants turn yellow and, on lifting them, you'll see a fluffy, white fungal growth on the bulb. The fungus is soil-borne, so it's wise to rotate crops each year.

Foot and root rots These occur in many species, showing as a blackening of the base of the stem and a general collapse of the plant. They're caused by soil-borne fungi and are difficult to control. Pull out affected plants immediately. Grow new crops in a different part of the garden.

Methods of chemical control

DISEASES OF FRUIT

As in the case of pests, diseases of fruit trees and bushes can be almost eradicated with a continued programme of spraying, but this is hardly necessary in the garden. Keep an eye open for the first signs of attack and take action then. Bear in mind, too, that it's possible to buy 'cocktails' to deal with both pests and diseases and that fungicides and insecticides can be mixed provided the manufacturers recommend it.

RIGHT **Grey mould** A very common and widespread fungus disease particularly attacking currants and strawberries, especially in wet weather. The fungus enters through the flowers but is not seen until it erupts on the fruit, covering it with grey fungal growths and rendering it useless. Remove infected berries as soon as the disease is seen and apply a fungicide containing carbendazim immediately the first flowers open.

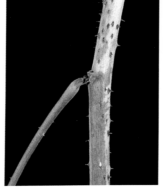

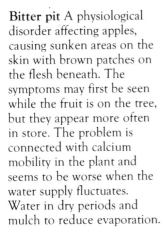

Bitter pit A physiological disorder affecting apples, causing sunken areas on the skin with brown patches on the flesh beneath. The symptoms may first be seen while the fruit is on the tree, but they appear more often in store. The problem is connected with calcium mobility in the plant and seems to be worse when the water supply fluctuates. Water in dry periods and mulch to reduce evaporation.

Cane spot and cane blight These attack raspberry canes. Cane spot shows up as small, purplish spots which spread and eventually split, while cane blight starts at the bottom of the canes as dark brown patches, followed by withering of the leaves and buds. Cut out affected canes and spray with carbendazim when the buds begin to unfurl and repeat at three-week intervals.

Coral spot This can affect all woody plants, including ornamentals. It gets in through wounds or pruning cuts and shows as bright red spots. Eventually the branch will die. Again, there's no chemical cure. Cut out affected branches and destroy them.

Fireblight A serious and increasing disease. Treatment normally involves cutting out infected branches or even removing the tree completely. The disease enters through flowers and rapidly spreads to the rest of the plant, which withers and turns brown. The leaves remain attached, giving the impression that the plant has been burnt.

Honey fungus A name that sends a chill down gardeners' spines. It will attack most woody plants, including ornamentals, and often starts on dead trees and spreads. It causes white fungal growths under the bark at soil level. Brownish-black threads may be seen on roots and in the soil, giving it its alternative name of bootlace fungus. The fruiting bodies, honey-coloured toadstools, may also sometimes be observed in autumn. Remove any dead or dying plants and treat the surrounding area with a phenolic emulsion. The best way is to make 60cm- (2ft)-deep holes with a crowbar at 60cm (2ft) intervals around the infected plant and pour the solution into those.

Canker A very common disease of apple and pear trees. It shows as sunken patches on the bark with white fungus growths appearing from the area in summer. The stem tends to swell around the wound, and if the canker girdles a branch it dies. Cut out diseased branches or, if they're large, cut out the canker and collect and destroy the diseased wood. Bacterial canker affects plums, causing round shot-holes in the leaves followed by an exuding of gum from the branch. The buds fail to open and the branch eventually dies back. Again, cut out infected branches and spray with copper fungicide in mid-summer and at monthly intervals until autumn.

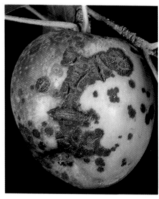

Brown rot A common sight on garden apple trees. The fungus enters through bird pecks or similar wounds and turns fruit brown and soft. It eventually becomes covered with rings of white mould which rapidly spread. The fruit falls and dries up. There's no control but, because the disease is rapidly spread by contact, pick off infected fruit immediately and, as it also attacks in store, store only perfect fruit.

Mildew Attacks most fruit trees and bushes, causing a silvery-white coating on shoots. On gooseberries it cloaks leaves, stems and fruits. Spray with a fungicide containing bupirimate and triforine when the flower buds have become green but before they colour, and then at two-week intervals. Some gooseberry varieties are resistant to the disease.

Peach leaf curl Attacks peaches, nectarines and almonds, causing red blisters to appear on the leaves which eventually turn black and fall. It's important to treat early with copper fungicide, giving the first spray in late winter and another two weeks later. Spray again in autumn. The organic control is more effective (see p. 298).

Scab Affects apples and pears, causing brown marks on leaves and fruit. Spray with bupirimate and triforine when the flower buds are formed but still tightly closed and again when they've turned pink (or white in the case of pears). Spray a third time when most of the petals have fallen and once more three weeks later.

Methods of organic control: general

Organic pest and disease control should really shun chemicals entirely. My instinct and experience tell me that to spray indiscriminately will upset nature's fine balance by killing gardeners' friends as well as their enemies. Then, without competition, the pests that remain will breed very fast indeed and cause an even heavier infestation and much damage.

My own methods, therefore, rely on attracting predators of known pests by planting a wide diversity of species (see p. 202), plus good husbandry to produce strong, healthy plants that have the best chance of withstanding any assault which does occur. Hygiene is important, too, so make sure that you avoid leaving rubbish lying around the garden, that you immediately confine thinnings from the vegetable plot to the compost heap and that you remove and destroy diseased plant material just as soon as you see the first signs of attack. Often onslaughts from pests can be controlled by simply picking the offending creatures off plants before large populations have the chance to build up.

All this should be coupled with a careful selection of plant varieties and some purely physical controls and deterrents against pests.

There's absolutely no doubt that these methods work and, indeed, much of the research into pest control is directed towards such methods. I do, however, have one word of warning. If you've been spraying your garden with chemicals, don't expect that, the minute you stop, your allies will come flooding in – they won't. It takes at least a couple of years to build up a balance of wildlife, in which time your plants will certainly suffer some damage. The only thing you can do is be patient: I promise you that it will sort itself out in the end. However, if you do weaken and return to chemicals just once, you will simply have to start again, right back at square one.

Hoverflies Some insect predators can be encouraged into the garden with suitable plants. Hoverflies, for example, need a feed of pollen before they lay their eggs. Since they have a short feeding tube, they look for open-structured flowers like that of the poached egg plant (*Limnanthes douglasii*). After feeding they lay eggs among colonies of aphids, and the resulting larvae eat up to 100 greenfly a day.

Frogs and toads These will feed on slugs in particular, and once they breed in your garden they'll come back year after year. So beg a little spawn from a friend (*don't* take it from the wild) for your own pond and provide them with plenty of water weed, especially when they're in the young stages.

Toads, like this old gentleman, live for a long time and breed very freely, so it's not difficult to build up a thriving colony quickly. Victorian gardeners would always keep one or two in the greenhouse as a recognised method of slug control.

Birds These eat slugs, snails, caterpillars, aphids and other pests too, so they should certainly be encouraged. Do this by providing a water source, trees in which they can perch, nesting boxes and, particularly, winter food plants like berrying shrubs and trees.

Physical barriers These are naturally very effective. New fabrics have been developed that can be used over cloche hoops to cover crops without significantly raising temperatures in summer. These will exclude all winged insects and are 100 per cent successful. I grow crops like parsnips, carrots, celery, celeriac and parsley in beds under a cover to protect against carrot fly.

Floating cloches are another form of protection against winged insects. These can be used without hoops to lift them above the crop. Their use is somewhat limited, however, since they often need to be removed from the crop before it matures.

Netting Birds are best controlled by physical barriers too, but here netting is generally used. It's important to stretch netting tightly over plants to prevent birds getting caught up in it.

Hedgehogs You can sometimes encourage these to stay in the garden if you provide them with a home in a pile of logs, but they're nomadic animals and may well move on. Putting out a feed of dog food each night should make them more interested in hanging around, though that'll stop them feeding on your slugs, so it rather defeats the object. You simply can't win them all!

Ground beetles All sorts of ground beetles are great allies of the gardener, so never kill them. They devour slugs and caterpillars in particular, feeding mainly at night. During the day they need to hide from their own enemies, the birds, so provide them with plenty of ground cover in the form of plants or, in a newly planted garden, pieces of wood or slate under which they can conceal themselves.

Other insect predators Various insects like ladybirds and lacewing larvae will also eat hundreds of insect pests, but I know of no specific plant that will attract them into the garden. Just provide a good selection of planting and they'll naturally follow.

Resistant plant varieties Plant breeders have made a significant contribution to organic pest and disease control by producing many resistant varieties. It's well worthwhile checking up on varieties of fruit, vegetables and ornamentals and growing only those that show some resistance. There are many roses, for example, that are a martyr to blackspot and mildew, while others are virtually free of both diseases. Obviously the latter are the ones to grow.

Methods of organic control: specific

The general controls listed on pp. 344–5 will deal with most garden pests and diseases, but there are some more specific measures that need to be taken to control the more awkward customers. All of these methods are quite specific to the pests concerned, so they'll cause no damage to other wildlife. With the exception of biological control all these methods are also much cheaper than using chemicals.

RIGHT **Clubroot** Impossible to control, and once land becomes infected it remains so. It's described on p. 341 and organic gardeners should also improve drainage and add lime as suggested there. In addition perfectly acceptable vegetables can be grown if they're started off in pots. Finally pot them into 10cm (4in.) pots of bought-in compost and plant out once a strong root ball has been formed. Plants will still be attacked, but the original clean roots will carry them through to harvesting. The one exception here could be cauliflowers which are more difficult to grow.

BELOW **Rabbits** The only effective way to keep these out is with a fence of 1m- (3ft)-wide wire netting with a 3cm (1¼ in.) mesh. Bury 15cm (6in.) of the netting and curve it outwards away from the garden to prevent burrowing.

Cabbage root fly The damage caused by this pest is described on p. 335. Complete control can be achieved by preventing the female laying her eggs next to vulnerable plants. This is done by slipping a disc of coated paper or foam-rubber carpet underlay around each stem immediately after planting. Note that the disc must fit snugly round the stem.

Caterpillars Some, particularly those of the cabbage white butterfly, can be controlled by spraying with a parasitic bacterium, *Bacillus thuringiensis*, which attacks the digestive system. It will harm nothing else.

Aphids in the greenhouse These can be controlled by introducing a parasitic wasp, *Aphidius matricariae*, which lays its eggs inside adult aphids (ABOVE). Most parasitic insects of this type are bought as eggs or larvae on leaves or pieces of card which are simply hung among the plants. There is also a fungus, *Verticillium lecanii*, which can be sprayed on to plants.

Codling moth This (see p. 337) can be partially controlled by killing males before they fertilise the females. A sticky trap is set up in fruit trees (one trap per five trees) with a capsule of the female sex pheremone. When males are attracted they stick to the pad, reducing fertile females by 80 per cent. The same control is now available for plum sawfly.

Earwigs These cause deformation of flowers by feeding on the buds. They feed by night and hide away by day, so provide a hiding place for them by stuffing a flower pot with straw or dry grass. Place this, inverted, on a cane among the crop and regularly remove and destroy the contents.

Red spider mite in the greenhouse The depredation of this pest is described on p. 334. It can be controlled first by raising the humidity. It prefers dry conditions, so keep the atmosphere moist by regular spraying with water. There's also a predatory mite, *Phytoseiulus persimilis*, which can be introduced to prey on red spider.

RIGHT **Slugs** Putting a plastic bottle around young plants helps, as does surrounding plants with lime, soot or ashes. I leave a few boards around for slugs to hide under at night and turn them over each morning for the birds. There is also a new biological control, a nematode called *Phasmarhabditis hermaphrodita*.

RIGHT **Whitefly** A persistent pest in the greenhouse (see p. 332). A sticky, yellow card makes an effective trap. However, once they start to feed, they ignore the trap, so shake plants once a day to get them flying. They can also be controlled with the parasitic wasp *Encarsia formosa*, which lays its eggs in the bodies of whitefly scale.

Winter moth A pest of fruit trees (see p. 336). The wingless females can be trapped with a sticky grease band, or grease applied with a special gun, as they crawl up the trunk to lay their eggs in early autumn.

Vine weevil The adults are all female and are wingless like the winter moth, so they can be trapped in the same way in greenhouses by putting grease on the legs of the staging. They can also be controlled biologically by watering on a preparation containing the parasitic nematode worm *Steinernema bibionis*.

Moles These make extensive tunnels below ground and sometimes create hills of excavated soil in the lawn. The only reliable way to get rid of them is to trap them with a barrel trap which is buried in one of the runs. It's a pretty barbaric method and only to be used as a last resort.

Weed control

Because weeds are natives they're ideally suited to the conditions in which they grow, so they'll always have an unfair advantage over other plants that come from different conditions. The gardener therefore has to referee a somewhat one-sided contest. Weedkillers can be used and there may be some justification for using them on paths and driveways, but I firmly maintain that hand pulling or hoeing is safer, cheaper and actually quicker. By the time you've got the sprayer out, measured the weedkiller and filled the tank with water,

I'll have probably finished the job by hand.

Good weed control can also be achieved by mulching. All plants need light to grow, and excluding it will eventually kill them off. The amount of time this takes depends on the weed and its ability to store food. Obviously perennial weeds like dock or oxalis take much longer than annuals. Use plastic sheeting, old carpets or even several thicknesses of newspaper held down with a thin layer of soil (see p. 77).

For advice on how to deal with lawn weeds see p. 169.

NON-CHEMICAL METHODS

RIGHT Rules of weeding
Weeding must be done regularly, and preferably while the weeds are still small. The bigger they're allowed to grow, the harder and more time-consuming they'll be to get rid of. Certainly you should never allow them to reach the stage where they seed, since this will multiply your problem several thousand times over.

RIGHT Hand weeding
A very satisfying job and certainly the most effective. Once weeds are pulled out and confined to the compost heap, they can cause no more trouble. Some weeds like groundsel and bittercress are continually in flower so they're best buried.

Using a Dutch hoe One of the quickest methods and much easier if it's done regularly. Choose a dry day and walk backwards to avoid treading the hoed weeds back in. Regular hoeing when the weeds are tiny will eventually kill off even the most persistent perennials, but perseverance is needed!

Using a swan-necked hoe This is good for larger weeds and is used with a chopping motion while walking forwards. In the best-regulated gardens it should never be necessary, because the weeds will have been dealt with while they were still small.

Using a wheel hoe A much quicker way of weeding in the vegetable area, where you have long, straight rows, is to use a wheel hoe. It has a blade at the bottom to slice off weeds and can be used with little effort at a slow walking pace provided the weeds are small.

CHEMICAL METHODS

Aerosols Some weedkillers are available in aerosol cans. Most are for use on weeds growing in paths or drives or for lawn weedkilling. The foam content is simply so that you can see clearly which weeds have been treated. It quickly disappears. Make sure you shake the container well before use and hold it a few centimetres from the weed.

Total weedkillers These must be used very carefully and you must ensure that they don't touch the leaves of any cultivated plants. Work on a completely windless day and use a shield on the sprayer. It's often helpful to cover plants with plastic bags or cardboard boxes or to get help to protect them with a piece of wood or cardboard.

Systemic weedkillers Those which contain glyphosate get into the system of the plant and prevent the roots storing food. They will kill perennial weeds and are most effective if the tiny droplets stick to the leaves, so put on a small amount with a sprayer. If the leaves are thoroughly soaked, the surface tension of the droplets is lost and the weedkiller runs off on to the soil where it loses its effect.

BELOW **Path weedkillers** Total in their effect, so again it's important to avoid plants in adjoining borders.

Contact weedkillers Only annuals are killed by the sort containing paraquat. They're designed to attack the chlorophyll in the leaves, so a good soaking is needed. It's equally effective to use a sprayer or a watering can.

The paintbrush method If you're troubled with perennial weeds in the borders and can't use a sprayer, you can do a very effective though time-consuming job with a paintbrush. Mix the weedkiller as recommended but add a little washing-up liquid to help it stick. Then, wearing rubber gloves, paint the leaves of the weeds with the solution, carefully avoiding cultivated plants. There are weedkiller gels designed for this job, but they're more expensive.

A guide to some common weeds

There are, of course, hundreds of weeds which might invade your garden. But bear in mind that what you call a weed, other gardeners might call a wildflower. Some are useful, some are very decorative, and all play host to other forms of wildlife. Wherever you can keep weeds, therefore, it's perhaps a good thing to do so. Nettles, for example, provide a breeding site for butterflies, while ivy is home to hundreds of insects and is also a favourite nesting area for birds. If you can reserve a corner for even just these two plants, so much the better.

However, most gardeners want to get rid of weeds in beds and borders and certainly wouldn't dream of playing host to some of the pernicious ones like ground elder or couch grass. Since the list is pretty extensive, I've included here only those which are going to give you trouble.

ANNUALS

RIGHT **Sow thistle (*Sonchus oleraceus*)** A tall plant which seeds prolifically. Deep-rooted, so dig it out well before it flowers.

Herb Robert (*Geranium robertianum*) A beautiful little plant worth keeping if there's not too much of it. Easily pulled out.

Chickweed (*Stellaria media*) Will flower and seed all year round. Hoe in hot weather and pull out where it's grown bigger.

Gallant soldier (*Gallinsoga parviflora*) An American plant, now worldwide. It seeds all summer, so don't let it get ahead of you.

Black nightshade (*Solanum nigrum*) A tall, bushy plant worth getting rid of quickly because the berries are poisonous.

Bittercress (*Cardamine hirsuta*) Often imported in container plants. Seeds very prolifically, so don't let it get a hold.

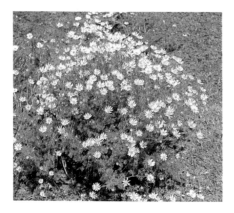

Stinking mayweed (*Anthemis cotula*) Another prolific seeder which must be hoed or pulled before it flowers.

Annual meadow grass (*Poa annua*) A rapidly seeding annual grass, sometimes difficult to pull out. Keep on top of it.

Groundsel (*Senecio vulgaris*) Seeds fast and furiously. Birds love the seed but in this case you can't afford to be charitable.

Shepherd's purse (*Capsella bursa-pastoris*) Seeds very quickly all year round, so keep on top.

Fat hen (*Chenopodium album*) Was once used as a vegetable. Seeds prolifically in late summer.

Annual nettle (*Urtica urens*) A smaller plant than most nettles which doesn't creep but seeds prolifically.

A guide to some common weeds

PERENNIALS

Perennial weeds are much more troublesome than annuals for obvious reasons. With most, the best bet is to dig out as much as you can and then keep the hoe going. Never put perennial roots on the compost heap, because they'll simply regrow there and you'll spread them again.

Creeping thistle (*Cirsium arvense*) Difficult because of its brittle, creeping roots. Use mulches or weedkiller, or hoe constantly.

Rosebay willow-herb (*Epilobium angustifolium*) Another plant with creeping roots and prolific seeds. Use mulches or weedkillers.

Pink oxalis (*Oxalis articulata*) A real headache because of the hundreds of tiny tubers below ground which are easily spread. Mulch with black plastic or use weedkiller.

Dandelion (*Taraxacum officinale*) A well-known weed with a fleshy taproot. The best way to eradicate it is to dig it out bodily.

Japanese knotweed (*Polygonum cuspidatum*) A real horror if it becomes established, because the roots go on forever. Dig it out as soon as you see it.

Horsetail (*Equisetum arvense*) Another very difficult weed to eradicate because of the deep roots. Mulching helps, or constant hoeing.

Bindweed (*Calystegia sepium* and *Convolvulus arvensis*) Both types have an extensive network of brittle roots. Leave just one piece in and it will rapidly re-establish. Much perseverance is needed.

Ground elder (*Aegopodium podagraria*) Much the same problem as bindweed. Use plastic mulches, weedkillers or constant digging and hoeing.

Couch grass (Agropyron repens) Shallower-rooting than ground elder, so it can be dug out more easily.

Stinging nettle (*Urtica dioica*) As already mentioned, this is a plant to keep where you can. Otherwise dig it out.

Creeping buttercup (*Ranunculus repens*) Here running stolons travel along the surface, but the plants root deeply and so they're hard to pull out.

Dock (*Rumex* spp.) Another broad-leaved weed with a fleshy root, this is also a prolific seeder. Dig it out before it gets too big.

JOBS FOR THE SEASON

THERE'S ABSOLUTELY no doubt that you simply can't garden by the calendar. While it's handy to have a list of jobs to be done in the garden just as a memory-jogger, at the end of the day it's the weather and soil conditions that will finally decide when you do things. The experienced gardener knows by the feel of the soil and the smell of the air, and there's no way of learning that from a book!

So please use my list just to remind yourself when to start thinking about what's got to be done, and do so in conjunction with the zone maps. These have been devised from statistics to show roughly when you can expect the first frost of the year and when you can safely plant out tender plants in the sure knowledge that you've seen the last one.

Having said that, better gardeners than me have been caught out in early summer when all the signs have shown that it was worth taking a risk, and everyone's lost tender plants at the other end of the year too. Always err on the pessimistic side and nine times out of ten you'll get it right. And never be too proud to take advice from experienced local gardeners.

Timings for all gardening work will vary according to your local conditions. I harvest my rhubarb, for example, a week later than my brother who lives further south, but a full fortnight before my friend in the north of Scotland.

Climate

It's quite impossible to forecast the beginning and the end of winter accurately, but these maps will give a good idea of the climate in your area. All frost-tender plants should be protected or brought inside a week or so *before* the date of the first frost of the winter and no plants should be planted outside until a good week *after* the predicted last one. Plants put out into slightly warmer conditions will always catch up, so it's much better to err on the side of caution. Remember too that seeds sown in cold soil could rot.

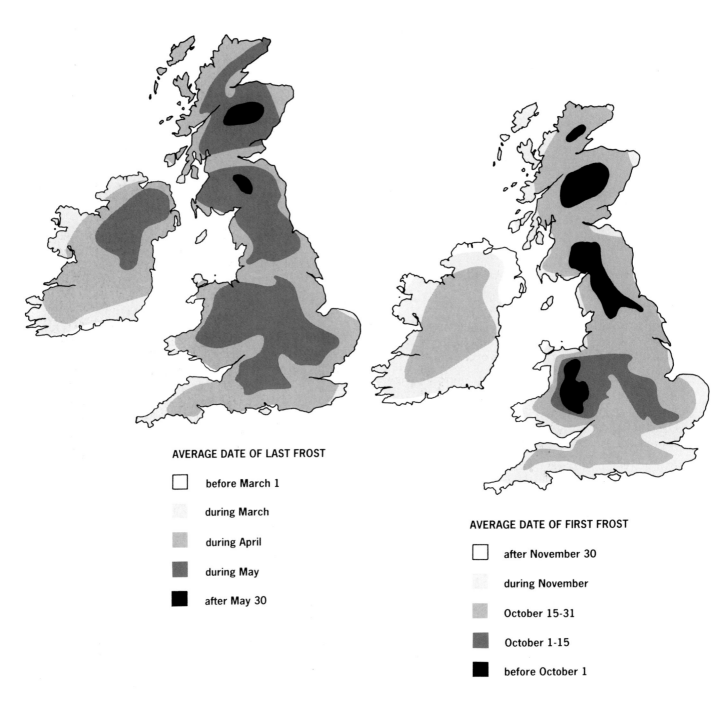

AVERAGE DATE OF LAST FROST

☐ before March 1

▫ during March

▪ during April

◼ during May

■ after May 30

AVERAGE DATE OF FIRST FROST

☐ after November 30

▫ during November

▪ October 15-31

◼ October 1-15

■ before October 1

Winter

Snapping leaves over cauliflower curds protects them from frost.

KITCHEN GARDEN

Protect all members of the cabbage family with netting against hungry birds.

Order seed catalogues.

Clear away debris and make regular slug- and snail-hunting sorties.

Plant fruit trees and bushes.

Lift a few parsnips and leeks and put them into a corner in garden compost in case the ground freezes hard.

Winter prune bush apples and pears.

Remove the top netting of the fruit cage in case of snow.

Keep strawberries in pots outside, but put them on their sides to prevent waterlogging.

Protect cauliflower curds from frost by snapping a few leaves over them.

Continue winter digging and manuring.

Remove all weeds to the compost heap.

Remove stumps of brassicas immediately after harvesting and shred them if possible

Plant new rhubarb crowns.

Cover a piece of ground with clear polythene for the early crops.

Plant new tubers of Jerusalem artichokes.

FLOWER GARDEN

Sweep up fallen leaves and put them into a container.

Cover alpines that resent winter wet.

Clear away all debris from the borders and lightly fork over, spreading manure or compost at the same time.

Winter prune deciduous shrubs.

Plant trees and shrubs.

Be prepared to protect plants in the coldframe against frost by covering.

Sow seeds of berried shrubs and alpines and put the pots outside or in the frame.

Check stakes and ties on trees and replace or loosen as necessary.

Brush snow off trees and shrubs if it threatens to damage them. Otherwise leave it on as insulation.

Remove all weeds to the compost heap.

Move shrubs that are in the wrong position.

Protect tender plants with cloches.

Take hardwood cuttings.

GREENHOUSE, WINDOWSILL AND POTTING SHED

Ventilate as much as possible during the day but leave only the smallest chink at night. Some heating may be necessary to maintain frost-free conditions.

Insulate with bubble polythene to save heating costs.

If you have border space, sow broad beans, early peas and winter lettuce.

Examine stored fruit and vegetables and remove any showing signs of rotting.

If your seed order arrives, store it in a cool, dry place.

Check dahlia tubers in store.

Sow cyclamen if you can maintain a temperature of 18°C (65°F).

Clean pots and boxes in very hot water with a little household bleach added.

Take advantage of sunny days to do any greenhouse repairs.

Plant figs, vines, peaches and nectarines and pot up citrus fruits.

Put grease bands on the staging legs to protect against vine weevils.

Set up potato tubers to sprout.

Towards the end of the period, sow hardy annuals in modules.

Sow broad beans, cabbage, carrot, cauliflower, celery, celeriac, lettuce, spinach, onion, peas, salad onion and turnip in trays or modules.

Take root cuttings of perennials.

GENERAL

Check tools, repair them if necessary and put them away.

Take the mower to be serviced.

Buy in manure and stack it.

Check the garden centre for winter bargains and try to buy the next season's requirements all at once while they're a bit cheaper.

Early spring

Use a forcer or a bucket to produce the earliest rhubarb.

KITCHEN GARDEN
Try to finish off the winter digging as soon as possible.

Put out cloches for early vegetables at least two weeks in advance of sowing or planting.

Plant potatoes.

Test for lime and spread it if necessary.

Feed fruit trees and bushes.

Plant Jerusalem artichokes.

Cover strawberries with cloches.

When the soil has warmed up sufficiently under cloches, sow broad beans, carrot, cabbage, cauliflower, lettuce, early peas, salad onion, spinach and turnip. If you sowed the same crops in the greenhouse, plant them out at the same time.

Plant onion sets and shallots outside if the weather and soil conditions are favourable.

Protect peaches from rain to avoid peach leaf curl fungus.

Prune autumn-fruiting raspberries.

Net black currants against bullfinches which eat the buds.

Feed spring cabbage with a high-nitrogen fertiliser.

Sow parsnip and Hamburg parsley.

Plant perennial herbs.

Towards the end of the period, sow winter cabbage, cauliflower, kale, Brussels sprouts, sprouting broccoli and leek in a seed bed.

Plant out globe artichokes and onion sets towards the end of the period.

Lift, divide and replant chives, garlic chives and sorrel.

Graft apples and pears.

FLOWER GARDEN
Prune deciduous shrubs that flower later in the year on the current season's growth.

Prune hypericums back to the ground if they were infected with rust disease.

Prune late-flowering clematis.

Lift and transplant snowdrops, snowflakes and aconites.

Sow sweet peas or transplant those raised inside from an earlier sowing.

Towards the end of the period, sow hardy annuals or plant out seedlings raised earlier inside.

Prune roses. Plant new herbaceous perennials and lift and divide congested clumps.

Replace rockery plants.

Hard prune shrubs grown for their winter bark colour.

Rake the lawn to remove old thatch. You may also be able to mow.

Lay turf lawns unless the soil is frozen.

Trim winter-flowering heathers as soon as they finish flowering.

Towards the end of the period, plant gladioli.

Plant lilies outside if the weather's favourable. If not, pot them up for planting later.

Feed all plants in the border, not forgetting the hedges.

GREENHOUSE, WINDOWSILL AND POTTING SHED
Ventilate on sunny days, but close up almost completely at night. Ventilate frames and cloches on sunny days.

Sow begonias and geraniums in a heated propagator.

Take cuttings of chrysanthemums, dahlias, fuchsias, geraniums and most tender perennials.

Towards the end of the period, sow cucumbers, melons and tomatoes for growing in the cool greenhouse.

Sow half-hardy annuals.

Repot fruit plants if necessary.

Begin liquid feeding potted plants.

Take basal cuttings of perennials.

Sow seeds of perennials for flowering later this year.

Sow tender perennials like salvia, eccremocarpus and rhodochiton for flowering later this year.

Take cuttings of heathers.

GENERAL
Put down tiles or slates to catch slugs and turn them over each morning.

Spring

Once seedlings are big enough you can water with a hose and a fine rose.

KITCHEN GARDEN

Sow maincrop varieties of beetroot, broad beans, carrot, chicory, Florence fennel, French beans, kohl rabi, lettuce, onion, peas, radish, salad onion, salsify, scorzonera, spinach, summer cabbage, summer cauliflower, Swiss chard and turnip.

Thin out or transplant seedlings as necessary.

Continue to plant early potatoes.

Prune cherries and plums.

Plant out onions raised in the greenhouse or frame.

Mulch with compost or manure around rhubarb.

Apply water in dry weather.

Sow dill, hyssop, parsley, rue, marjoram and thyme.

Plant asparagus.

During the day remove cloches from strawberries to allow access by pollinating insects. Tuck straw underneath ripening fruit.

Towards the end of the period sow swede.

When weather conditions permit, plant courgette, tomato, cucumber, French beans, runner beans and squash under cloches and sow the same vegetables outside.

Pinch out the tops of broad beans attacked by blackfly.

Protect carrot, parsnip, celeriac, Hamburg parsley and parsley against carrot fly attack.

Put out codling moth traps.

Earth up potatoes and protect them against frost.

Plant leeks and brassicas from the seed bed.

Plant self-blanching celery and protect against carrot fly.

Take cuttings of mint and rosemary.

Take measures to control apple and pear scab.

Tie in new growth of briar fruits as they develop.

FLOWER GARDEN

Thin out hardy annual seedlings sown earlier.

Plant acidanthera, crocosmia, galtonia, gladioli, nerine and ornithogalum.

Plant evergreens and shift large plants if necessary.

Plant out sweet peas.

Plant out chrysanthemums, argyranthemums and euryops.

Mow the lawn regularly and feed and weed.

Turf or sow new lawns.

Take conifer cuttings.

Finish lifting, dividing and transplanting hardy perennials.

Prune spring-flowering deciduous shrubs as soon as they finish flowering.

Stake hardy perennials.

Plant aquatic and bog plants and remove blanket weed from the pond.

Towards the end of the period sow hardy perennials and biennials in a seed bed outside.

Prune early-flowering clematis after flowering.

Lift, divide and replant polyanthus.

Lift bulbs that have finished flowering where space is needed and heel them into a corner of the vegetable plot.

Plant out hardy perennials raised from seed.

Trim alpines if they're spreading beyond their alloted space.

GREENHOUSE, WINDOWSILL AND POTTING SHED

Ventilate the greenhouse as much as possible and keep floors and staging moist.

Sow sweetcorn and tomatoes for planting outside.

Continue to prick out and repot plants as necessary.

Continue sowing half-hardy annuals for outside planting and for pot plants.

Take dahlia cuttings.

Take conifer cuttings.

Plant tomatoes and cucumbers in the border or in growing bags and pot up peppers and aubergines, all in the cold greenhouse.

From the middle of the period, shift half-hardy plants to the coldframe to harden off before planting out.

Cover the frame if frost is threatened.

Plant up hanging baskets and tubs and keep them inside until after the last frost.

Remove side shoots from tomatoes and start feeding them, together with cucumbers, peppers and aubergines.

Sow calceolarias, cinerarias and primulas for pot plants.

Start to prune grapes.

GENERAL

Keep topping up the compost heaps.

Keep on top of the weeds by hoeing or hand pulling.

Check all new plantings and water regularly.

Early summer

After flowering, flag irises can be lifted and divided.

KITCHEN GARDEN

Plant out runner beans, tomatoes, cucumbers, courgettes, marrows and sweetcorn.

Continue sowing radish and spinach, but now in a shady spot.

Peg down runners of strawberries to make new plants for forcing.

Control greenfly and other pests.

Continue sowing beetroot, carrot, chicory, endive, lettuce, swede and turnip.

Sow chicory for forcing and spinach beet for autumn use.

Sow Chinese cabbage, French beans, Swiss chard, rhubarb chard and spring cabbage in a seed bed.

Net fruit bushes against birds.

Pick the first gooseberries for ripening and leave some to eat fresh later.

Protect newly planted brassicas from cabbage root fly.

Harvest and store shallots and harvest early potatoes.

Remove flower spikes from rhubarb.

As tomatoes grow, take out the side shoots from the upright growers and tuck straw underneath the bush varieties.

Pick and dry herbs as they become ready.

Sow carrot, turnip and beetroot for winter storage.

Harvest globe artichokes before the flowers start to open.

At the end of the period start to sow some early varieties of vegetables for lifting in autumn.

Sow a few broad beans for the harvest of green tops they provide in autumn.

After strawberries have finished cropping, cut off the old leaves and clean the beds.

Pinch out the tips of runner beans when they reach the top of the canes.

Harvest and prune raspberries as they ripen.

Summer prune pears towards the end of the period.

FLOWER GARDEN

Plant out half-hardy annuals and tender perennials.

Put out planted tubs and hanging baskets and start watering daily and feeding weekly.

Take softwood cuttings of shrubs.

Prune brooms that have finished flowering.

Continue to trim and tie herbaceous plants, cutting them down after flowering unless you intend to save seed.

Divide and replant *Iris germanica* rhizomes.

Plant corms of *Anemone coronaria*.

Take stem cuttings of pinks.

Tie in climbers regularly.

Top up the pool and bog garden in dry weather.

Propagate climbers by layering.

Plant perennials and biennials sown earlier into a nursery bed.

Stake gladioli and other tall summer bulbs.

Disbud chrysanthemums and dahlias for larger blooms.

Mound up alpines that are going bare in the middle, dropping a little compost into the bare areas.

Prune summer-flowering deciduous shrubs.

Dead-head roses and annual bedding to extend flowering.

Take cuttings of hydrangeas.

Layer border carnations.

Collect and sow seed of some perennials.

Take half-ripe cuttings of shrubs.

Cut back straggly growth of arabis, aubrietia and violas.

Plant autumn-flowering bulbs.

GREENHOUSE, WINDOWSILL AND POTTING SHED

Ventilate freely, all night if necessary, and keep damping down the floors and stagings. Shade the glass.

Prick out seedlings of pot plants sown earlier.

Trim and feed cucumbers and tomatoes regularly and feed peppers and aubergines.

Put those greenhouse plants that prefer lower temperatures outside, but don't forget to water.

Pinch back vines regularly and feed fruit in pots.

Take cuttings of regal pelargoniums.

Sow more half-hardy annuals for pot plants.

GENERAL

Keep the sprinkler going if it's allowed.

Turn the compost heap to accelerate rotting.

Continue hand weeding.

Summer

Now the gardener reaps the benefit of his (or her) hard work.

KITCHEN GARDEN
Prune raspberries and tie in new canes.

Support autumn-fruiting raspberries with a single string round the whole row.

Sow an autumn variety of lettuce.

Prune cordon gooseberries, red currants, apples and pears.

Cut off potato haulms showing symptoms of blight and harvest the crop.

Remove old wood of briar fruits after harvesting and tie in new.

Sow winter-hardy salad onion, winter-hardy spinach or spinach beet and winter radish or mooli.

Sow spring cabbage in a seed bed if not already done.

Towards the end of the period sow early carrot, lettuce, radish and turnip in the coldframe.

Harvest early apples and use.

Support heavily laden branches of fruit trees.

Protect autumn-fruiting raspberries and strawberries from birds.

Allow a few French beans to ripen and collect and bottle them.

Plant strawberries and pot up runners for forcing.

Cut and dry herbs.

Begin harvesting onions.

Set up marrows in the sunshine to ripen.

Begin to lift and store root vegetables.

Remove debris from peas and beans to the compost heap, but leave the roots in the ground to release nitrogen.

Prune peaches and nectarines.

Continue picking apples and pears.

Earth up celery, celeriac and leeks to blanch them.

Control cabbage white butterflies.

FLOWER GARDEN
Take clematis cuttings.

Take cuttings of alpines, especially those that are short-lived.

Trim conifer hedges and cut back those that have reached the required height.

Continue mowing the lawn, but leave the grass longer in dry weather.

Sow or turf new lawns, but be prepared to water.

Continue to feed plants in pots and baskets, but change to a high-nitrogen feed.

Cut gladioli, but leave some foliage to build up the corm.

Take half-ripe shrub cuttings and softwood cuttings of geraniums, fuchsias and other tender perennials.

Continue to dead-head roses, annuals and herbaceous perennials unless you wish to save seed.

Continue to cut back herbaceous perennials after flowering, but also continue to harvest seed where required.

Prune rambler roses after flowering.

Early in the period, plant autumn-flowering bulbs.

Plant narcissi.

Pot up a few narcissi to fill gaps next spring.

Sow biennials where they are to flower.

Plant evergreen shrubs towards the end of the period.

GREENHOUSE, WINDOWSILL AND POTTING SHED
Maintain continuous night ventilation and damp down to keep up the humidity.

Harvest vegetable fruits regularly, keep up regular feeding and remove dying leaves from the bottom of the plants.

Sow calceolarias, schizanthus, cyclamen and primulas for pot plants.

Pot up prepared hyacinths for Christmas flowering and plunge them outside.

Sow winter lettuce for growing in the cold or slightly heated greenhouse.

Repot cyclamen corms that have been resting.

Towards the end of the period remove shading.

Take stem cuttings of coleus, begonias and impatiens.

Autumn

Leaves are far too valuable to be wasted and easy to turn into leafmould.

KITCHEN GARDEN

Harvest and put into store onions, garlic and root crops.

Plant lettuce for later cloching and spring cabbage outside.

Harvest and store apples and pears.

Bring ripened marrows inside to store.

Take hardwood cuttings of gooseberries.

As patches of soil become vacant, manure and dig them.

Prune black currants and gooseberries.

Prune plums when they've finished cropping.

Protect the last of the autumn-fruiting strawberries with cloches.

Check tips of apples and pears for mildew and cut it out.

Divide and replant rhubarb.

Plant garlic.

Take hardwood cuttings of currants.

Start lifting and forcing chicory.

Cut down tops of Jerusalem artichokes.

Cut down asparagus and mulch with compost.

Put grease bands round apple and cherry trees.

Continue to pick and store apples.

Remove any leaves that start to go yellow from Brussels sprouts.

Sow broad beans.

FLOWER GARDEN

Plant herbaceous perennials and evergreen shrubs.

Plant deciduous trees and shrubs as soon as leaves have fallen.

Lift, divide and replant perennials.

Remove and compost summer bedding and replace with spring-flowering biennials.

Replant polyanthus.

Lift gladioli and dahlias and store the corms/tubers.

Lift tender perennials and box them up for winter storage.

Plant spring-flowering bulbs and lilies.

Stop mowing the lawn. Rake out the thatch, spike and top dress.

Continue laying turf.

Take cuttings of fuchsias, chrysanthemums, heathers and hydrangeas, together with tender perennials.

Cut down all perennials that are over and clear away debris.

Clean up the pool and cover with netting to prevent leaves falling in it.

Prune climbing and rambler roses and weeping standards.

Cut back the old leaves of hellebores.

Clip over loose-growing conifers like *Chamaecyparis pisifera* 'Boulevard'.

Pick up fallen rose leaves to remove any infected with blackspot.

Take hardwood cuttings of deciduous shrubs.

Sow sweet peas in the coldframe.

Plant containers with bulbs and biennials.

GREENHOUSE, WINDOWSILL AND POTTING SHED

Start to close the greenhouse at nights and reduce watering and damping down.

Pot up a few root cuttings of mint and sow a pot of parsley for the windowsill to give a winter supply.

Alternatively bring a tub of herbs into the greenhouse.

Pot up and plunge bulbs for spring flowering.

Bring inside any plants that have been standing out for the summer.

Clear out all vegetable fruits and give the greenhouse a good clean with a solution of household bleach.

Start a regular inspection of pot plants and remove leaves attacked by fungus.

Pot up a few roses for early cut flowers next year.

Pot up some early-flowering herbaceous plants from the garden to make good, cheap pot plants.

Bring in pot-grown chrysanthemums and feed regularly.

GENERAL

Clean up the garden as much as you can for the winter, removing dead leaves and weeds to the compost heap.

Spread compost or manure on vacant soil and prick it in with a fork.

INDEX

PICTURE CREDITS

BBC Books would like to thank the following for providing photographs and for permission to reproduce copyright material. While every effort has been made to trace and acknowledge all copyright holders, we would like to apologise should there have been any errors or omissions.

Key: a – above, b – below, c – centre, l – left, r – right.

A-Z Botanical Collection pages 15 (r), 49 (bl), 160, 176 (l), 250 (cr), 254 (ar, br), 260 (ar), 261 (al, ar, bl), 275 (3), 276 (4), 277, (1, 2, 3), 290 (r), 291 (acl), 293, (c, bl), 294 (bc), 313 (ar), 332 (br), 337 (bcl), 339 (bc), 340 (a, bcl), 351 (cl, bl), 352 (l, ar), 353 (al, ac, cl, cr, bl, bc); **Brogdale Horticultural Trust/Crown Copyright** pages 293 (ar, cl, cr), 294 (a, bl), 295 (al, cl), 296 (bl, bc, br), 297 (bl), 303 (c), 305 (ar, cl); **Bruce Coleman Limited** page 223 (a, b); **Liz Eddison** pages 25 (bc), 157 (br), 172 (John Chambers), 173 (bl, Sonning Herb Farm), 200 (b, Chelsea 90), 207 (br), 228–9, 231 (bl, bcl Garden Artefacts, bcr, br), 268 (l), 274 (4, 5), 277 (4, 5); **Ron & Christine Foord** pages 337 (bcr), 352 (br); **The Garden Picture Library** pages 126 (Brian Carter), 133 (Ron Sutherland), 133 (bl, Steven Wooster), 153 (br, Alan Bedding), 215 (r, l, John Glover), 255 (ar, Mayer Lescanff), 271 (b), 299 (bl, br, Brian Carter), 301 (a, Brian Carter), 309 (a, Ann Kelley), 322 (a, Steven Wooster), 326 (br, Brian Carter), 327 (bcr, David Russell); **John Glover** pages 18 (ar)–19, 162–3, 173 (al), 176 (r), 177 (b), 198 (al), 243 (a), 258 (bl, br), 260 (bl, br), 275 (2), 281 (al, ar), 291 (acr, ar cr), 293 (bc), 310–11, 312 (a), 324 (r), 325 (acl), 326 (l, ar), 327 (bl, bcl, br); **Jerry Harpur** pages i, 131 (l, r), 140–1 (designer Simon Fraser), 145 (ar, designer Christopher Masson), 152 (ar), 157 (ar), 159 (a), 161 (l, designer Michael Balston), 174–5, 180 (b), 187 (br), 188 (ar, Park Farm, Great Waltham), 190 (l), 193 (r), 196 (a), 206, 207 (bl), 214 (a), 240–1, 262–3, 266 (a), 280 (a); **Holt Studios International** (Nigel Cattlin, except 297r Inga Spence and 334bl Duncan Smith) pages 17 (bl), 251 (al), 332 (bc), 334 (al, cr, br), 335 (ac 1, 2, ar, cr, bl, br), 336 (bl, bc), 337 (al, ac, ar), 338 (al, ac, bl, bc), 339 (al, ac, ar, bl, br), 340 (br), 341 (al), 342 (br), 343 (ar, br), 353 (c); **Horticulture Research International, Wellesbourne** pages 16 (bl), 17 (al), 281 (bl); **ICI Garden Products** pages 16 (bc, br), 17 (ac, ar, bc, br); **Andrew Lawson** pages 2–3, 14 (l), 149, 179 (a), 180 (a), 201 (b), 204–5, 216 (bl, br), 223, 255 (ac), 258 (ar), 259 (al), 265 (b), 272 (5), 274 (1), 292 (r), 293 (br), 333 (acl), 337 (br); **The Lindley Library** page 24; **Peter McHoy** pages 4 (al, bl, ac, bc), 25 (ar, br) 48, 49 (al), 73 (br), 96 (al), 181 (br), 216 (bcl), 218–19, 250 (ar), 252 (al, ar), 253 (a), 334 (ar), 335 (al), 338 (ar); **Ken Muir** pages 302 (a), 303 (ac, cl, cr), 305 (ac, ca, c, bl, bc), 306 (bl, bc, br), 307 (bc), 308 (bl, br), 309 (cl, c, bc); **Natural Science Photos** pages 216 (bcr, P. & S. Ward); **Nature Photographers** pages 332 (ac, Paul Sterry), 333 (al, Derick Bonsall, ar, E. A. Janes, bl, Paul Sterry, bc, N. A. Callow, br, Nicholas Brown), 334 (cl, Paul Sterry), 335 (cl, Owen Newman), 336 (a & br, Paul Sterry), 353 (ar, Jean Hall, br, Paul Sterry); **Clay Perry** pages ii, vi, 12–13 (l), 26–7, 28, 31, 33, 35, 37, 39, 41, 43, 47, 52 (l), 60–1, 66, 84, 94–5, 113, 168 (a), 202 (r), 203 (l), 210 (r), 225 (br), 226 (ar), 244 (a), 246 (a), 328–9, 355; **Photos Horticultural** (Michael Warren) pages 324 (l), 325 (al, acr, br); **The Harry Smith Collection** pages 14 (r)–15, 25 (al, bl), 73 (bl), 130, 152 (al), 156 (r)–157 (l), 158 (a), 176 (c), 177 (a), 201 (cl), 243 (bl, br), 250 (ac, bl, bc, br), 251 (ac, ar, c, bl, bc), 252 (bl, br), 253 (bl, bc), 254 (al), 255 (al, bl, br), 256 (al, ar, bl), 257 (al, br), 258 (al), 260 (al), 272 (1, 3), 273 (1, 2, 4), 274 (2, 3), 275 (1), 276 (2, 3, 5), 281 (br), 290 (l, c), 291 (al, cl, ccl, ccr, bcr, br), 294 (br), 295 (ac, ar, c, cr), 296 (ac, ar), 297 (al), 299 (al, ac, ar), 300 (br), 301 (c, b), 303 (ac), 309 (cr), 316 (a), 325 (ar), 327 (ac), 332 (bl), 333 (acr), 337 (bl), 340 (bl, bcr), 341 (ac), 351 (bc, br); **Solardome** page 313 (l); **Trip** pages 67 (Sefton Photo Library), 128–9 (Glyn Davies), 146 (c, R. Whistler), 272 (2, Eye Ubiquitous), 273 (3, Ed Buziak), 275 (4 & 5), 276 (l), 278–9, 288 (a), 292 (l) (all, Eye Ubiquitous); **David Ward** pages 4 (ar, br), 5, 6–7, 8 (ar, br), 9 (al, ac, bl), 10, 62–3, 68–9, 70, 82–3, 327 (bl).

All other photographs were specially taken for BBC Worldwide Ltd on location at Barnsdale by Stephen Hamilton